# REASON AND VIOLENCE

## Philosophical Investigations

# Contributors

Robert Audi
Timothy Binkley
Harry Girvetz
Rubin Gotesky
Philip P. Hallie
John O'Neill
M. Lionel Rubinoff
Sherman M. Stanage

**The Nation** for an excerpt from *What Violence Is* by Newton Garver, The Nation, June 24, 1968.

**The New York Review of Books** for excerpts from *On Violence* by J. M. Cameron, The New York Review of Books, July 2, 1970.

**The New York Times** for excerpts from *Report of the National Advisory Commission on Civil Disorders* by Otto Kerner © 1968 by The New York Times Company. Reprinted by permission; for an excerpt from *The Shadow of Hitler* by Gert Kalow © 1967 by The New York Times Company. Reprinted by permission; and for excerpts from *Political Terrorism* by Irving Howe, The New York Times Magazine, April 12, 1970, © by The New York Times Company. Reprinted by permission.

**W. W. Norton & Company, Inc.** for an excerpt from *Civilization and Its Discontents* by Sigmund Freud, (translated by James Strachey). W. W. Norton & Company, Inc. © 1961 by James Strachey; for an excerpt from *Our Inner Conflicts* by Karen Horney, W. W. Norton & Company, Inc. © 1945; for an excerpt from *Power and Innocence: A Search For the Sources of Violence* by Rollo May, W. W. Norton & Company, 1972; and for an excerpt from *Power, A New Social Analysis* by Bertrand Russell. W. W. Norton & Company, Inc., New York, N.Y. George Allen & Unwin, Ltd., London.

**Open Court Publishing Company** for an excerpt from *The Philosophy of Rudolph Carnap*, P. A. Schilpp, ed., Open Court Company, La Salle, 1964.

**Penguin Books** for an excerpt from Plato, *Gorgias*, trans. W. Hamilton, Baltimore: Penguin Books, 1960. Reprinted by permission of Penguin Books, Ltd.; and for an excerpt from Plato, *The Republic*, Book II, trans. H. D. P. Lee, Baltimore: Penguin Books, 1955. Reprinted by permission of Penguin Books Ltd.

**Prentice-Hall, Inc.** for an excerpt from *Ethics* by William K. Frankena © 1963. By permission of Prentice-Hall, Inc., Englewood Cliffs, N.J.

**Princeton University Press** for excerpts from *The Devil's Share* by Denis de Rougemont, trans. by Haakon Chevalier, Bollingen Series II, copyright 1944 by Bollingen Foundation. Reprinted by permission of Princeton University Press.

**Random House** for an excerpt from *Tradition and Revolt* by Robert A. Nisbet, Random House, Inc. 1970; and for an excerpt from *Love's Body* by Norman O. Brown, Random House, 1966.

**Russell and Russell** for an excerpt from *The Genealogy of Morals*, Vol. 13 of The Complete Works of Friedrich Nietzsche, General Editor, Oscar Levy, translated by H. B. Samuel [1909–1911] New York: Russell & Russell, 1964.

**Sidgwick & Jackson Ltd.** for an excerpt from *I Cannot Forgive* by Rudolph Vrba and Alan Bestic, London: Sidgwick & Jackson, 1964.

**Simon & Schuster, Inc.** for excerpts from *Do It!: Scenarios of the Revolution* by Jerry Rubin, Simon & Schuster, 1970.

**University of Chicago Press** for excerpts from *The Human Condition* by Hannah Arendt, University of Chicago Press, 1958.

# REASON AND VIOLENCE

## *PHILOSOPHICAL INVESTIGATIONS*

*edited by*

### SHERMAN M. STANAGE

1975

**ROWMAN AND LITTLEFIELD**
Totowa, New Jersey

Library of Congress Cataloging in Publication Data

Stanage, Sherman Miller
  Reason and Violence

  Bibliography: p. 241.
  1. Violence—Addresses, essays, lectures.
  I. Title.
  HM291.S78    301.6'33'01    72-85273
  ISBN 0-87471-603-9

*Printed in the United States of America*

The authors and the publisher gratefully acknowledge the following
sources for permission to quote passages from the works indicated.

**Addison-Wesley Publishing Company** for an excerpt from sections 12
and 13 of *The Feynman Lectures on Physics*, Volume I by Richard P.
Feynman, et al. Copyright 1963, Addison-Wesley, Reading, Mass.

**American Psychiatric Association** for an excerpt from *Diagnostic and
Statistical Manual of Mental Disorders*, 1963.

**Basic Books** for excerpts from Chapter XXIV of *Collected Papers of
Sigmund Freud*, edited by Ernest Jones, M.D. Volume IV, Translation
supervised by Joan Riviere. Published by Basic Books, Inc., 1959 by
arrangement with The Hogarth Press, Ltd.

**Beacon Press** for an excerpt from *Humanism and Terror* by Maurice
Merleau-Ponty, Beacon Press, 1969.

**Basil Blackwell Publisher** for an excerpt from *An Essay Concerning the
True, Original, Extent and End of Civil Government* by John Locke,
Oxford: Basil Blackwell & Mott, 1946.

### ACKNOWLEDGMENTS

**The Bobbs-Merrill Company, Inc.** for excerpts from *Thomas Hobbes:
Leviathan*: Parts I and II, edited by Herbert W. Schneider, copyright
1958, by The Liberal Arts Press, Inc. Reprinted by permission of The
Bobbs-Merrill, Company, Inc.

**The Bodley Head** for excerpts from *The Professor* by Rex Warner, London: The Bodley Head, 1936.

**Brandt & Brandt** for an excerpt from *Nineteen Eighty Four* by George
Orwell, copyright, 1949 by Harcourt, Brace & World, Inc. Reprinted by
permission of Brandt & Brandt.

**Curtis Brown Ltd.** for an excerpt from *Intimate Journals* by Charles
Baudelaire, translated by Christopher Isherwood, Methuen & Co. Reprinted by permission of Curtis Brown Ltd.

**The Clarendon Press** for excerpts from *The New Leviathan* by R. G.
Collingwood, Oxford: The Clarendon Press, 1942.

**Doubleday & Company, Inc.** for an excerpt from *The Social Construction of Reality* by Peter L. Berger and Thomas Luckman, Doubleday
and Company, Inc. 1967; and for excerpts from Goethe's *Faust* translated by Walter Kaufmann, Doubleday Anchor, 1962.

**Grove Press, Inc.** for an excerpt from Jean-Paul Sartre's Preface to *The
Wretched of the Earth* by Frantz Fanon, copyright 1963 by Presence
Africaine. Reprinted by permission of Grove Press, Inc.

**Publishers-Hall Syndicate** for an excerpt from Sydney J. Harris' *Strictly
Personal*, May 1, 1972.

**Harcourt Brace Jovanovich, Inc.** for excerpts from *On Violence* by
Hannah Arendt, Harcourt Brace & World, 1970.

**Harper & Row, Publishers, Inc.** for an excerpt from *Sociology as a Skin
Trade* by John O'Neill, Harper & Row, 1972; and for an excerpt from *On
Caring* by Milton Mayeroff, Harper and Row, 1971.

**Harper's Magazine Co.** for an excerpt from *The Future of American
Violence* by Richard Hofstadter from the April, 1970 issue of Harper's
Magazine.

**Holt, Rinehart and Winston, Inc.** for an excerpt from *The Theory of
Inquiry* by John Dewey, Henry Holt & Co., 1938.

**Humanitas: Journal of the Institute of Man** for an excerpt from *Violence
and Love* by R. D. Laing, Humanitas, Fall, 1966.

**Journal of Philosophy** for excerpts from *On Violence* by Robert Paul
Wolf, Journal of Philosophy, LXVI (1969), and for an excerpt from *On
Violence* by Francis Wade, Journal of Philosophy, LXVIII (1971).

**McGraw-Hill Book Company** for an excerpt from *Soul On Ice* by Eldridge Cleaver, McGraw-Hill Book Company, 1968.

**Macmillan Publishing Co., Inc.** for excerpts from *Reflections On Violence*
by Georges Sorel, Free Press, 1950; and for excerpts from *The Ramparts
We Guard*, Encyclopedia of the Social Sciences, 1st edition Vol. 14, and
new edition Vol. 13.

**David McKay Company, Inc.** for an excerpt from *Violence and the Rule
of Law* by Bernard Harrison, David McKay Company, Inc. 1971; and
for an excerpt from *Violence, Force, and Coercion* by Ronald Miller,
David McKay Company, Inc. 1971.

**The University Press of Hawaii** for an excerpt from *Violence: A Christian Perspective* by Rev. Peter J. Riga, *Philosophy East and West*, Vol. 19, No. 2, 1969.

**Viking Press, Inc.** for an excerpt from *Power* by Bertrand de Jouvenal, copyright 1949 by The Viking Press, Inc. Reprinted by permission of The Viking Press, Inc.

**The Wall Street Journal** for an excerpt from an editorial, *The Dilemma That Is Greece*, published by The Wall Street Journal on January 12, 1970.

ACKNOWLEDGMENTS

*To all who have
suffered from man's
inhumanity to man.*

# CONTENTS

# PREFACE

There are few phenomena more widespread today than violent acts and violent events, and few occurrences within the total span of recorded history so seldom understood or explained. In fact, the human condition is perhaps most tellingly manifested in persons' violations of themselves, their neighbors, and their environments. The wonder is that so few philosophers have directed their attention toward the investigation and exploration of the phenomena of violence. Indeed, this same conclusion can be drawn with reference to all of the disciplines that might be expected to pursue such investigations.

Whether or not we all agree with the judgment that violence is omnipresent depends upon our perceptions of certain acts and events. Surely in our lives we have all, in some form and degree, experienced a good deal of what we call violence; some have experienced this much more fundamentally and encompassingly than others. But judgments about which acts and which events are the violent ones are judgments based upon the widest latitude of interpretation—and misinterpretation—of what constitutes violence.

*What is violence? When does violence occur? Why does violence occur? Who are the victims of violent acts and events? Who are the agents of violent acts? And who can remain the spectators of violence today?*

The philosophical investigations in this volume focus upon these central questions and many others. They explore technological violence, economic violence, business violence, political violence, radical violence, and police violence. Sexist, racial, and ethnic violence are also discussed. Personal, anomic, and psychogenic violence; assassination, terrorism, and political murder are treated. Moreover, the essays analyze at some length questions of violence perpetrated or accepted in the name of equality, justice, and law; and they explore questions of religious violence and violence in the name of order and morality.

Although the authors of these essays employ differing philosophical methods and sets of presuppositions and present a variety of theses about the forms and degrees of violence, there are several points of identical focus. All of them discuss the location and dislocation of reason with respect to violence. All are concerned with fundamental philosophical investigations toward answering the question of what violence is. All propose definitions of violence, or characterize some of its dimensions. All of the authors are concerned with questions of the theory and the practice of violence. All discuss in some degree the language of violence, and most discuss the contemporary violence of language. Moreover, many practical questions such as the questions of legal sanctions, law enforcement, and the justification of force are taken up. All of the questions to which the authors address themselves are of the utmost importance to philosophy, to the social sciences, to the emerging human sciences, to the humanities, to education, and to the law.

The eight essays clearly fall into two parts. *Part One* is concerned with the larger questions of violence, technology, and culture. The first two essays focus upon the body politic, upon the problems of a culture undergoing awesome technological changes, and upon the consequences of violence for culture, both today and tomorrow. The third and fourth essays trace some of the traditions of violence through history from accounts found in mythic and religious sources, particularly those involving Satan. They also draw heavily upon some of the Western literature of violence and upon the psychological literature.

*Part Two* focuses upon violence and persons and upon the language we use and abuse in speaking of violence, for example the concepts of force, power, harm, and strength. It is also concerned with the larger questions of the language of violence —questions that have to do with classifying the articulations of kinds and degrees of violence. One of the essays discusses the question of consensus and the justification of force and another examines social force, social power, and social violence. The final two essays speak to the problems of classifying violence in ways useful for further research.

This volume is concerned with both the theory and the practice of violence. The practice of violence will hardly come to an end with this volume; *the* theory will surely not be settled upon in any final manner. It is enough to hope that these essays will challenge all those persons—lay folk and specialists alike—who are interested in these questions to set about the difficult work of understanding violence *better* than the present authors have. Thus it is hoped that these essays will put persons, societies, and cultures more firmly to the task of investigating the problems of the human condition—or more specifically, the problems of human bondage. Violence manifests itself in the all-too-human ways, and it is surely the case that all disciplines must cooperate in investigating and exploring violence toward the end of understanding and explaining it. And yet it is not enough merely to understand and to explain. Through the further understanding of what it means to be human in the human worlds, violence—in most of its forms, if not all—must be rendered less pervasive. Only by cutting down violence, *and by cutting it down still further*, can our civilization be enriched and move away from barbarism—if we still have the time to do so.

Indeed, as we look about and fashion our future, and go about civilizing our young, we should ask ourselves what are the legacies of violence that we have already willed upon them.

The editor expresses his warm thanks to the other authors of the essays, whose work in philosophy is already widely respected and who now add further chapters in philosophy relevant to the human condition; to John Wieboldt of Littlefield, Adams & Company, whose early encouragement sustained this project and whose patience has surely helped it become a better statement; to Pat White, whose editing has evidenced a most orderly mind and sensitivity to language, and to whom we are more grateful than we have ever admitted; to Gregory Harris, who assisted in the preparation of the extensive bibliography; to Northern Illinois University, which following the violent spring of 1970 funded an institute in philosophy on Reason and Violence. Special appreciation is reserved for my wife, Diane, who has long been associated with the book in love and care, and for our daughters, Ruthe, Deborah, Kelley, Lisa, Suzanne, and Christine, whose acceptance enriches our work and whose love transcends it.

*Guernica, Spain*                                                          S.M.S.
*March, 1974*

# PART ONE

# Violence, Technology, and Culture

# Violence, Technology, and
# the Body Politic

JOHN O'NEILL has taught at York University (where he has chaired the Department of Sociology), the New School, Stanford University, and San Jose State College. He studied at the London School of Economics and Political Science, the University of Notre Dame, and Stanford University, where he was awarded the Ph.D. in 1962. He has served on the editorial boards of the *International Journal of Comparative Sociology*, the *International Journal for Contemporary Social Theory, Philosophy of the Social Sciences*, and *The Human Context*. Professor O'Neill's more than fifty books, articles, and reviews in philosophy, sociology, and related disciplines include the books *Perception, Expression and History: The Social Phenomenology of Merleau-Ponty* (1970), *Sociology as a Skin Trade: Essays towards a Reflexive Sociology* (1972), *Making Sense Together: An Essay in Social Ontology* (1973), and *Politics and Art* (1974). He has translated and edited *Studies on Marx and Hegel* by Jean Hyppolite (1969, 1973), and several works by Maurice Merleau-Ponty: *Humanism and Terror: An Essay on the Communist Problem* (1969), *Themes from the Lectures at the Collège de France, 1952–1960* (1970), and *The Prose of the World* (1973).

# Violence, Technology, and the Body Politic

## by John O'Neill

A political community must always find and sustain a symbolic expression of its beliefs concerning the sources, mechanisms, and potential threats to the orderly relationships and exchanges between its members. The symbolism of the body politic is a recurring expression of the nature of order and disorder in the political community. In the modern period the concept of rationality has provided the dominant imagery of the production and maintenance of institutional order, making alternative conceptions of society seem utopian and irrational. However, the repressive function of modern rationality has inevitably led to a search for a new political symbolism which I believe can be understood in terms of a more articulated notion of the body politic.[1] The body politic is the fundamental structure of political life. It provides the ground of ultimate appeal in times of deep institutional crisis, of violence and terror, of hunger and exploitation, when it is necessary to renew the primitive grounds of political authority and social consensus.

The crisis of political authority, and the critique, emerging from the campuses and the streets, of the legitimacy of technological rationality, may be approached in terms of an argument based upon the dialectic between common-sense and libidinal knowledge versus the technical knowledge of bureaucratic institutions. The dramatic articulation of the organic and libidinal needs of the body politic, which is so often violent and anarchic at first, is a representation of the political lifeworld of its poor and oppressed members in the cities, ghettos, and colonies. The dramatization of the everyday political practices of a community will be considered here in terms of a phenomenological reflection on the symbiosis between rationality and violence which is always reduced to a form of irrationality to suit interpretation by the dominant political authority. We shall proceed from the phenomenological variety of our experience with violence to its dominant modes in the social structure of war and colonial exploitation. Tne method of understanding will be to adopt a basically Marxist analysis of the infrastructure of violence, making it for the most part inseparable from exploitation, together with an analysis of the symbolic expressions of violence developed around the presentation of Hannah Arendt's essay, *On Violence*.[2]

The experience of violence tests in us the sense of our own humanity. It may provoke in us the cry of our own anger, rage, and sorrow felt for the very first time. In some it will lead to despair and silence. Terror commits its deepest injury when it tempts us to silence. Yet this, surely, must be the first reaction to acts of terror which rip into the fabric of the simple human expectation that our life is our own within the circle of those we love, or that the day we have begun will close peacefully on the scenes we have projected for ourselves—a day's work, a walk, or a picnic. This is not to overlook the fact that the everyday presumption of the goodness of the world is held in the face of the cruelty and oppression that we encounter in the world. But this presumption lies deeper than the rhetoric of civil liberties, and we should hesitate in the name of those liberties to rebuke the hurt and anger that terrorism arouses in us. Violence tears into the flesh of our humanity. But like the flesh of Hiroshima, in unknown ways and untold agony the human flesh heals and its tissues are rebuilt. A new life forms, and also a new city, tracing out the endless repetition of human wants and needs through which men are pitted and caught together. At the same time, terror raises in us an outcry. Yet it is not easy to say what we feel in the face of terror, for at such times to speak at all is to depend upon precisely the human motives and situations that terror destroys. Thus terror hollows and empties our language, threatening it with destruction and ultimate silence.

How, then, are we to speak of terror and violence, which obliterate the human landscape and wither the look of man? We need to dwell among men even to begin to understand how it is we find violence among our other experiences like love and disappointment, joy and anger. We know about violence just as we know about famine and floods, or the coming of the jumbo jet and thalidomide babies. We know that there is violence in the streets in which whites and blacks and police and students are involved in our own towns: in Berkeley, Tokyo, Paris, and London—even Toronto. What child does not know of Vietnam? What parent does not know of Hiroshima, Auschwitz, and Biafra? Our common awareness of violence easily draws distinctions within the forms and modes of violence as it affects our daily practices. We distinguish between war and revolution, political violence and criminal violence. We also distinguish between personal violence and institutional violence, between the blow on the head and the hunger and disease that result from foreign trade. We know of these things from life in the family, from the hurts of love, and in general from the very business of living that ties the world together in a patchwork of wealth and misery. We know of racial violence, urban and colonial violence, and what we know in general of these is not much less than the knowledge of the experts whom these phenomena produce.

We have through everyday language a capacity for living with violence. Even Hiroshima was not experienced in the same way by everyone, and so there were some left to help, to pray, and to rebuild. Indeed, the phenomenon of violence is curiously revealing of the nature of human space and human time, that is to say, of the human world as the frame and flesh of violence and imagination. Every day we turn away a poor man. Every day we ride through ghettos on overhead expressways in automobiles for which the exploitation of the world's natural resources is the primary symbol of affluent pride and colonial indignity. Every evening we watch living death and destruction on newsreels just as all day long, day in and day out, we and our children, but especially our children, watch hours of violent action as the medium of a primitive sense of right and wrong, the code of criminal justice. And yet we celebrate, as we must, the great tissue of human understanding woven out of common need of each other's love and labor. We need to believe that the contiguity of space is human, that our neighbour fares no worse than ourselves. And still we live next door to misery. We need to believe that the fullness of time is human and supports the hopes and dreams of others as much as our own. And yet we know that our brothers are dying right now, that there are children without futures, not far away like the African babies of the missions, but like those in our own towns.

Violence is not simply any threat to the stability of the political and social order. For in everyday politics change and reform are as much sought after as stability and entrenchment. Under ordinary circumstances we do not speak of 'violence' to convey the expectation of the legitimate enforcement of political mandates. We understand the power of government, and we trust that it will carry out its will with due regard for humanity and with provisions for appeal. Nor are these conventional understandings in any way naive. They are the very fabric of political order. For this reason they are provided for in the institutions of law, parliamentary practice, democratic election, and freedom of speech and publicity. The conviction that government is not naked force, that justice is not terror, and that democracy is not merely a sham elitism is not to be regarded as a mere article of political faith unless it can be shown that none of the institutions of political life serve their purpose, and that there is no public domain in which this faith can be acted upon through political deeds and public speech to which men attend.

We are concerned here with an alternation in the nature of technical knowledge which moves between the rule of reason and the violence of reason. Hannah Arendt has argued that conflict between technique and Eros has plagued Western knowledge and its political tradition since Plato.[3] In modern times this conflict appears in the struggle between technical-scientific rationality and what I call *libidinal politics*, or the symbiosis between rationality and violence which distorts and destroys our political culture. In these terms I propose that we read Miss Arendt's essay, *On Violence*, as a phenomenology of the basic vocabulary of politics—that is to say, an essay motivated by the tendency of violence to destroy the foundations of political speech and action and to undermine the world or realm of politics. To this purpose I suggest the following reading of her essay, conscious that it is not to be found there except as a further exercise in political imagination, hopefully within the spirit of her own reflections and without conceit.

Confronted with the scope of modern destruction and its technological amplifications, we are tempted to identify the rationality of science with the rationalization of war. This is especially a danger in the science-fiction-like production of war scenarios written up in the think-tanks of desert America. It is precisely here, where science tempts us with inevitability and with the passionless contemplation of the future as world destruction, that Miss Arendt enters the most profound objection to such a construction of the nature of knowledge and its utopian politics.

We cannot speak of knowledge outside of the context of human action and purposes, that is to say, outside of human initiatives and the bonds of promise and forgiveness. The accumulation of modern knowledge, the self-infinitizing labors of the man of culture as well as the man of property, is the labor of modern self- and world-alienation. As Kafka puts it, modern man "found the Archimedean point, but he used it against himself; it seems that he was permitted to find it only under this condition." The modern age is built upon the paradox that its expansion of technological, economic, and social activity has produced a massive world-alienation, an attitude of world-domination and universal migration motivated by what Weber called "innerworldly asceticism." The release of these forces was preceded by the collapse of the ancient and feudal conceptions of the world as a political realm of public deeds and public speech resting upon the citizen's or the lord's control of his own household and its private economy. So long as the household economy was embedded in the political order, men's labor served to produce objects whose value was subordinate to the social values created by the thoughts, deeds, and speech of political man. The modern world, however, is built upon a inordinate expansion of individual utilities that subordinates labor or production to a cycle of consumption and destruction disembedded from the political order. This is the source of the modern conception of "society" as a field of individual interests solely, a conception that inspired Hobbes's nasty vision and whose essentially contradictory features were later explored by Hegel and Marx.

Although Miss Arendt considers Marxist knowledge a contributing factor, the self-infinitizing world logic of modern production and consumption was seen prophetically in Marx's *Communist Manifesto*. But there the internal logic of world-alienation is attributed to the class struggle without reference to the underlying dialectic of recognition that is the real source of Marx's historical vision. The inherent world-alienation of capitalism and its innerworldly asceticism is due to the classical utilitarian reduction of the world to a world of utilities from which it could not save man himself as an ultimate standard of value. Kant's categorical imperatives raised a standard of action and person conduct that had no foundations in the context of class inequality and exploitation which reduced most men to the status of a means only and never an end. Marx drew from Hegel the essence of modern subjectivity in the notion that man produces himself. But what Hegel also pointed out in *The Phenomenology of Mind* is that modern subjectivity also consumes itself in an unstable utilitarianism that destroys the substantive rationality of things and the orders of nature and society at the same time that it represents the greatest release of subjective rights and freedoms.

We need to presume this background in order to understand what Miss Arendt means by the processes of world-destruction and the cycle of meaningless labor and "science" which designs the landscape and invents the scenarios of modern violence. The disenchantment of the world and the devaluation of nature are the results of a consistent utilitarianism driven by the rational asceticism of modern subjectivity guessing at a hidden God. Once man no longer has an end beyond himself, nothing stops him in the relentless exploitation of the world and himself. In this project the vocabularies of liberal individualism and progress provide motivational supports for the privatization of world resources and the unthinking pollution of alternative human environments. It is no longer possible within this ideological framework to separate the processes of production and destruction. For modern labor is the inspiration of a divine madness working upon a promised land where abundance feeds rapacity and denies conservation. We need to generate a counter-myth to the ideology of world domination. To achieve this, it is necessary to separate the notion of work from the self-infinitizing logic of utilitarianism.

The human world is an artifice built upon everyday passions but also against time and eternity. Much of human labor is incessant, and consumes life in the simple reproduction of life and in the tending to bodily needs. This labor consumes a good part of the mental energies of men, so that it is necessary, Arendt argues, to distinguish that "science" which serves wants from *thought*, whose aim is non-utilitarian. Thought serves no obvious purpose; it considers the riddle of human activity, and is the source of religion, magic, myth, and art. Thought produces objects for their own sake; pre-eminently in art, it draws from time and destruction a world of essence, an edifice, an immortal home for mortal men. Of itself, thought produces nothing without human hands, eyes, ears, and tongues, which materialize thought and embody its creations—creations which would otherwise lose man in reflection, dream, and imagination. Thought transcends science, logic, and intelligence; it can never be expropriated by computerized homunculi which merely aid mental labor in the service of wants. This, however, is a view that depends upon the reversal of modern utilitarianism and the subordination of economics to politics. Upon this reversal hangs the question of the humanization and conservation of the world not as an emporium but as a public space in which men's words might be memorable and their deeds glorious. Without such a space, history and politics are polluted and the human story reduced to an insane series of commercials. As Miss Arendt says,

> If the *animal laborans* needs the help of *homo faber* to ease his labor and remove his pain, and if mortals need his help to erect a home on earth, acting and speaking men (*political man*) need the help of *homo faber* in his highest capacity, that is, the help of the artist, of poets and historiographers, of monument-builders or writers, because without them the only product of their activity, the story they enact and tell, would not survive at all. In order to be what the world is always meant to be, a home for men during their life on earth, the human artifice must be a place fit for action and speech, for activities not only entirely useless for the necessities of life but of an entirely different nature from the manifold activities of fabrication by which the world itself and all things in it are produced. We need not choose here between Plato and Protagoras, or decide whether man or a god should be the measure of all things; what is certain is that the measure can be neither the driving necessity of biological life and labor nor the utilitarian instrumentalism of fabrication and usage.[4]

We cannot understand the predicament of modern knowledge and its capacity for world violence and destruction apart from Miss Arendt's analysis of the essence of modern political economy. In the essay *On Violence* she challenges the pseudo-rationality of the extrapolation of futures designed by those who "think the unthinkable" on the ground that these exercises do not involve *thought* at all.[5] Here her argument is that scientific politics is based upon the same world-view generated by the utilitarian reduction of life and labor to process and species—existence, which in turn makes behaviorism a threat precisely because it is a plausible reduction of the future of human action. In this sense, behaviorism and the paramilitary objectivism of the new sciences of the future describe utopias in which the contingencies of human conduct are removed and, with them, the field of politics and history. A somewhat similar argument applies in the case of the revolutionary fiction of futures that have been generated by colonial violence. Here (in a significant reappraisal of her own earlier analysis) Arendt takes Sartre to task for his misunderstanding of the Marxist future through his equation of violence with creativity (in his Introduction to Fanon's *The Wretched of the Earth*). She points out that the basis of Marxist humanism is that man produces his world through work and language, and, it will be remembered from *Capital*, through thought which distinguishes the work of man from the labor of the bee.

I think it is necessary here to develop briefly the Hegelian-Marxist phenomenology of thought, language, and work in the development of the human world.[6] Without such an understanding, Marxism is too easily identified with a utopian conception of violence as social and political world innovation. In *Phenomenology of Mind*, Hegel described the history of consciousness as the social organization of the unity of the self and the world, which it first discovers abstractly in the unity of the mind and its objects. The humanization of the world is mediated by desire and the production of utilities which reveal the world as human praxis. So long as desire rules the mediation of consciousness, things, and other selves, human life becomes a struggle to the death. But this means that human consciousness can never be satisfied through the desire for objects and the servitude of others. In this, consciousness could only consume itself, whereas it needs a common world in which things and other selves reflect consciousness in order for consciousness to realize its human potential in the creation of a common world of recognition, language, and work. The universalization of culture and human sensibility implicit in the expressive activity of work and speech is progressively articulated through the special languages of history, politics, economics, and sociology. This progression is reflected in the ideal typical constructs of nature and convention, or of community and society, which reflect the fundamental alternation of freedom and alienation in the growth of modern subjectivity.

The question which lies at the core of the social sciences is the question of the meaningfulness of the subjectivization of the bases of need and utility once these are disembedded from their political matrix. The problem that focuses the sociological tradition through Marx, Durkheim, and Weber, is what Hegel would have called, not unlike Hobbes, the truth of subjectivity in search of itself and inter-subjectivity in a world where the bonds of traditional sentimentality have been destroyed through the machinery of rights, exchange, and property.

Marx portrayed the vast release of human energy made possible by bourgeois civil society and its capitalist economy as a series of cataclysmic conflicts which would result in its overthrow by the proletariat and the creation of a socialist society in which the rule of utilitarianism could be replaced by the humanization of human wants and social relations. It was part of this vision that the reversal of capitalism would be a revolutionary event. Meanwhile, the socialist revolution in advanced capitalist countries is becalmed. Marcuse has argued that affluent slavery is fun mediated by the techniques of repressive desublimation— the executive pink shirt, and that ambiguously available Mary from the Royal Bank.[7] This is an argument that makes violence tempting to Miss Arendt, inasmuch as the resulting smoothness of progress and the inevitable widening of the gap between contrived and human needs invites violence as the only possible means of interrupting a course of events that threatens to automate dehumanization. Although this is only a remark she makes in passing, it must be pointed out that it serves more to identify the violence of affluent student youth or American despair than the violence of worker strikes or of the ghetto and colonial poor. Indeed, Arendt has herself pointed to the essence of modern experience among the masses as the pain of bodily labor (in language that resembles Marx's description of the alienation of the worker not just from his product, but from his other sensory and intersubjective possibilities). She says,

> The development of the modern age and the rise of society, where the most private of all human activities, laboring, has become public and been permitted to establish its own common realm, may make it doubtful whether the very existence of property as a privately held place within the world can withstand the relentless process of growing wealth. But it is true, nevertheless, that the very privacy of one's holdings, that is, their complete independence "from the common," could not be better guaranteed than by the transformation of property into appropriation or by an interpretation of the "enclosure from the common," which sees it as the result, the "product," of bodily activity. In this

aspect, the body becomes indeed the quintessence of all property because it is the only thing one could not share even if one wanted to. Nothing, in fact, is less common and less communicable, and therefore more securely shielded against the visibility and audibility of the public realm, than what goes on within the confines of the body, its pleasures and its pains, its laboring and consuming.[8]

Labor's desire to break with the privatization of experience through bodily pain is surely the most basic cause of the revolutionary violence that Miss Arendt would recognize as essential to the cause of humanity, although in her formulation of the privacy of the body she seems to cut it off from the inter-subjective dimensions of the body-politic and its revolutionary poetics. Meanwhile, the political culture of affluence built upon the over-privatization of social resources worked by monopoly capitalism results in a stylization of the issues of power, class, and public indifference in a fun-culture riddled with violence, racism, and colonial wars.[9] The basic class conflict underlying the social order of monopoly capitalism is distorted, through the techniques of repressive desublimation, into the sentimentalities of charity, social reform, and colonial aid, which are the vicarious counterparts of affluent fun-culture and its white liberal politics. In such a contest, it becomes very difficult to speak of justice and outrage that calls for unavoidable violence, because this is a response that has been made "irrational" through the passive "rationalization" of motives worked upon the card-carrying members of the fun-culture, the political future of whom has been mortgaged by this very same process. It belongs to this same context that violence is made to appear "senseless," just as the exploitation which causes it, for want of any adequate sociological analysis, is considered "unnecessary," in part because cynics consider that the class system can be sustained without overt exploitation, and for the rest because the "solution" of the production problem reduces exploitation to a problem of improved patterns of social consumption. Violence, however, can also be made part of the "realism" of capitalist fun-culture. By this I mean that the split between domestic peace and international violence can be reproduced as the split between the animal and rational nature of man. The colonies, ghettos, and now the prehistory of man provide marvelous scenarios for the dramatization of the destructive potential of a superficially harmless fun-culture.

Fanon and Cleaver have shown how well the rhetoric of mind-body dualism is suited to the expression of racial exploitation and colonial revolt, and thus how the vocabulary of violence is essential to the lifeworld of the body politic. In his book *Soul on Ice*, Eldridge Cleaver understands instinctively the contemporary reversal of the ideal and material orders in American civilization. Since Cassius Clay affected poetry, the Word is no longer white property to teach blacks the lesson of submission, the great white dualism of class and the mind-body split. Worse still for American white male supremacy, it was a black muscle-man who betrayed their fears—Muhammad Ali spouting poetry, floating like a butterfly, stinging like a bee. But Cleaver himself understands deepest of all the demon of black poetry, the blinding white Circe of the black soul. In his allegory of the black eunuchs, Cleaver looks into the face of his own·anger and what he sees there should give us pause lest we speak too easily of reform or revolution. He sees the hatred between whites and blacks so twisted into the roots of the black family that there can be no love that isn't warped by the black's lust for a white woman or the black woman's secret admiration for the white man unbroken by the system. In a racist context the class struggle roots itself in the individual's split self, dividing the black male and female against themselves and destroying the natural unit of a black society, a black nation or homeland. Thus the black man suffers a socially imposed self-hatred of his manhood compounded by the sterotypification of the black as brute strength, body without mind. In terms of this analysis the black revolution can only succeed if it involves a deep psychic transformation, the rebirth of black pride, of the black spirit, of the black family and black culture. This is not to deny the place of violence in the black revolution. But I think Cleaver means to say that there is much potential violence that is the violence of twisted souls who must also pass through their own dark night before the blood flows in the streets and before anyone can be sure he is building the new Africa.

The same profound diagnosis of the black experience is developed in Frantz Fanon's essays on colonial social structure and the psychology of slavery and revolt. Fanon makes it clear that the way oppression works is through the black man's dreams, through his sexual and family life, and through his language, which teaches him the contours, the touch, and the taste of self-hatred and oppression. Here, too, the medium is the message. Language, knowledge, beauty, power, money, and the land are all *white*, and the black man who uses or looks upon any of these instinctively warns himself off as a thief, a violator, a brute negativity. To be in the world at all is for the black man to leave his home and his woman and even his senses for the white man's world. This is a daily routine, a journey of the soul made every time the black man leaves the ghetto for work in the morning and passes a policeman, a home, or any white man whose look tells him that there is another way but it is not for blacks. Fanon has the marvelous gift of revealing the structure of racial neurosis as a landscape, a country, a language, a dream, a vision of the body in which black and white confront each other as themselves. In the white man's neurosis, the black man figures as the force of life that is drying up in himself. In his own dream, the black man dreams of white civilization.[10]

Miss Arendt remarks on the irony of interpreting the violence generated by the world's most complex industrial technology as due to man's basically animal need for violence which if frustrated by culture then takes such "irrational" forms as world destruction rather than the more natural periodic displays of war and violence. It is in her reply to the attempt to place the definition of the uses of violence in the hands of the new political zoologists that Miss Arendt's conception of *the essentially human nature of violence* is set forth.

I remarked earlier that while Miss Arendt is critical of Sartre's formulations of the political role of violence, we should not fail to understand her own argument on the human or humanizing nature of violence. The attempt to reduce violence to an irrational factor, to deprive it of any place in the vocabulary of politics, can only be successful where the processes of dehumanization have reduced men to abject slavery and victimization. It is only where men see no prospect of action that their sense of injustice and rage at alterable human conditions atrophies or is turned against themselves. In short, violence and rage must be understood as integral motives so long as the institutions of political conduct are open to human initiative and the call for freedom and justice. Miss Arendt warns against the tendency to place the human emotions in opposition to "rationality" when in fact these emotions only become "irrational" when they sense that reason itself is distorted. Indeed, so much of what outrages contemporary rationality is nothing but the outrage of a more humane reasonableness driven to expose the sham of establishment rationality. It is in this context that we must understand the rhetoric of creative violence as the attempt to connect with the humane roots of reason, which have been progressively destroyed by technological rationality and the myth of progress.

Miss Arendt is critical of the attempt to reduce violence to a biological concept that is then reintroduced as a dangerous metaphor in the vocabulary of revolutionary politics. Here, however, I think she is not always in touch with the language of revolution, which belongs to a general cultural revolution and is first of all the work of poets and artists who restore language and perception to playfulness, say what is unspeakable, and make the word flesh once more.

The language of revolution reaches naturally for the language of the body because its experience is the awareness of the body starved, brutalized, and ready to kill or be killed—the body tired of having the shit kicked out of it, tired of being fucked for a living. This is the conviction that underlies Jerry Rubin's comments on the fate of language:

> A dying culture destroys everything it touches.
> Language is one of the first things to go.
> Nobody really communicates with words anymore.
> Words have lost their emotional impact, intimacy, ability
> to shock and make love.
>
> Language *prevents* communication.
>
>    CARS LOVE SHELL
> How can I say
> "I love you"
> after hearing:
> "CARS LOVE SHELL."
>
> Does anyone understand what I *mean?*
>
> Nigger control is called "law and order." Stealing is
> called "capitalism."
>
> A *"REVOLUTION"* IN TOILET PAPER.
> A *"REVOLUTION"* IN COMBATING MOUTH ODOR!
> A *"REVOLUTIONARY"* HOLLYWOOD MOVIE!
> *Have the capitalists no respect?*
>
> But there's one word which Amerika hasn't destroyed.
> One word which has maintained its emotional power
> and purity.

Amerika cannot destroy it because she dare not use it.

It's the last word left in the English language:

FUCK ! ! !

One bright winter day in Berkeley, John Thomson crayoned on a piece of cardboard "FUCK WAR," sat down with it and was arrested within two minutes. Two more people sat down with signs saying "FUCK WAR." *They* were arrested.

The Filthy Speech Movement had been born.[11]

While the poet of the body politic is Norman O. Brown, its playwright is Jerry Rubin, the author of revolutionary street theater. Muhammed Ali, Eldridge Cleaver, and Frantz Fanon are the artists of black soul politics. Between them they have taught us to understand the deep political structures of sex, language, and the body. They have reduced conventional politics to biological warfare in order to renew love's body. Brown sweeps away conventional reality as illusion, mystification, and dream. We reenact our past, the primal scene; and all politics is infantile regression, the overthrow of genital tyranny directed by identification with the father's penis, which is our soul enslaving our body. The head of the state is the erection of the body politic (Tricky Dick) sublimated in his official person. In the language of Norman O. Brown:

Erect is the shape of the genitally organized body; the body crucified, the body dead or asleep; the stiff. The shape of the body awake, the shape of the resurrected body, is not vertical but perverse and polymorphous; not a straight line but a circle; in which the Sanctuary is in the Circumference, and every Minute Particular is Holy; in which

> Embraces are Cominglings from the Head even
> to the Feet,
> And not a pompous High Priest entering by a
> Secret Place.[12]

The aim of the revolution is revelation—to take words out of the marketplace, to renew the word, to renew vision, to declare the Pentagon a public urinal. Norman O. Brown drives radical thought to the limits of cynicism and madness in order to pass through the cave culture of the Protestant ethic and spiritless capitalism. The argument between Marcuse and Brown is the Left's version of the generation gap. Marcuse's civilization of Self, Person, and Property balks at Brown's communism based upon the theory of libidinal use-value.[13] Meanwhile, while the ideological Left tortured history in order to deliver the revolution, and when it came, missed it (in Russia, China, and Cuba) due to the law of uneven development—or while it puzzled over whether the proletariat was any longer a revolutionary agency— Jerry Rubin was in the revolution business, casting parts for thousands of middle-class kids in street scenes that packed them in in Berkeley, Chicago, and Washington. His techniques were exaggeration and the co-option of the police, the Pentagon, the House Un-American Activities Committee, NBC, George Wallace, and color TV. Rubin turned the revolution into a youth movement, which survived the failure of the civil rights movement by making pot *the* civil rights issue of America and the real bond between blacks and whites in their struggle against the pigs and the status quo.

In America, religion, politics, and business are alike in being serious business. There is no joy in them, and thus their very seriousness is inverted into the vulgarities of worship, democracy, and money-making. We must, however, understand that profanity or vulgarity can only be what it is in the light of its fall from the sacred. Politics, religion, and business are equally holy works of man. It is the task of the rebel, the clown, and the practical joker to remind us of the dialectics of the holy and the profane, of godhead and manhood. Thus Jerry Rubin was a consummate street artist engaged in constructing apocalyptic scenarios in which the world of business and politics was consumed in its own fires. Rubin built take-out kits for the revolution. Consider the beginning of his Chapter 22:

> ### 22: *Money Is Shit—Burning Money,*
> ### *Looting and Shoplifting*
> ### *Can Get You High*

> The Stock Exchange official looks worried. He says to us, "You can't see the Stock Exchange."
>
> We're aghast. "Why not?" we ask.
>
> "Because you're hippies and you've come to demonstrate."
>
> "Hippies?" Abbie shouts, outraged at the very suggestion. "We're Jews and we've come to see the stock market."

VISION: *The next day's headlines:*
NEW YORK STOCK MARKET BARS JEWS.

We've thrown the official a verbal karate punch. He relents.

The stock market comes to a complete standstill at our entrance at the top of the balcony. The thousands of brokers stop playing Monopoly and applaud us. What a crazy sight for them—longhaired hippies staring down at them.
We throw dollar bills over the ledge. Floating currency fills the air. Like wild animals, the stockbrokers climb all over each other to grab the money.
*"This is what it's all about, real live money!!! Real dollar bills! People are starving in Biafra!"* we shout.
We introduce a little reality into their fantasy lives.

While throwing the money we spot the cops coming. The cops grab us and throw us off the ledge and into the elevators. The stockbrokers below loudly boo the pigs.
We find ourselves in front of the stock market at high noon. The strangest creeps you ever saw are walking around us: people with short hair, long ties, business suits and brief cases.
They're so serious.
We start dancing "Ring Around the Rosey" in front of the Stock Exchange.
And then we begin burning the things they worship: dollar bills!
Straight people start yelling: "Don't! Don't do that!"
One man rushes to get a burning $5 bill out of Abbie's hand, but it's too late. The money is *poof!*
A crowd assembles; emotions are high. The police come to break it up. We split into the subway.

Three weeks later *The New York Times* reports: "The New York Stock Exchange last night installed bullet-proof glass panels and a metal grillwork ceiling on its visitors' gallery for what an exchange spokesman said were 'reasons of security.'
"Last August 24 a dozen or so hippies threw dollar bills from the gallery—a display many exchange members do not want to see repeated."[14]

Rubin's method is political theater, in which it is essential for the audience to participate in the staging of their own myths. By participating in the Amerikan myth, the yippies succeeded in making Amerika strange to itself in ways that the politics of alienation and withdrawal could never do. "Up against yourselves, motherfuckers." Rubin gathered the Coca-Cola tribes of Amerika in the cities, in the streets, and in the parks in order to resurrect the body politic. What they exposed was not themselves but the obscenity of the American dream turned on to radios, pop-up toasters, and the Huntley-Brinkley Report.

These observations, however, imply no endorsement whatsoever of the use of biological metaphors that propose violence as the cure for a sick society, sick with white guilt and black rage. Violence may serve as a means to the dramatization of the political condition, but the risk in resorting to violence is that it proposes itself as a solution to racial and ethnic differences to which liberal society refuses to give a genuine political definition. So long as these interests lack the vocabulary of class politics, violence can be reduced to crimes against property as a purely criminal or police concern. The anti-political character of violence regarded from the standpoint of law and order in turn feeds back into anti-political violence, driving racial violence into terrorism in ever more desperate attempts to expose the political and social segregation of the issues of poverty, race, and war. This cycle is only aggravated where the establishment power is organized in bureaucracies that increasingly privatize the contexts of meaning and action at the expense of the political realm. The result is a certain pathological symbiosis between bureaucratic rationality and the resort to vocabularies of creative violence, to internal migration, and to communal utopias which destroy genuine political speech and public action.

Bureaucracy destroys the political realm because it treats individuality as equality: it thereby destroys the sense of "individuality" as the uniqueness that brings into being the necessity for human speech and expression. Bureaucracy stylizes differences as fads or fashions, thus creating the political paradox of conformist freedoms. Corporate capitalism in particular parodies human initiative through the engineering of responses to the inevitability of annual novelties. It drowns the question of who a man is in the litanies of what he has or what he can acquire in order to construct an image. These effects of bureaucracy are perfectly geared to the liberal minimization of the public realm of common action—a realm that was once inspired by collective identity and a tradition in which character and history interwove. The modern world systematically destroys the spatial and temporal dimensions of public conduct through the privatization of the resources of action and of public discourse.

This is a condition which, as I have tried to show from her earlier argument, Miss Arendt attributes to the "labor movement," that is to say, to the subordination of politics to economics. However, it is essential to see that her argument is not confined to a critique of Marxist knowledge but rather aims at the very foundations of Western political knowledge. In her analysis of the crisis of authority, Miss Arendt shows how the problem of violence is inherent in the philosophical basis of political knowledge in the Platonic or utopian tradition. The historical source of the crisis of authority lies in the tension between the authority of philosophical knowledge and the violence of the rule of technical knowledge. She argues that Plato's experience of the hostility of the *polis* toward philosophy as he witnessed it in the death of Socrates drove him to invent a standard of knowledge built upon the hierarchy of the ruler-ruled relationship, which in the Greek experience was a pre-political relationship. To achieve this standard of knowledge, Plato was obliged to subordinate the first city, in which the body politic is ruled by the Form of the Beautiful, to the politics of the second city, ruled by an expert politics based upon the Form of the Good and the sanctions of the Er-myth.

The vocation of western knowledge for domination establishes modern science as the paradigm of social and political knowledge. Its behavioral assumptions invent plausible utopias of colossal world violence and destruction, while alienating the human responses of outrage and violence as appeals against their injustice and insanity. The *Report from Iron Mountain*[15] is in many ways a paradigm (as well as a parody) of the modern literature on violence and of the objectivity of liberal scholarship that Chomsky has attacked in his *American Power and the New Mandarins*. It is a recipe for the production of domestic and international violence—the blueprint for numerous other scenarios of collective psychosis, bloodletting, ecological destruction, and faceless cynicism. The *Report* represents the last stage in the development of the literature of violence from the primal scenes of victim and assailant to the impersonal, modern landscapes of violence of which the concentration camp is the perfect image. In the escalation of modern violence, the agents, whether aggressor or victim, are less essential to the

action than the massive horror constituted by the very scene of
the action—the landscape as violence.

Modern techniques of violence are of such an enormous
scope and impersonality that it strains every metaphor of language by which we might tie events to their authors and victims.
In turn, there is less in the action to report since there is no one
to speak about. The scene of violence—the camp, the bombed
area, the riot—overwhelm the categories of character, intentionality, and action so that not even the writer can situate
himself, far less construct a conventional story. There remains
only the author's guilt over his own survival, which reduces his
language to the barest medium of tactual account. Modern armies obliterate a village or town before they can enter it, and
when they do, the village is empty or littered with dead and
maimed bodies with no other story to tell than the ravages of
overkill and napalm whose meaning is reduced to the scene
itself. As Frederick J. Hoffman puts it in his *The Mortal No*:

> The final stage in the literature of violence describes the assailant
> as landscape; it is not only dehumanized, but chaotic. As in the
> Guernica painting of Picasso, the bodies and sensibilities are
> twisted, misshapen, and fragmented, and they blend with the
> contours of the blasted landscape. In such a setting man relies on
> neither courage nor a sense of the right, but upon a busy (even at
> times, a frenetic) earnestness to define himself. In his soul are
> contained both the energy of the assailant and the masochistic
> receptivity of the victim.[16]

Modern violence destroys human time and human space; its
aim is sheer obliteration, whether through genocide, overkill, or
defoliation. The modern literature of violence is forced to dwell
upon the bits and pieces of the world that are all that remains of
man himself. We must understand what Erich Kahler calls the
"new factism" in modern sensibility as a re-invention of language through the reconstitution of the deed and its relation to
the assailant and victim. Mass violence reduces writing to the
zero point of factual description because of the need to reestab-
lish the bonds between action and responsibility, suffering and
understanding. Once the new factism has passed through this
zero point, then it may once again make possible genuine metaphor and poetry, and thus save language from delirium. But
there can be no question of starting with poetry or science
before the claims of our humanity are set down in plain lan-

guage. We cannot expect to endure the burning of our cities and the destruction of minds and bodies and still expect our language to escape these ravages.

Language is the soul of our lives together. Today we must work to restore language, to speak where violence puts an end to speech. Miss Arendt's essay *On Violence* begins the work of renewing political speech, of defining its basic words and the contexts of public and private usage which generate their meaning. In this task the only resources we have are the same words which condemn a man to death, or to prejudice and exploitation. There are times when words must take refuge in songs, jokes, and prayers. But the soul of language is never broken while men still have on their lips the words "freedom," "justice," "faith," and "revolution."

It is in times like these that we need our poets, that we need to dramatize political life, for we cannot entrust cultural revolution solely to Marxists and social scientists. Some will prefer the cool, clear voice of a Chomsky and his merciless exposure of the behavioralist assumptions in the logic of the American war in Vietnam. Each of us, however, must speak on these things as we can, with an honest intention to discern in the present some hope for the future, some hope for the renewal of love's body.

As I see it, the eroticism of modern economic and political life is the fundamental feature of the major events or happenings of the body politic. The counterparts of the happy, healthy, integrated executive and his suburban family are the long-haired visionaries of flowers and rainbows who are the soul brothers in the sit-ins, lunch-ins, ride-ins and love-ins that are the renewal of the libidinal body politic. The phenomena of violence in the ghettos, mass demonstrations, and sit-ins in the offices of authority are all grounded in the basic logic of the body politic not to endure the unendurable, not to suffer inhuman denials of recognition, and in ultimate crises to "come together" so that the authorities can "see" what they are doing to the people. The underlying logic is a logic of demonstration that is pre-ideological: it rests upon the simple faith that men have in the renewal of justice and community. It contains a simple logic that challenges the constitutional authority of the body politic. For once, the injustice of life in the ghetto goes beyond the limits of tolerance; then the ghetto becomes a natural armory of stones, bottles, sticks, and crowds with which to beat the conventional police system. Once the inanity of administrative authority is exposed, it is defenseless against the belly-laugh, the clap-in or sing-in. Where is the official who will explain to children and to young men and women with flowers the necessity of the war that will cripple them or blow them to bits?

It may be that we are engaged in a new meta-politics in which the Burkean identification of temporality and political community is destroyed in the politics of the generation gap and the street happenings of what Leslie Fiedler calls the "new mutants."[17] The new style of political demonstration destroys the *polis* as an organization of need and wants, of life and against death, by pushing death into the erotic economy of male-female, black-white, rich-poor, expert-layman organization. The politics of unisex, nudity, camp, and pop art exhibit the reversibility of organization, artist and audience, leader and mass, whose own self-improvisation and abandonment is the supreme anti-political act.

The flight from *polis* to *thiasos* is at the same time a new direction of political knowledge which surpasses the Victorian misgivings of Lionel Tiger's genetic code of male-bonding no less than Fiedler's own anxiety over the post-Jewish antics of the anti-male. The new politics is Dionysian, achieving form only in the moment of self-destruction. Because it maintains control through improvisation, the new politics cannot presume upon any rationalization or ideological interpretation of sensory experience. Its audience is therefore part of the art, the music, the lesson, and the political platform. The new politics invents a destruction of vicarious experience through becoming children, playing with toys, dressing up, mocking, loving, and raging in the streets. Its destruction of vicarious experience is simultaneously the creation of community groups, circles, and games in which experience is opened to feeling, magic, and mysticism in the search for a workable and communicable truth. The way of this truth is often stark and violent. It differs from the established truth in its search to become a truth—a search founded upon the gift and the exigency of the human body.

# Notes

[1] John O'Neill, "Authority, Knowledge and the Body Politic," *Southern Journal of Philosophy* 8 (1970): 225–64. I have drawn on this essay at various points in the present argument.

[2] Hannah Arendt, *On Violence* (New York: Harcourt, Brace & World, 1970).

[3] Hannah Arendt, "What Is Authority?" in *Between Past and Future: Eight Exercises in Political Thought* (New York, Viking Press, 1968).

[4] Hannah Arendt, *The Human Condition* (Chicago: University of Chicago Press, 1958), p. 153.

[5] Arendt, *On Violence*, p. 6.

[6] See John O'Neill, "History as Human History in Hegel and Marx," in Jean Hyppolite, *Studies on Marx and Hegel*, trans. with notes and bibliog. by John O'Neill (New York: Basic Books, 1969).

[7] Herbert Marcuse, *Five Lectures: Psychoanalysis, Politics and Utopia,* trans. Jeremy J. Shapiro and Shierry M. Weber (Boston: Beacon Press, 1970).

[8] Arendt, *The Human Condition*, p. 97.

[9] John O'Neill, "Public and Private Space," in *Agenda 1970: Proposals for a Creative Politics*, ed. T. Lloyd and J. T. McLeod (Toronto: University of Toronto Press, 1968), pp. 74–93.

[10] Frantz Fanon, *The Wretched of the Earth*, trans. Constance Farrington, preface by Jean-Paul Sartre (New York: Grove Press, 1968).

[11] Jerry Rubin, *Do It!: Scenarios of the Revolution*, intro. by Eldridge Cleaver (New York: Simon & Schuster, 1970), pp. 109–10.

[12] Norman O. Brown, *Love's Body* (New York: Random House, Vintage Books, 1966), p. 137; Brown quotes William Blake, *Jerusalem*, pl. 69, lines 39–44.

[13] Herbert Marcuse, "Love Mystified: A Critique of Norman O. Brown," and Norman O. Brown, "A Reply to Herbert Marcuse," in Herbert Marcuse, *Negations: Essays in Political Theory,* trans. Jeremy J. Shapiro (Boston: Beacon Press, 1968).

[14] Rubin, *Do It!* pp. 117–19.

[15] Leonard C. Lewin (pseud.), *Report from Iron Mountain: On the Possibility and Desirability of Peace* (New York: Dial Press, Dell Publishing Co., 1967).

[16] Frederick J. Hoffman, *The Mortal No: Death and the Modern Imagination* (Princeton; Princeton University Press, 1964).

[17] Leslie A. Fiedler, "The New Mutants," *Partisan Review* 32 (1965): 505–25.

# Violence, Legal Sanctions, and Law Enforcement

ROBERT AUDI has taught at the University of Nebraska—Lincoln and the University of Texas at Austin. He studied at Colgate University and the University of Michigan, where he received the Ph.D. in 1967. He was a Woodrow Wilson Fellow and is a member of Phi Beta Kappa. In 1970, Professor Audi was a co-winner of the Council for Philosophical Studies essay competition on the subject of violence. His numerous articles and reviews in philosophy are principally on the topics of violence, the philosophy of action, and the philosophy of the social sciences.

# Violence, Legal Sanctions, and Law Enforcement

## by Robert Audi

Violence is one of the most commonly deplored phenomena of modern life. Nearly everyone would like to reduce or eliminate it. But there is very little consensus on just what constitutes violence. People differ widely in the examples of violence they single out for attention, and there is bitter controversy over what should be done to reduce violence, whether in the streets of our cities or in foreign countries in which we have diplomatic commitments or financial interests. My concern, however, will not be with violence in American foreign policy, nor even directly with violence in America. I shall explore two more general questions, neither of which seems to have received adequate attention in recent discussions of violence. In a democratic society, what role should legal sanctions have in controlling violence? And what role, if any, should violence play in law enforcement in a democracy? The notion of a democratic society is far from clear. To say that a democratic society is one in which political power lies ultimately with the people is only a beginning. But this rough notion will suffice in this paper, and for convenience I shall simply assume that contemporary American society can be taken as an example of a democracy. I shall also assume—though this is not entailed by the concept of a democracy—that a democratic society aims at being a free society, at least in the minimal sense that its laws prohibit only certain actions which would, or might, harm someone other than the agent.

29

The first part of the paper will attempt to clarify the notion of violence. This is especially important because the notion seems to be often distorted or unwarrantedly extended. Without some clarification of it, the kinds of moral, social, and legal questions I want to take up cannot be satisfactorily answered. Part II will pursue the question of what legal sanctions it is reasonable to institute in a democratic society for the purpose of controlling violence. And Part III will be devoted to the question of what rules should govern the use, if any, of violence in law enforcement.

## I.  DIMENSIONS OF VIOLENCE

Except possibly in the waging of war, most violence to persons or property violates someone's moral rights. This, together with the verbal and etymological kinship of 'violence' and 'violation', makes it natural to suppose that the notion of violation of at least one moral right is part of the concept of violence. Thus, one writer has held that

> Violence at its root definition is any violation of the basic human rights of a person. These violations can be social, economic, moral and political.[1]

A similar notion is proposed by Newton Garver, who holds that "What is fundamental about violence is that a person is violated," and that "violence in human affairs amounts to violating persons," where the violation may be "personal or institutionalized," "overt or covert."[2] F. C. Wade also seems to think that violence entails some kind of violation. He says that some form of "infringement" is "a factor" in violence, the other factor being "strong force."[3] Neither Garver nor Wade does much to clarify the concepts of violation or infringement. It is not clear whether, for Garver, violation of a person entails the violation of at least one moral right, nor whether, for Wade, infringement of, say "the holiness of a church, or the sovereignty of a country" (Wade's examples) entails such violation. But they talk as though they believe this entailment holds.

Even if it should be true, however, that violence entails the violation of at least one moral right, it does not clearly follow that it is never justified. For it would seem that sometimes one moral right conflicts with another and overrides it, and, if so, the action which is in accord with the overriding right would be justified though it violates the second right. For instance, perhaps Smith's moral right to a fair trial could conflict with and override Jones' moral right to mention, in a conversation with a juror in the case, non-defamatory details of Jones' past relations with Smith. The former right might override the latter where the details in question, though non-defamatory, would tend to influence the juror. I state these points guardedly because one can plausibly argue that Jones' right to mention such non-defamatory details is only conditional and does not extend to cases of the sort envisaged, since the right might hold only on the condition that mentioning the details violates no other moral right. One can extend this reasoning to all cases of apparently conflicting moral rights and thus argue that no moral right is ever overriden by another: instead, ostensibly conflicting moral rights simply limit one another's scope. This seems to me less plausible than supposing that some moral rights can override others; but I shall not try to settle the issue here, nor is it clear that it is of great significance. My point is simply that unless we have reason to think that the notion of violation of a right is taken by Garver, Wade, and others to entail that the action in question is unjustified, we should not conclude that they believe violence is by definition unjustified.

Some philosophers do seem to believe this, however. For example, Robert Paul Wolff maintains that "Strictly speaking, *violence is the illegitimate or unauthorized use of force to effect decisions against the will of others.*" Wolff does not mean by 'illegitimate or unauthorized' simply 'illegal or forbidden'. He says that "on this interpretation the concept of violence is normative as well as descriptive, for it involves an implicit appeal to the principle of *de jure* legitimate authority."[4] Thus, for Wolff it appears that violence is by definition unjustified. Nor is this view uncommon.[5]

I want now to assess the above characterizations of violence. I shall argue that (1) so far as one can gather what is meant by the somewhat metaphorical notion of violation of a person, even violence to persons does not entail violation of a person; (2) violence does not entail, though it usually involves, violation of at least one moral right; and (3) violence is not by definition unjustified, though *most* forms of it are prima facie unjustified.

In connection with (1), we should first of all bear in mind that violence may be done to animals and inanimate objects. But presumably Garver was simply ignoring this in saying that

violation of persons is fundamental in violence. Yet his claim
seems too strong even as applied to interpersonal violence.
Imagine two friends wrestling vigorously though by the standard
collegiate rules. They throw each other about furiously and
sometimes fall to the mat with a loud thud. They are engaged in
violence, yet neither need be injured or even suffer pain. Under
these circumstances, surely, neither need "violate" the other.
There is a distinction between merely doing something violently,
e.g. shouting with furious but harmless gestures, and on the
other hand *doing violence to* someone or something. One might
argue, then, that neither wrestler does violence to the other and
that it is doing violence *to* someone which entails violating him.
But imagine that one of the wrestlers is far superior to the other
and throws him around violently, repeatedly thrusting him hard
against the mats, though without injuring him. Here it becomes
plausible to say that the superior wrestler is doing violence to
the other. But it is not plausible to say he violates him. This is
partly because the latter has consented to the match and implicitly to its continuation, and partly because none of his rights
is being violated.

If I am correct in thinking that violation of at least one of a
person's moral rights is a necessary condition for "violating"
him, then the many forms of violence that seem justified in self-
defense, e.g. punching a would-be mugger, are also cases of
doing violence to someone yet not cases of violating that person. It is true that often, and especially in such figurative
phrases as 'do violence to the poem' and 'do violence to his
good name', the expression 'do violence to' is used with the
implication that there is a violation of either a moral right or
some other standard of correctness. This makes it initially
strange to say that one can do violence to a person without
violating him (or his moral rights). But that one can is surely
evident when one reflects on the great force and vigor with
which, say, a boxer's punch can be delivered. To say that such
things are merely acting violently is to ignore the violence that is
suffered; and surely if violence is suffered by someone at the
hands of another, it is done by the latter to the former. I conclude that violence, even doing violence to someone, does not
entail violating him. Nor does the latter entail the former, since
one may violate a person by injecting a heavy sedative into him
against his will, even if one does so with a tiny and virtually
imperceptible needle, and with a gentleness quite untinged by
violence.

But let us not dwell on the vague notion of violating a person. I want now to show that violence does not entail the violation of at least one moral right, not even when the violence is done to a person. My examples of vigorous collegiate wrestling and of punching in self-defense seem to me to show this. But there is a different way to make the point. If we leave aside secondary senses of 'violence', such as those illustrated by violence to someone's character or an interpretation's doing violence to a poem, it seems that the notion of violence is an observational notion. That is, roughly speaking, whether violence is being done by a particular agent, at a given time, to a particular person or object, can be ascertained, if at all, by closely observing what the agent is doing at that time with respect to that person or object (there will be borderline cases because the notion of violence is vague, but this applies even to such paradigmatic observation terms as 'red', 'bitter', and 'smooth'). We need not postulate any reason why the agent is doing violence, nor need we interpret his behavior in terms of a rule, such as a moral rule to the effect that one ought not to beat people. But clearly the notion of violating a moral right is not observational in this way: to know whether, in doing $A$, someone is violating a moral right, we must typically know, or at least have good reason to believe, more than can be grasped simply from closely observing the action. The following contrasts illustrate the distinction between violence as an observational notion and the violation of a moral right as a non-observational notion. If, upon rounding a corner, we see one man sharply club another, we know he is doing the other violence; but since we might have no idea just from closely observing the clubbing by itself whether it is an unavoidable act of self-defense or, say, an act of aggression, we do not know whether it violates the sufferer's moral rights. And if we glimpse a man forcefully slapping a woman's face, we know he is doing violence to her; but since for all we know he may be arresting a fit of hysteria in the only way anyone knows how in her case, we do not know whether he is violating any of her rights, and as in the case of the clubbing we may not (from a very brief look) even have *good reason* to believe the sufferer's moral rights are being violated. Or, consider an example cited in the *Random House Dictionary*: "to take over a government by violence." Surely one could arrive in Saigon just as a contingent of citizens were taking over the government by violence and know by mere observation that they are doing violence; but clearly it is a *further* question whether they are violating anyone's rights in using that violence. But if the writer of the Random House entry were correct and violence (in the sense that occurs in the example) were by definition (morally) unjustified, then it would be contradictory to say they were justified in taking over the government by violence. Thus, if we saw them doing violence it *could* not be a further question whether they were violating anyone's rights.

The point is not that the applicability of an observational notion cannot entail the applicability of a non-observational notion. For the applicability of 'burning', which is an observation term, entails the applicability of 'flammable', which is not an observation term. But in cases like this, the terms are related in a special way: the non-observation term simply designates the disposition to manifest the event or process which the observation term designates, so of course the latter entails the former. But many non-observation terms, including "violation of a moral right", are not related to any observation terms in this simple way. Violation of a moral right is not a disposition, on the part of the violating agent, to manifest some one observable event or process, nor to perform one or more acts of violence. Indeed, it is not a disposition at all. But my argument is not that violence does not entail the violation of any moral right just because the former is an observational notion and the latter not. This contrast merely supports my main argument, since it appears that except in the kind of case just cited the applicability of an observation concept does not entail the applicability of a non-observation concept. The main argument is that if violence by definition entailed the violation of at least one moral right, then we could not know just from closely observing an act whether it is an act of violence; for most acts of violence are such that what we can know just from closely observing them leaves open the question whether they violate anyone's moral rights. But what we can know from closely observing them does *not* leave open the question whether they constitute violence. If violence by definition entailed the violation of at least one moral right, then once we observed that an act was one of violence, it could not be an open question whether it violated any moral rights, any more than, once we know that an animal is a vixen, it is an open question whether it is female.

It may be that some violent acts do necessarily violate the victim's rights, e.g. flogging an infant. If so, then merely observing such an act would suffice to tell us that it violates at least one moral right. But few acts are such that merely observing just those acts suffices to establish that they violate a moral right; and most acts of violence, including some that do violate moral rights, are not of this sort.

One might argue, however, that just as some violations of moral rights can be known simply from observing the acts constituting the violation, some cases of doing violence are not observable. Suppose, for example, that one sees a man push a button which causes the dynamiting of a building. One would not know from observing him push the button that he is doing violence. This objection is irrelevant to my thesis, which is that whether or not a particular action, $A$, constitutes doing violence to someone or something is ascertainable by closely observing the agent's doing of $A$ (where closely observing implies observing from a suitable distance and angle, and under suitable conditions). In the above case one observes the agent's pressing of the button but not his destroying the building, which is the violent act. It is not the *same* act as his pushing the button; for the latter act is a means to, and is completed before, the former. To observe the agent's destroying the building, one would not only have to see the agent push the button; one would also have to perceive the destruction of the building, knowing it was caused by the agent's pushing the button. And if one observed all this, one would know the agent was doing violence, even if one had no idea whether he was violating anyone's rights.

It is not important here to develop the notion of observing an action. My distinction between observational and non-observational notions is intended mainly to help *explain* why doing violence does not entail the violation of at least one moral right. *That* the entailment does not hold is shown by the examples I have given and diverse others. Now it seems clear that the same sorts of cases show that neither violence simpliciter, nor even doing violence to someone or something, is by definition unjustified. For just as we can know whether an action we are closely observing is a case of violence while it is an open question whether or not it violates any moral rights, we can know whether an action we are closely observing is a case of violence while it is an open question whether or not the action is justified. If this can be plausibly denied, it is only on the assumption that, *independently* of the claim that violence is by definition unjustified, all acts of violence are unjustified. But this assumption is surely unreasonable. At least in certain kinds of self-defense, such minimal violence as shoving the aggressor away is sometimes justified. Even if one is unqualifiedly dedicated to the idea that we should turn the other cheek, it is not clear that this doctrine rules out all forms of violence in all cases of self-defense. But if it does, then it is simply not plausible for our world, however appropriate it might be on the eve of the Day of Judgment, when all such sacrifices are to be rewarded.

Perhaps there are some people who are careful not to speak of violence being done to someone unless they believe his moral rights are being violated. But not everyone talks this way; and I suspect that even if one resolves to use the term 'violence' this way, it would be difficult to hold to the resolution or to have one's meaning generally understood. For the word 'violence' has many central uses in which violation of moral rights is clearly not entailed, and these uses would constantly tend to exert an influence on one's special use of 'violence'. These central uses would be particularly likely to alter one's special use of the term if the accused perpetrator of violence were oneself.

There is an important reason why I am so concerned to refute the view that violence is by definition unjustified. This is that the view paves the way for a callous disregard for the enormous amount of violence that most people think is justified. This includes domestic violence done in the name of the law, and violence abroad done in the course of purportedly just wars. I am not saying that most such officially sanctioned violence is unjustified. The point is that it *is* violence, and since so much violence is not justified and causes great suffering, most violence is at least prima facie unjustified and the word itself has connotations that lead people to question the justifiability of the actions to which they apply it. Thus, so far as one thinks violence is by definition unjustified and that what one's government does is by and large justified, one finds it that much easier to give a neutral or even misleading description to what is really extreme violence: violence by police is, say, "rigorous law enforcement"; and napalming may be just "protective reaction." And since the enemy abroad and violators of the law at home are thought of as *not* justified, it tends to be they who are singled out as perpetrators of violence. One can thus easily come to be neither adequately self-critical nor adequately critical of those one tends to approve of.

To be sure, the realization that violence is not necessarily unjustified might lead some people to dismiss as acceptable some violence that ought not to be done. But this is unlikely to be the result of accepting such a weak thesis as that violence is not *necessarily* unjustified, particularly when it is realized that it typically *is* unjustified. By contrast, if we accept the strong thesis that violence is by definition unjustified, then we cannot ask such questions as "Should we be using violence in Southeast Asia?" since what is unjustified should of course not be done. But surely such questions are both intelligible and important.

But if there are dangers in taking the notion of violence too narrowly, there are also dangers in taking it too broadly. For instance, Garver says that

> There is more violence in the black ghettos than anywhere else in America—even when the ghettos are quiet. . . . A black ghetto in American society operates very like any system of slavery. Relatively little overt violence is needed to keep the institution going, and yet the institution violates the human beings involved because they are systematically denied the options given to the vast majority in America.[6]

There are also many who, as Wolff says, "will defend rent strikes, grape boycotts, or lunch counter sit-ins with the argument that unemployment and starvation are a form of violence also."[7] This statement is especially to the point because it indicates both that some people regard even (non-violent) strikes, boycotts, and sit-ins as violence (presumably because they seem to be unjustified uses of force), and that others regard starvation and unemployment as violence when these seem to them to be caused by certain kinds of injustice. Garver, for example, seems to think that white society is doing violence to blacks insofar as it unjustly maintains conditions under which they cannot achieve equal opportunity with whites.

Now it seems to me that these institutionalized violations of human beings Garver speaks of—meaning such things as widespread inequalities in opportunity—should be called injustices; and the unemployment and starvation Wolff mentions may be forms or results of unjust economic arrangements. These various injustices may be as serious as most forms of violence; but they are different from violence, and it confuses the issue to use the emotively loaded word 'violence' when the grievance can be better described and treated under another name. The term 'injustice' also has much emotive force; but those who want to call (non-violent) injustices violence *also* tend to apply the term 'injustice', so the use of 'violence' here is often not an alternative, but an addition to what is already heated discourse. More important, if such things as (non-violent) social injustice are

termed violence by their critics, this opens up the possibility
that, at least some of the time, their charges will be dismissed as
unfounded by those who point out, rightly, that little or no
violence is being done in the disputed cases. Misnaming the
disease can lead to the use of the wrong medicine—or none at
all.

If discussions of violence are not to ignore much of what
governments do in the name of protection of their people, or on
the other hand, to spill over into the broad area of social justice,
then we need a definition of 'violence' which enables us to avoid
both the tendency—especially common among conservatives
and reactionaries—to regard as violence only what are believed
to be unjustified uses of force, and the tendency—especially
common among liberals and radicals—to apply the term 'violence' to a host of non-violent, though, in their view, serious,
social injustices. Conservatives, it seems, tend to miss some
salient perpetrations of violence in the world; liberals tend to
find more violence than there is.

Our definition must also take account of something we have
not so far mentioned: psychological violence. Clearly a person
can do violence to someone (or even to an animal) by sufficiently vigorous and highly caustic verbal abuse. Psychological
violence may also take the form of piercing verbal attacks on
someone's sensitive spots. It may take the form of a loud, vehe-
ment, nerve-shattering recitation of a person's failures. And
there are other forms.[8] The following definition of doing violence is meant to capture both psychological and physical violence:

> Violence is the physical attack upon, or the vigorous physical
> abuse of, or vigorous physical struggle against, a person or ani-
> mal; or the highly vigorous psychological abuse of, or the sharp,
> caustic psychological attack upon, a person or animal; or the
> highly vigorous, or incendiary, or malicious and vigorous, de-
> struction or damaging of property or potential property.[9]

The "core" notion in this definition is that of vigorous abuse:
all the cases that fit the definition either involve vigorous abuse
or at least suggest a fairly clear potential for it. This core notion
helps to capture what is valuable in Garver's idea that violation
of a person is fundamental in violence to persons; for typically
—though not always—vigorously abusing a person does in
some sense violate him. The definition also helps to explain why

we consider violence prima facie unjustified; for clearly, attacking or vigorously abusing persons, and even most violent destructions of property, are prima facie unjustified. Yet the definition does not entail that doing violence is unjustified, or even that doing it entails violations of any moral rights. The definition has several points of serious vagueness, though this seems unavoidable given the vagueness of the notion of violence itself. I shall not have space to take up further problems in the analysis of violence, but the definition will be adequate for the discussion to follow.

## II. VIOLENCE AND LEGAL SANCTIONS

Suppose that someone observing a noisy political rally from his window were to say, in disgust at the pushing, yelling, and fist-raising, "Why don't we just outlaw violence?" A moment's reflection makes it clear that this would be unreasonable, at least in a democratic society. For this would prohibit boxing, wrestling, football, and even violence done in self-defense. It would also excessively restrict law-enforcement officers. Nevertheless, violence is both so widely deplored and so often destructive that it is worth asking whether there are at least some forms of it which should be singled out by the law and made punishable.

It is true that many kinds of acts of violence are already prohibited by the laws of most nations, though mainly because they are, say, harmful, rather than mainly because they are violent. But often a given wrongful act, such as kidnaping, violates more than one law, for example both state and Federal laws; and other acts, such as obstructing traffic, might be illegal both under that name and because they fall within the scope of another law, prohibiting disorderly conduct. This kind of legal overdetermination of an offense could be argued to be an advantage both in law enforcement and in deterrence. Such an argument for illegalizing certain forms of violence so designated might be supported by the claim that current laws, in America at least, are insufficient to give law-enforcement agencies the power they need to control violence. Thus, it is well worth asking whether legal sanctions against certain forms of violence should be instituted, even if most or all of the acts proscribed are already punishable under some other law.

One might think we could at least outlaw non-defensive, non-athletic *bodily* violence to persons. But this proposal will not bear scrutiny. Presumably there are such people as masochists, and they might enjoy having certain kinds of bodily violence, such as whippings, inflicted on them. One might try to deal with this case by making an exception of "consensual" bodily violence, i.e., bodily violence to which the sufferer has consented. But this will not do. For one thing, outlawing non-athletic, non-defensive, non-consensual bodily violence would tend to give the impression that all consensual bodily violence was legally permissible. Yet some of it, for example that resulting in death or certain injuries, should surely be illegal even if the sufferer has consented to it knowing its probable consequences. It would be very difficult, however, to specify with adequate clarity what these excepted dangerous acts are. Moreover, suppose one person knows through a second that a third, who is an acquaintance of both, enjoys a certain kind of bodily violence, say being vigorously thrown around. If the first then throws around the third, who enjoys this and makes no protest, should the former be liable to prosecution because the latter has not consented to the abuse? Surely not. We may say that the third person *would* have consented and that 'consensual bodily violence' could be construed as bodily violence to which the sufferer consented *or* would have consented had he been asked. But this is dangerously vague, and it might be abused by some who want to fight at the first hint that their victim *would* consent. Moreover, even if we could specify a form of consensual bodily violence with mild enough effects to make it a reasonable exception to the proposed prohibition of bodily violence, any such law would surely infringe on the segment of private behavior that should be the business of individuals and not the law. Suppose that during a family quarrel a woman becomes angry with her husband and sharply slaps his face. Should this be considered a violation of the law, because the husband, though forgiving, would not have consented to it?

A further difficulty for the proposed illegalization of non-athletic, non-defensive bodily violence is the vagueness of even the notions of defensive and athletic bodily violence. Suppose that someone delivers a series of the most scathing and demeaning insults to an inarticulate person who then, in speechless rage, clamps his hand over the former's mouth to stop him. Is this defensive violence? Or should the victim have fled the scene and avoided physical contact? And when two boys who are competing for leadership in the neighborhood voluntarily engage in a serious but "clean" wrestling match on the ball field, is that athletic violence, or would they be violating the law we are imagining? It would be easy for these and similar cases to be construed as violations of the kind of law we are considering. But even if they represent behavior that is undesirable or even immoral, in a democracy they should probably not be subject to legal sanctions. It appears, then, that the notion of bodily violence is simply too vague to be a basis for imposing legal sanctions in a democracy. To be sure, many of our laws are vaguely worded. But few are as vague as a prohibition of bodily violence would have to be; and it is recognized at least by most higher courts, for example the United States Supreme Court, that when certain statutes are seriously vague, they should be struck down. However many seriously vague laws remain in democratic societies, we should try not to add to their number.

One might think that we could at least introduce a statute prohibiting violence to property and thereby give the law additional muscle to prevent such violence. But we certainly could not simply prohibit violence to property in just those words. This would presumably make it illegal for a man to burn down, bulldoze down, or dynamite away a structure which is on his own property and which, for some good reason, he needs to dispose of quickly. Nor would it do to say instead that one may not do violence to others' property without their consent. For if this were the law, then demolition teams hired to demolish others' property would either be in danger of prosecution (in case they were allowed by the owner to demolish only non-violently) or given too much freedom (in case they were granted permission to demolish violently). For 'non-violent demolition' is terribly vague, and it would be easy for even conscientious workers to transgress the limits it might seem to impose; and 'violent demolition' surely encompasses modes of destruction far too dangerous to be legal in a modern city. We are much better off, then, with specific ordinances governing the protection and demolition of property. The notion of consensual violence to property is simply too vague to specify a form of conduct that should be prohibited by law in a democratic society.

To some people, there might seem to be better prospects for the legal use of the notion of political violence in a democracy. After all, it is widely held that in a democratic society the people govern by orderly, peaceful, electoral processes. Why, then, should we not outlaw political violence, i.e., violence aimed at changing laws or government policies, or at influencing the political process? Political violence would include such things as certain riots; forcible interferences with communication, transportation, and production; politically motivated incendiarism; and perhaps certain kinds of obstructive picketing. What right do people have to use such means of achieving political or social change when there are electoral and other peaceful procedures of achieving such change?

It seems to me that even if there were a way to specify all the offenses which a prohibition of political violence would be intended to prevent, and even if it were reasonable in a democratic society to prohibit all those offenses, it would still be unreasonable to institute a "political violence act." For even if we restrict the notion of violence in accordance with the definition I have proposed, the concept is still liable to unwarranted extension. However clear we make the offenses listed under the heading of political violence, so long as we do not close the list—in which case the heading would be unnecessary and a set of more specific statutes preferable—there would be a serious danger of punishing acts which should be permissible, or even protected, in a democracy. Surely there are people who would regard as political violence even a noisy political gathering with shouts and chants endorsing the proposals of the speakers. Yet clearly this kind of gathering need not constitute or produce violence and must be protected in a democratic society. Picket lines, too, would be considered political violence by some, especially some people of conservative orientation; and, as some of my quotations suggest, various purportedly unjust but non-violent policies and institutions would be considered political violence by others, especially some people of liberal or radical orientation. In general, it would be too easy for those in power to construe as political violence many forceful though non-violent tactics by their opponents.

To many, it may be obvious that no prohibition of political violence would be reasonable in a democracy. But I want to make it clear why this would be unreasonable. Moreover, there is a related point that is not so obvious. The very notion of political violence is not even a helpful category of description and assessment. This is in part because the word 'violence' is so emotively loaded that it often clouds what is at issue. But more important, the notion of political violence is, as I have tried to show, dangerously open to conflicting interpretations. Those who tend to think of violence as the unjustified use of force—and there are many who think of it thus—will tend to apply the term 'political violence' to any protest against the status quo which they think forceful and unjustified; whereas those who think of violence as extending to the perpetration of social injustice will tend to apply the term 'political violence' to various policies and (non-violent) actions aimed at maintaining social arrangements they disapprove of. For these reasons, the notion of political violence is likely to hinder opposing groups in communicating; and it is too vague and too likely to be stretched in conflicting directions to be a viable legal concept or a useful category of social criticism.

The positive point that emerges from this discussion is that in a democracy the role of the law in prohibiting dangerous behavior is primarily to proscribe certain specific acts; and in a democratic society there is far more danger of specifying them too broadly, thus making punishable acts which citizens have a right to perform, than of specifying them too narrowly, thereby requiring that new provisions be added to existing statutes. In a free and democratic society the presumption must be in favor of the liberty of the citizen, and there is usually much more danger of legislating it away than of extending it too far. It is true that a law can suffer from excessive specificity, which will limit its scope and thereby its usefulness. It may sometimes be desirable to use phrases such as 'reasonable care'. But especially in legislation that makes certain conduct punishable, phrases like 'political violence' (and indeed 'disorderly conduct') are so liable to unwarranted extension that they should generally be avoided in a democracy, in favor of clearer terms.

## III.  VIOLENCE AND LAW ENFORCEMENT

One might think that the domain of law enforcement, being considerably narrower than the area of behavior of ordinary citizens, is more likely to be one in which a democratic society could reasonably institute laws or other kinds of rules to curtail violence. Certainly this is to be hoped for. We often hear of police brutality, and whatever the extent to which it has occurred, there is evidence that police actions, in America at least, have been a major factor in setting off urban violence. This is documented in detail by the *Report of the National Advisory Commission on Civil Disorders*. It says, for example, that

Almost invariably the incident that ignites disorder arises from police action. Harlem, Watts, Newark and Detroit—all the major

outbursts of recent years—were precipitated by arrests of Negroes by white police for minor offenses.[10]

The wording of the report suggests that the police have often
used violence in making arrests in the ghettos, sometimes unnecessary violence.[11] But the report also appreciates the dilemma of police in American cities:

> One side, disturbed and perplexed by sharp rises in crime and
> urban violence, exerts extreme pressure on police for tougher law
> enforcement. Another group, inflamed against police as agents of
> repression, tends toward defiance of what it regards as order
> maintained at the expense of justice.[12]

It would surely be desirable, then, to be able to formulate some
general rules governing the use, if any, of violence in law enforcement in a democracy.

Let us first note that even in a democratic society committed
to according its members maximum freedom and high respect. it
is unlikely that law-enforcement officers can do their job if they
are never permitted to use violence. They may need it for self-
defense, to apprehend a dangerous person who would otherwise
escape, or to subdue a struggling captive. I shall not argue the
point further. The more pressing question is what sorts of restrictions on the use of violence in law enforcement should be
imposed in a democracy.

If the points made in Section II are sound, then it should be
obvious that those enforcing the law cannot reasonably be prohibited from using bodily violence or violence to property. They
should not even be expected always to abstain from homicidal
violence, e.g. in battles with snipers, since both the protection of
the public and self-defense may require it.

One possible restriction is suggested by the practice that has
been followed by police in England, namely carrying firearms
only on special assignments. But there are some democratic
countries, such as the United States, in which criminals are
already so heavily armed that even if disarmament by law-
enforcement officers would eventually reduce the level of violence, it would doubtless initially lead to increased crime, including higher police mortality. It is not clear, then, that in
countries like the United States we can reasonably impose, except on special assignments, a prohibition of violence by firearms on the part of law-enforcement officers. If we could

somehow go back to the beginning, this would seem to be a good rule, and presumably some attempt should be made to phase out the use of firearms on both sides of the law. But no major change is a realistic hope for the near future.

It may be, however, that police should follow a rule of never firing on someone unless in self-defense or because it is the only way to apprehend a dangerous person—though 'self-defense' and 'dangerous person' are sufficiently vague to make the restriction in effect dangerously broad. In any event, my chief concern is not with what rules law-enforcement officers should follow in specific segments of their official conduct, but with what general prohibitions of violence as such it might be reasonable to impose on them in a democracy.

The broadest principle that suggests itself is that in a democratic society law-enforcement officers should use violence only when and to the extent that it is necessary for either self-defense or the apprehension of an apparent lawbreaker. This presents several difficulties. For one thing, how much prima facie evidence against a person is required before he qualifies as an apparent lawbreaker? It seems impossible to say with any precision, and for that reason the principle would create a danger to citizens who, though acting within their legal rights, arouse police suspicion because of certain kinds of unconventionality. Moreover, the infringement of some laws, e.g. laws against jaywalking, is not always serious enough to justify the use of violence to apprehend the offender. The vagueness of the notion of violence also makes the principle difficult to interpret; for example, is taking a firm hold of someone and pulling him, as gingerly as possible, into a police car doing him violence? And is it necessary for his arrest, even when he refuses to enter the car when told to do so by the arresting officer? After all, it would usually be enough just to threaten violence, e.g. a clubbing, to get him to enter the car on his own. This brings out the difficulty of allowing only violence *necessary* to apprehending an apparent lawbreaker: in many cases in which violence is not necessary, the alternative, for instance a severe threat, or the use of non-violent force (for example, by gently administering a tranquilizer with a tiny needle), may be worse than the kind of minimal violence required to accomplish the arrest. It appears that even when violence is not necessary, some form of it may be *called for* as the most reasonable expedient.

It begins to look as though there is no way to control police violence by any prohibition of violence as such. It seems that we must instead count on a humane disposition and, on the other hand, specific rules in which the word 'violence' does not appear, e.g. rules forbidding firing guns into a crowd.

But the situation may be somewhat better than this. For unlike the case of the ordinary citizen, whose behavior is open-ended and can be justifiably restricted only in order to protect others from quite concrete dangers, law-enforcement officers have a set of specific tasks to carry out, in some of which we may be able to prohibit violence categorically. For instance, democratic societies should and sometimes do outlaw the use of violence (and force, too) by law-enforcement officers in obtaining confessions. Violence should also be prohibited in obtaining testimony. And there may be other areas of behavior on the part of law-enforcement officers in which violence as such should be prohibited.

Notice that we have not found a *kind* of violence which they should be prohibited from using, but rather *areas* of their official conduct in which violence of any kind should be proscribed. But perhaps there are kinds of violence that they should not use. Indeed, it may appear that they would never be justified in using *psychological violence*. If this is so, it is quite important, in part because psychological violence is often neglected, especially by advocates of "law and order," both in discussions of violence and in proposals to reduce it. There is also evidence that psychological violence on the part of police has played a significant role in generating urban violence, at least in America. For instance, the National Advisory Commission on Civil Disorders reports that such things as police harassment of interracial couples and the stopping of Negroes without obvious basis, "together with contemptuous and degrading verbal abuse, have great impact in the ghetto."[13] The Report does not mention psychological violence by name in this context, but there is little doubt that some of the abuses it cites would warrant the term.

But can psychological violence be reasonably outlawed in the practice of law-enforcement officers? A good case can be made for this. For one thing, it is not obvious how psychological violence, e.g. vigorous, caustic verbal abuse, could be required for either self-defense or the apprehension of an apparent law-breaker. And if in a democracy a person is to be treated as innocent until "proven" guilty, he should suffer no harsh treatment at all by law-enforcement officers other than that called for by self-defense or in order to apprehend him. Secondly, the indignity often caused by psychological violence to a person frequently exceeds even that caused by physical violence and should certainly be avoided. Despite the importance of these points, one can imagine cases in which law-enforcement officers might be justified in using psychological violence in self-defense. If a policeman who is in a dangerous position with respect to an armed man knows that a certain kind of violent tirade will reduce the latter to tearful helplessness, it would seem preferable for him to use this violence rather than risk the life of either of them. In similar situations, the apprehension of a dangerous person might also justify psychological violence.

There are other serious obstacles to instituting, and backing with legal sanctions, the rule that law-enforcement officers may not use psychological violence in carrying out their work. For one thing, there is the possibility that a person who is arrested is so deviant that he responds to even routine questioning by authority figures only if they prod and finally scream at him, in which case they could be accused of psychological violence. One may protest that here it is not clear that they would be doing any violence. But that brings us to the major difficulty of the proposed rule: though we do have a sense of the difference between psychological violence and mere psychological abuse or, say, the psychological intimidation that may be inevitable in some arrests, the distinction is not sharp, and a law prohibiting psychological violence would tend to jeopardize law-enforcement officers. It would probably become too easy for people arrested to argue that they had suffered psychological violence; and doubtless the psychological effects of arrest and imprisonment might be difficult—especially for sympathetic psychiatrists —to distinguish from those of psychological violence.

Certainly a principle prohibiting psychological violence in the normal assignments of law-enforcement officers would be a very good guide and should be enforced by their superiors in appropriate ways. But like the principle that law-enforcement officers should use violence only when and to the extent that self-defense or apprehension of an apparent lawbreaker calls for it, the rule is suitable only as a guide to conduct. It is too vague to merit the status of law in a democracy. In a few areas, such as those of obtaining confessions and testimony, it seems reasonable to make it illegal for law-enforcement officers to use violence as a means. Yet even here the vagueness of 'violence' makes it a less reasonable choice than 'force', though that, too, is subject to such difficulties as arise when there is a question whether the police are offering inducements for a confession, say in the form of assurances of a lighter sentence, or are really using threats, e.g. by suggesting a heavier sentence, and thus employing force.

The prohibition of violence so designated, whether in specific forms, such as psychological violence, or in particular areas of conduct, such as obtaining testimony, should probably not be backed by legal sanctions in a democracy, though other measures should of course be undertaken to reduce it. This applies even more to prohibitions of violence in the behavior of ordinary citizens than to its prohibition in law enforcement. For in the former case it is even more difficult to specify just what actions are to be ruled out, and there is even greater danger of ruling out too much.

## IV.  CONCLUSION

We began by examining various common conceptions of violence. I argued that violence, even to persons, does not entail their "violation"; that violence does not entail the violation of anyone's moral rights, though it typically does this; and that it is not by definition unjustified. I pointed out serious dangers in conceiving violence too narrowly, especially by supposing it to be by definition unjustified, and in conceiving it too broadly, especially by using 'violence' as an inflammatory term for various forms of injustice, bigotry, and hatred that are not instances of violence, however severe they may be. Positively, I suggested that violence is the physical attack upon, or the vigorous physical abuse of, or vigorous physical struggle against, a person or animal; or the highly vigorous psychological abuse of, or the sharp, caustic psychological attack upon, a person or animal; or the highly vigorous, or incendiary, or malicious and vigorous, destruction or damaging of property or potential property. I indicated some respects in which this definition is superior to others we considered; but it must still be emphasized that the notion of violence is seriously vague, and any correct definition will reflect this to some degree.

In discussing the question of what legal sanctions might, in a democracy, be instituted against violence so designated, it became clear that the concept is simply too vague, too inflammatory, and too liable to distortion to be a suitable basis for legal prohibitions. This is not to imply that, as Wolff maintains, "The concept of violence is inherently confused," since it depends for its "meaning in political discussions on the fundamental notion of legitimate authority, which is also inherently incoherent."[14] A vague concept need not be confused; and once it is seen that violence, even political violence, is not by definition unjustified, one can dismiss the argument that the concept rests on the distinction between legitimate and illegitimate authority. But though the concept of violence is not confused and is useful in certain contexts, it is both too broad and too flexible to delimit a type of conduct that should be proscribed by law. Various informal rules governing the use of violence so designated may be reasonably instituted, particularly in the domain of law enforcement. But they are too vague to merit the status of laws making certain kinds of conduct punishable. In certain kinds of civil laws, such as those indicating conditions under which contracts and wills become invalid, vagueness is less serious. I am also aware that there are criminal laws which may be about as vague as some of the prohibitions of violence I have explored. But I am certainly not supposing that all the criminal laws on the books in democratic societies are justified. I am instead pointing out some dangers of excessively vague statutes, particularly those limiting the freedom of the individual; and I suspect that these dangers are often underestimated.

If all this is true, then it would seem that, in a democratic society, at least, we cannot legislate violence away, though we can—and usually do—make illegal, under various descriptions, a great many of the acts constituting it. Beyond and alongside the enforcement of such laws, what is required to reduce the violence of life in countries like America is, I believe, something even more difficult to achieve than adequate law enforcement: the cultivation of a humane disposition on the part of both citizens and law-enforcement officers; effective channels for dealing expeditiously with grievances; and the establishment of equality of opportunity and some minimum level of well-being for all segments of society.[15]

# Notes

[1] Peter D. Riga, "Violence: A Christian Perspective," *Philosophy East and West* 19 (1969): 145; quoted by Ronald B. Miller, "Violence, Force and Coercion," in Jerome A. Shaffer, ed., *Violence* (New York: David McKay Co., 1971), p. 12.

[2] Newton Garver, "What Violence Is," *The Nation*, 24 June 1968, reprinted in Thomas Rose, ed., *Violence in America* (New York: Random House, Vintage Books, 1969), pp. 6, 7.

[3] See Francis C. Wade, "On Violence," *Journal of Philosophy* 68 (1971), esp. p. 370.

[4] Robert Paul Wolff, "On Violence," *Journal of Philosophy* 66 (1969): 606.

[5] For example, the Second Edition of *Webster's New International Dictionary* defines 'violence' as "the unjustified or unwarranted exercise of force, usually with the accompaniment of vehemence, outrage or fury." (This definition is given in the entry for 'force', with which 'violence' is there compared.) A similar idea appears in the recent *Random House Dictionary of the English Language*. Their third entry under 'violence' reads "an unjustified or unwarranted exertion of force or power, as against laws, rights, etc.: *to take over a government by violence.*"

[6] Garver, "What Violence Is," pp. 12–13.

[7] Wolff, "On Violence," p. 614.

[8] For a discussion of psychological violence, see my "On the Meaning and Justification of Violence," in Jerome A. Shaffer, ed., *Violence* (New York: David McKay Co., 1971), esp. pp. 54–55.

[9] Ibid., pp. 59–60. This definition is defended and extensively discussed in Part II of that paper. The phrase 'potential property' in the definition is meant to refer to objects that do not but could belong to someone. I should also mention that the notion of malicious destruction or damaging in the third clause should be construed as an observational notion. This would sometimes require calling destruction of property malicious when the agent did not actually act with malice. But surely we would say that someone's destruction of a museum's paintings with a blowtorch was malicious destruction, even if we never found the perpetrator and assumed nothing about his motives. The definition may need other glosses or some revision. But that is too special a task to undertake in this paper.

[10] See Otto Kerner et al., *Report of the National Advisory Commission on Civil Disorders* (New York: New York Times Co., 1968), p. 206.

[11] Ibid., esp. pp. 302–5.

[12] Ibid., p. 300.

[13] Ibid., p. 303.

[14] Wolff, "On Violence," p. 602.

[15] This paper has benefited from discussions I have had on the subject with Joseph J. Bien, Hardy E. Jones, and Robert E. Mathews.

# Satan, Evil, and Good in History

PHILIP P. HALLIE has taught at Vanderbilt University, Oxford University, and the University of California at Santa Cruz. He has served both as chairman of the Department of Philosophy and as acting director of the Institute for Advanced Studies at Wesleyan University, where he is Griffin Professor of Philosophy and Humanities. He has studied at Grinnell College, Oxford University, and Harvard University, where he was awarded the Ph.D. in 1951. Professor Hallie has received many fellowships and awards, including election to Phi Beta Kappa and appointments as Harvard Traveling Fellow, Fulbright Scholar, and Guggenheim Fellow. His many publications include the books *Maine de Biran: Reformer of Empiricism* (1959), *Scepticism, Man, and God* (1964), *The Scar of Montaigne* (1966), and *The Paradox of Cruelty* (1969).

# Satan, Evil, and Good in History

## by Philip P. Hallie

At the beginning of the prologue to *The Wife of Bath's Tale*, Chaucer has that passionate, powerful woman say: "Experience, though no authorities were in this world, is right enough for me." For thousands of years philosophers have been writing about good and evil in high abstractions; what I want to do here is to deal with good and evil in terms of experience, examples, not paper-thin philosophic terminology. Philosophers usually write about good and evil in just those terms—"good and evil": evil is an afterthought. A definition of goodness comes first; and then evil, they say, is just an *absence*, missing the bull's-eye, of goodness. But the millions of children and other innocents who were killed for religion or for power or for gold or for simple sadistic satisfaction are not an absence, not a "privation," they are hard reality, at least to the victims—the blacks, the Jews, the Gypsies, the Indians. And so let us consider evil and good (not good and evil) in terms of experience, and particularly in terms of the experience of the victims of evil, of those who have suffered harmdoing at the hands of their fellow men.

But instead of using the old philosophical terminology, let us use images *to see* this experience of evil. If philosophers are goody-goodies, looking at goodness abstractly and then dismissing the evils men do to each other, literature does just the opposite (and by literature, for the moment I mean not only novels, plays, etc., but the literature of faith, the Bibles of the world). Chaucer, I understand, tried to write a *Legend of Good*

*Women,* and couldn't finish it. I don't know how many writers have tried to write about goodness, but very few have succeeded. Literature is mainly about harmdoing, evil: the name of a novel or play is usually the name of somebody in trouble or the name of a sort of trouble, *Oedipus the King, King Lear, The Brothers Karamazov, Crime and Punishment.* If philosophers treat evil as an afterthought, the writers of literature think of it first. The plot of a play or novel is usually the story of how some people deal with the trouble in their lives.

And so let us turn to literature for help. Specifically, let us turn to the images in literature, the *pictures* of people and deeds that literature offers us. Pictures are more concrete, richer, closer to experience, and more memorable than abstract words. And let us use these images the way scientists use *models.* For instance, psychologists use the image of a theater to study people's behavior: they sometimes say that a person acts according to visual and auditory *cues,* and they say that he plays different *roles* in different situations (I am a father with regard to my children, a friend and lover with regard to my wife, a reliable colleague with regard to my fellow teachers at Wesleyan, etc.). Cues and roles—the image of the theater. Similarly, let us take some images from literature and use them for the sake of understanding our experience of evil, and see if we can get some understanding of goodness out of it, too. We'll take some images, and tell how these images can be applied to understanding experience. Then we'll talk about a vast human experience of evil and good, Nazi Germany, and apply those images mainly to this experience. Now a map has a picture, a legend, and a use. We shall take some images as our maps, offer a legend that will tell us how to use those images, and then we'll use them to understand a few massive examples of evil and good.

In a book, *The Paradox of Cruelty,* I used the image of the castle—the medieval castle of Count Dracula, actually—to understand the horrors of America's black slavery before the Civil War. Now I want to use a set of images from the Bible. I shall use a few images from the first four chapters of Genesis as maps, so to speak, or, if you will, mirrors, of evil and good—as ways of seeing the life-or-death matter of evil and good concretely. The main image will be that of the serpent in the garden of Eden, who, according to rabbinic tradition (and according to some Christian traditions, too), is Satan.

But our main character enters late, as you remember, and we must get ready for him before he twists himself around that tree and starts tempting Eve. To set the stage, let us begin with the Creation story:

> And God created great whales, and every living creature that moveth, which the waters brought forth abundantly . . . and God saw that it was good.
>
> And God blessed them, saying, Be fruitful, and multiply, and fill the waters in the seas, and let fowl multiply in the earth. . . .
>
> And God saw every thing that he had made, and, behold, it was very good. [Gen. 1:21–22, 31]

The legend for this map is: What the Jews call *ḥayyah* ("living") is good. The fullness of life is good, precious, a gift. For some people it takes imagination to see the goodness of life—and I pity you if it is beyond your powers. But Aristotle says philosophy began in wonder, and the wonder it began in must have been wonder that there is life at all—grateful wonder. Imagine or remember a moment when the air was as lively and sweet as the feeling of your own body. In "Spring," Hopkins wrote:

> Nothing is so beautiful as spring,
> When weeds in wheels shoot long and lovely and lush.
> . . . . . . . . . . . . . . . . . . . . . . . . . . . . . . . . . . . . . . . . . . . . . . . . .
> What is all this juice and all this joy?

If such positive joy evades you, imagine what it must be like to have your life slowly crushed by cancer or by the brutality of another human being. Most people I know who are not aware of the joy of living are not aware of the horror we feel when that living is being crushed out of us, sucked out of us. For many of us, we have to imagine this if we would begin to feel joy in the gift of life: we have to hold our breaths, or imagine holding our breaths, if we would know how valuable fresh air is.

But there is a bit more legend I must give you before we move into the garden. The first chapter of the Bible implies that there is no evil in the world—it is all "very good," in God's words. The killing, the eating of plants, the course of nature is "good." Before man brought evil into the world there was no evil. Nature, red in tooth and claw as it is, has the goodness of innocence. It took man to bring *evil* into the world. The Oriental peoples, especially the Hindus, see that death itself is not evil—it is part of life. Eating is part of life.

The goodness of the world is a goodness that I shall call "pure." Pure goodness has nothing to do with temptation, nothing to do with words (the serpent, Satan, will be a tempter using words to do his tempting). The goodness of a lion, a tiger, or a cat is a goodness that does not say: "This ought to be done, and despite all temptation I'll do it." Pure goodness often does not say anything: it acts, apart from all "oughts," apart from all words, apart from all temptations. It enjoys and it acts wordlessly.

Now let us move into the garden of Eden, as God gives Adam and Eve their first *mitzvah* (to use the language of the Rabbis), their first commandment:

> of the tree of the knowledge of good and evil, thou shalt not eat of it: for in the day that thou eatest thereof thou shalt surely die. [2:17]

This is the real beginning, the first important stage of the Temptation and Fall scene. God has given an "ought," a *mitzvah*, and we are out of the first chapter and into a world where pure goodness is not all there is. "Don't eat." I shall not join the many speculative people who have tried to give *the* meaning of the tree and of the knowledge of good and evil that comes from its fruit. Let others do theology; I am interested in the actions of Adam and Eve as maps for us to find our way through experience.

Now, after the "ought" and "ought not" comes the serpent (3:1–5). According to the rabbinic tradition, which I am using more than any other for hints to help us refer this model to human experience, the serpent is Satan himself. As Maimonides tells us in his *Guide of the Perplexed*, "The Hebrew *satan* is derived from the same root as *s'teh*, 'turn away' . . .; it implies the notion of seducing and moving away from a thing."[1] Satan is the seducer who tempts us to move away from the *mitzvah*, the commandment. He leads us away from the straight path. Now, according to Maimonides, the Talmud also says that Satan is the same as the evil inclinations (*yetzer ha-ra*) inside a human being. Let us brush aside the question, "Does Satan exist outside of us as personal, actual being?", and read these five little verses as referring to the inclinations within human beings (whatever there may be outside them in the form of demons shaped like snakes or goats or terrifying men). Our interest is in this "turning away" tendency in man, the tendency to turn away from a commandment, the tendency to be tempted.

Now if you look at those verses you will see that temptation has two major aspects: let us call them "objective temptation" and "subjective temptation." Objective temptation is *what* it is that tempts—the object and the seductive arguments that draw you to turn away from the *mitzvah*. (Later we shall talk of the subjective temptation, the feeling that one should turn away from the command.) In the garden, the object was of course the fruit of that tree (a fig, according to some rabbis). The seductive arguments, the tempting words that the serpent utters to Eve, involve the serpent's claim that God will not in fact kill them if they eat of the fruit:

> And the serpent said unto the woman, Ye shall not surely die:
> For God doth know that in the day ye eat thereof, then your eyes shall be opened, and ye shall be as gods, knowing good and evil. [3:4–5]

The seductive arguments minimize the danger and maximize the happy effects of eating that fruit. What they do is promise that "Ye shall be as gods" with power to do whatever you want to do. In the rabbinic tradition the main temptation of Eve was to rival, even displace, God—the temptation to be proud and to determine by command matters of life and death, good and evil.

One day a woman in Lille, France, happened to be standing at her open window when Hitler was coming by in triumph. *"Voilà le Diable!"* ("Behold the Devil"), she said. I like to think that Hitler heard her and smiled up at her. In the history of man's temptations to destroy his fellow man—to violate the commandments of law, religion, or ordinary humane sympathy—the temptations to destroy our fellow man have taken many forms. Sometimes those temptations are not presented to a person or a people by a dramatic figure or a seductive personality. But always the temptation—whether merely in the minds and hearts of the tempted ones, or also in their political leaders —always the temptation involves a juicy, attractive object, and a persuasive argument that we turn away from preserving human life and toward smashing it. When that great conquistador, Francisco Pizarro, was asked why his fellow Spaniards had come across the ocean to subdue the Indians in the New World, he brushed aside the suggestion that God had told him to convert the heathen. The frank soldier said, " 'I have not come for any such reasons. I have come to take away from them their gold.' "[2] And when the slaveholders, especially in the cotton kingdom of the deep South before our Civil War, justified the horrors and indignities of owning and using black women, children, and men as one wished, they sometimes used profit as a justification, sometimes the inferiority of the blacks, and sometimes the words of the Bible. The main object was profit, I think: the main justifications flowed from that. But there was no dramatic seducer here to tempt men to be humane—only objects and arguments, and the capacity of men to swerve from being humane to doing evil when tempted by sweet fruits and cunning words.

But Hitler was the Devil, not only as the inward inclination of the Nazis. He was a personal leader of immense magnetism. And what he used to tempt the German people was a certain kind of object: the Third Reich, the thousand-year empire of pure-blooded Aryans totally subjugating the *Untermenschen*, the Jews, the Gypsies, and the Slavs. He told his people they could be as gods—with no moral or other restraints but the restraints they themselves lay down. This was the object he presented the German people, and he presented it with such consummate oratory and such a dynamic personality that he drew the people of Goethe, Beethoven, Kant, Brahms, and so many other geniuses of the human spirit to do the things they did: he seduced them into swerving from the commandment we all get with our mother's milk, the commandment not to kill other human beings.

In the early stages of the Third Reich, Hitler was the hypnotic, sexually attractive "Drummer," as he was sometimes called. He aroused immense enthusiasms, even faintings and screamings, in his audiences. He promised the knowledge and the power that would make Germans be as gods. These were the political years of the National Socialist Party. Later, when he had political power securely in his hands he became the Führer, no longer the Drummer who hypnotized and drew people like a sideshow barker, but an emperor, a general of the Reich whose absolute command regimented the people of Germany. Now his *commands* drew them to subjugate and destroy their fellow men.

Let me now mention the second major aspect of temptation:

subjective temptation. Right after the serpent has spoken, Eve reacts as follows:

> And when the woman saw that the tree was good for food, and that it was pleasant to the eyes, and a tree to be desired to make one wise, she took of the fruit thereof, and did eat, and gave also unto her husband with her; and he did eat. [3:6]

The delightful object and the cunning words are neither delightful nor cunning if the tempted one is not ready for them, is not ready to be tempted. The inclination was in Eve and Adam, the possibility was in them, or there would have been no temptation —only a snake muttering to himself. The German people were ready for Hitler, just as he was ready for them. Poverty and unemployment following the First World War, together with the long history of antisemitism in Germany—these and many other factors made the object tempting, the arguments persuasive, and the Devil attractive.

One does not do evil out of the blue. One does it out of the depths of one's being and in response to one's environment. One does it under many pressures. It is not a simple swerving of a neat little mechanism called a "will." It is a part of personal and public history, a resultant of many forces, as they say in physics. The tempter is within you, deeply rooted in you, or he is no tempter. Bismarck once said: give a German a half bottle of Champagne and he suddenly gets ten feet tall. Hitler, his Reich, and his arguments were that half bottle of champagne—in the very hearts and beings of the German people.

And just as there were two stages in Hitler's seductiveness— the stage wherein he hypnotized, exhilarated the German people, and the stage in which he commanded them with absolute power by way of his so-called *Führerprinzip*—so there were two stages in the seductiveness felt by the German people: first they were exhilarated, and then they were regimented, commanded absolutely. These two stages overlapped but they were as real for the German people as they were in the history of Hitler's rise and power. First they were tempted to do what they did by an exciting personality and by arguments and hopes; then they were tempted to do what they did by orders from above, orders that allowed many to say, "Well, this was not my responsibility —it was the Führer who did it, who ordered it." This, of course, was Eichmann's argument. The temptation of exhilaration, and the temptation of command.

But it would be a lie to say that Satan tempts only those in command, the Eichmanns, the plantation-owners, and the like. Let us call those in power "victimizers," and those in weak positions—the Jews under the Nazi regime, the blacks in the South before the Civil War—let us call these the "victims" of evil doing. Satan (a picture we use to depict all those forces that draw us to commit and help us to justify harmdoing), Satan also tempts the *victims* of harmdoing.

In *I Cannot Forgive* Vrba and Bestic tell about a little Jew, Yankel Meisel, who as a prisoner in a Nazi concentration camp had forgotten to sew his buttons on his uniform before an inspection tour by Heinrich Himmler. He was dragged into the barracks block and beaten to death while the whole camp was standing at attention waiting for Himmler. And while he was being beaten, while he was screaming under those blows, his fellow prisoners "all hated Yankel Meisel, the little old Jew who was spoiling everything, who was causing trouble for us all with his long, lone, futile protest." They were waiting for their chief executioner to appear, waiting with the Germans' love of order, and they did not hate that fatal order—they hated the dying man who was threatening to disrupt it.[3]

Victims are tempted by many forces to let their victimization continue. One force is our human fascination with orderliness, business as usual, a smooth machine, even if that machine is crushing us slowly. Another force is self-hatred. Running through the history of man's harmdoing to man is the victim's envy of and admiration for his victimizers. Some Jews were ashamed of their hooked noses and their names and wanted to be taken for neat, powerful Aryans. Some blacks formed the Brown Fellowship of Charleston, South Carolina, and put blacks with lighter skins on the top rank of their hierarchy: the more you looked like a white the "better" you were, to the blacks. And the Indians in the New World took the conquistadors to be gods on earth, at least for a while, and many continued to admire their destroyers.

This temptation to lie down and die under the beautiful strength of your victimizer did not come as an accident into the minds of the victims. Often victimizers deliberately set up ways of making their victims contemptible in their own eyes. For instance, the slaveholders would get their slaves deplorably drunk by making bets with each other that a certain slave could drink more than the others. And the slaves would be induced by this moment of pseudo-liberty to rival each other in degradation. As a result, there would be many slaves stretched out, after such a cunningly contrived debauch, drunk and sick, "helpless and disgusting" as Douglass puts it in his autobiography. And when they would sober up they would see more clearly than ever how despicable they were, how kind their masters were, and how they themselves deserved continuing degradation. Their brutishness justified—*in their own minds*—any ends their noble masters chose to attain.

In short, Satan tempts the victims of harmdoing as subtly as he tempts the victimizers. Moreover, he also tempts you and me as spectators to see the whole process as Hegel's "march of history," a necessary product of irresistible historical forces. Marx and Engels often fell under this temptation, and so have many who have only a biased, partial way of reading history. History is not neutral, free of good and evil because "what had to be, had to be." If you read those sparse first-hand accounts of slaves and other victims in history, you see their misery as something they sometimes sought to avoid, and among both the victims and the would-be victimizers you see good men who resist evil. You see decency and misery in history if you look closely and do not imagine blindly that you are studying simple, billiard-ball types of organisms according to some nineteenth-century pile of materialistic, metaphysical half-truths masquerading as science. If you as a spectator would avoid the Devil's temptation to be indifferent to harmdoing, read Frederick Douglass's *Life and Times* to see whether *he* was indifferent; read F. L. Olmsted's *The Cotton Kingdom* (an account of slavery in the South before the Civil War) to see if the slaves were indifferent; read Victor Frankl's *Experiences in a Concentration Camp* to see if the Jews were indifferent to the "march of history." No, we must all—victimizers, victims, and spectators—resist the Devil's temptation to gloss over harmdoing in some way or other.

After Adam and Eve fell, swerved from the *mitzvah*, the Bible says:

> And the eyes of them both were opened, and they knew that they were naked; and they sewed fig leaves together, and made themselves aprons. [3:7]

The notion of concealment as essential to a knowledge of good and evil has been interpreted by scholars in many ways. Let us read the fig leaves as follows: when one flatly violates a deep commandment, one tries to conceal it—one isolates one's victims in secret concentration camps or in plantations surrounded by waste land, swamps, poor-white patrollers, and other devices, and one keeps any communications from going out or coming in. This is what I meant by the castle in my book, *The Paradox of Cruelty*: concentration camps, plantations, and missions in the New World are examples of sequestering, of hiding the harm you do.

As far as Hitler was concerned, at first he and the Nazis were frank about their purges, their killings of opponents. This candor helped get them support: the German people were tired of hypocritical moralities and underhanded viciousness; they were grateful, even if harm was being done, as long as there was no mealy-mouthed hypocrisy. But with the rise of the concentration camps of Category III, the mills of death, the Nazis resorted to many types of concealment. The final solution of the Jewish problem was the result of the most secret political talks possible, the *unter vier Augen* talks between Himmler and Hitler. Even the Gestapo could not get into or out of a Category III camp without very strict security measures, and all communications among Nazis concerning extermination were done under the now famous *Nacht und Nebel* code—"night and fog," concealment. Kant once said: so act that the maxim of your action could readily become a universal, open law. Concealment is vital to evil; people must be kept ignorant of blatantly vicious deeds if they are to allow a destructive regime to continue. Or to put it more positively: when according to their own deepest insights people know they are doing evil, they feel a strong need to stop. Evil is, whatever else it may be, the discovery that there is something to conceal. Not all concealed things are evil (one's home, one's sexual practices, one's bank balance); but all evil things are concealed. Kant saw this when he said that we should act according to the golden rule: do as you would have done unto yourself and unto all others. Do what you would not hide. With all those persuasions and delectable objects we still have to hide the destruction of human beings, even though the persuasions help us to hide what we're doing under neutral terms like "extermination," which suggests the killing of rats and roaches.

But we have not yet finished reading those first four chapters of the Bible for modes of evil. After the Fall, there is the story of Cain and Abel:

And Cain talked with Abel his brother and it came to pass, when they were in the field, that Cain rose up against Abel his brother, and slew him. [4:8]

The central kind of evil we are considering here is that of the destruction of human life, the destruction of our brothers and sisters. Dante in his *Commedia* makes violence only one part of Hell—he makes sensual lust and fraud other parts. I here am emphasizing massive cruelty and killing, violence, but you have already seen how sensuality and fraud, lying to oneself and others, are a part of violence: Eve yearned for the taste of that apple and for the feel of that power, just as the Nazis yearned for total power over the weak. And, after all, concealment of evil is a type of fraud.

This is no place to summarize what happened in the Category III concentration camps, the mills of death, and later in Poland and elsewhere in Nazi-dominated Europe. Elie Wiesel has written about it very beautifully in his little novel, *Night*. Victor Frankl has written about it in detailed terms in *Experiences in a Concentration Camp*, and so has Eugene Kogon in *The Theory and Practice of Hell*. And there are hundreds of other books. Children's brains smashed out before the eyes of their mothers; fathers forced to choose which one of their family would die first, and having to live with that choice—the story seems endless. I shall not rehearse it. I cannot bear to do so again, but I urge you to read one of these books from time to time, painful as it is, or the word "evil" will lose its meaning, and so will the word "good," the love of life received and of life growing.

Right after the slaying we read:

And the Lord said unto Cain, Where is Abel thy brother? And he said, I know not: Am I my brother's keeper? [4:9]

But this verse does not stand alone, for the next verse is crucial to its meaning, at least for us. The Lord says:

What has thou done? the voice of thy brother's blood crieth unto me from the ground. [4:10]

To me, these two verses, especially the latter, are the most important and useful models for understanding evil in the book of Genesis. The main purpose of ethical discourse, like the words I am uttering to you now, is to urge you to develop the capacity to *hear* "the voice of thy brother's blood [that] crieth" unto you. Evil, massive evil, is falling under the temptation to maim and destroy human beings for great objects and under cover of cunning persuasions. Satan's task is simple: to keep us from seeing and hearing the smashing of victims. To see and to feel the evil in these destructions, these maimings, is to see the face, hear the voice, even sometimes, when you can bear it, feel the feelings of the victims. Some people cannot do this— they are either purely good, prelapsarian innocents, or they are perfect candidates for doing or permitting evil. Literature can help us to develop the capacity to hear the voice of that blood; so can history; so can ethics. Without that capacity, ethics is empty words, and history is a quaint, mildly comforting story of cozy, pleasant castles. With that capacity, history becomes a nightmare, and ethics a reality.

But history, for those aware of the victim's voice and face, is not only a nightmare. It is also an account of dignity and courage. The other reading I urge you to make of the phrase "the voice of thy brother's blood crieth unto me from the ground" is this: victims resist in many ways the indignities and destructions that evil brings. Frederick Douglass, the great black American abolitionist, kept his dignity and his life by all the means available to men: self-respect, physical power, penetrating intelligence, courage, love of life (human and other kinds), and luck. He escaped from slavery and helped make America free of the old forms of slavery (though we still have Jim Crow). The conquistadors found resistance—especially from some of their own number, for instance from saints like Bartolomé de Las Casas. And there were so many resistance groups in Nazi Germany that I cannot begin to summarize them. I often wonder whether, in similar circumstances, this beautiful country of ours with its great ideals would produce as many resistance groups against a Hitler as the Germans produced. I wonder.

I always think of one particular group who resisted evil and who made the blood of the victims cry up from the ground unto men's ears. They called themselves "The White Rose," and they were young people who resisted the temptations Hitler and their times laid upon them. They were students, and one philosophy teacher, all from the University of Munich. The White Rose bloomed for a little while, celebrating a joyous, free life and attacking Hitler's destructive, evil acts. And then they were all beheaded, young men, one young woman, a lovely girl named Sophie Scholl, and their professor. Their efforts to awaken Germans and the world to that cry were, in a sense, futile. But they did something, and what they did was infinitely better than no effort, no indignation, no dignity to resist those indignities. It was resistance to almost overwhelming temptation, and it was infinitely better than the practical, "logical" silence and ineptitude, the pointless self-torture of conscience-stricken Germans who said and did nothing. There are many ways to fall into doing evil, and these unhappy Germans exhibited those many ways. The White Rose was impractical, perhaps, but these young people and their professor heard the voice of the blood cry up from the ground, and they took up the sound of those anguished voices and made others hear them.

All of those whose dignity resisted the indignities of evil exhibit the second major kind of goodness I wanted to mention: not pure goodness, but "resistant goodness," let us call it. They were all tempted, but they would not fall. Of course resistant goodness requires skill, power, and luck. And some resisters of the conquistadors or the plantation owners or the Nazis lacked some of these valuable possessions. But all of them heard the voice of that blood, and we doom ourselves to passive complicity with evil if we do not see this. We must ourselves hear that voice clearly, strongly enough to help us resist temptations to turn away from it.

But there is one more verse in Genesis that I must scan with you as a model for understanding evil in terms of human experience. God has laid down his punishment on Cain:

> And Cain said unto the Lord, My punishment is greater than I can bear. [4:13]

If we understand this verse sensitively, we can go some distance toward avoiding the temptation to destroy in the name of punishment. Many people, not only Jews, hate the German people now. I am convinced that ethics is the enemy of hate, just as it is the enemy of destruction of all sorts. Sometimes, in order to get out from under destructive evil, we must do harsh things, like fight the destroyers. But when the evil deeds are done, when the victim is freed by either death or resistance, we dare not forget that life is good—German lives, too. Life must not be the scene of bitter, pointless retrospective hatred. If such hatred does not escalate harmdoing it often makes us would-be killers, little would-be killers. And killers—isn't it *obvious*?—are the enemies of life, no matter how righteous they are.

I know a man who was in the Nazi army in the last world war. The first day he met me he picked up my little Jewish son and threw him up into the air, saying, "Well, a few years ago we would have known what to do with you." The non-Jewish people present, including my non-Jewish wife, were horror-stricken at this apparently brutal statement. But it was my son he was throwing up, and I am Jewish, and he knew it. I knew the horror and anguish that that man felt when he said and did that in front of me. He was telling me that he had been guilty of evil, and he was drawing hatred onto himself. But he was not concealing anything—he was open, candid, and he was begging for forgiveness in ways I cannot here explain, but that some of you may understand. He is now one of my very dearest friends—we deeply need each other, though we fear each other a little. If we do not hold hard onto the preciousness of living, Satan will get us, not by tempting us to fall from pure goodness into evil, but by tempting us to fall from resistant goodness into evil, into destructive hating.

Let me insist on this point by being personal again. As a student interested in the Prince of Lies, the Prince of Darkness, I have, of course, studied much in the Middle Ages, when the Devil was more real than at any other time in the history of Western civilization. In those studies I have come across, again and again, vicious, destructive hatred on the part of Christians —hatred of the Jews. Not only have I come across it in history, with the murders of so many Jews in Europe, and, by the Crusaders, in the Holy Land—all in the name of Christian love— but I have also come across it again and again in Christian literature, or at least literature written by Christian persons. The Jews are deicides—they killed Jesus—therefore they should be slain like dogs wherever you find them. How many times I have come across this argument! Even my darling Chaucer, in *The Prioress's Tale*, says:

> Our first foe, the serpent Satan
> Has his wasp-nest in the hearts of Jews.

From this hatred, real and fictional (but always real), there is a straight line, at least for Jews who are sensitive about threats to their own lives and to the lives of their children, a straight line to Hitler's extermination camps. (In fact, Hitler in his youth was appalled at how the Medieval people treated Jews. Hitler! But he learned.) Now, knowing all this, *I* am tempted to fear and even hate professed Christians (fear and hate are often Siamese twins, as you know). And, after slavery, blacks are tempted to hate all whites. I am convinced that these temptations can be fought by reaffirming in one's mind and heart the preciousness of all life. I have no formula for resisting that temptation to hate and fear while keeping commonsensically alert so that pogroms in God's name won't happen again. All I can say is that it takes effort, character, and lots of weapons to do the job.

Of all the men who have resisted such temptation, I think Frederick Douglass late in his autobiography, *Life and Times*, seems to have done it with the greatest dignity and honesty. Remember, he had been a slave and had seen and felt in his flesh the misery and ignominy of slavery. Having been accused, in effect, of being kind to his enemies, this is what he said, and meant, late in his life:

> If any reader of this part of my life shall see in it the evidence of a want of manly resentment for wrongs inflicted by slavery upon myself and race . . . so it must be. No man can be stronger than nature, one touch of which, we are told, makes all the world akin. I esteem myself a good, persistent hater of injustice and oppression, but my resentment ceases when they cease, and I have no heart to visit upon children the sins of their fathers.[4]

Such a deeply felt "yes" to life can be acquired only painfully after one has watched much evildoing, and especially when one identifies with the victims of that evildoing. But the "yes" *must* be said, and we must always be willing and eager to hear others say it, and believe in them, while we must always be willing to say it ourselves, and mean it. As I have said: to fear and hate a life is—to fear and hate a life, no matter what the justification.

A person who understands the images from Genesis that we have discussed feels the joyous preciousness of all life, while at the same time he is ready to resist with dignity the indignities of evil. He must be ready for both roles or stances in life, or he has fallen under the spell of Satan. Sometimes it seems impossible to rejoice in all life and resist the temptation to do evil. There were times during the last World War when I was fighting the Nazis that this was the case. But ethics deals with ideals, not techniques. I do not know a formula for resisting evil while loving life; I know only that ethics must have this as its ideal or it becomes just one more of the Devil's temptations.

Let me conclude with a quotation from a letter. This letter was written by a young Sudetenland German boy on February 3, 1944. While you read it, notice how good and evil are sometimes deeply interwoven with each other. He was doing good, resisting temptation, and yet he was bringing evil, that is, misery, on himself and on his parents. The letter to his parents is a letter of apology. I suspect that it will forever be the best statement I know, not only of the intertwining of good and evil, but of the immense need for loving life and goodness while resisting evil:

> Dear Parents: I must give you bad news—I have been condemned to death, I and Gustave G. We did not sign up for the SS, and so they have condemned us to death. You write me, indeed, that I should not join the SS; my comrade, Gustave G., did not sign up either. Both of us would rather die than stain our consciences with such deeds of horror. I know what the SS has to do. Oh, my dear parents, difficult as it is for me and for you, forgive me everything; if I have offended you, please forgive me and pray for me. If I were to be killed in the war while my conscience was bad, that too would be sad for you. Many more parents will lose their children. Many SS men will be killed too. I thank you for everything you have done for my good since my childhood; forgive me, pray for me. . . .[5]

Satan never had a stronger adversary and the terms "evil" and "good" have never received so palpable and plain a meaning as they did in this young man's words and death.

# Notes

[1] Moses Maimonides, *The Guide of the Perplexed*, trans. Morris Friedländer (New York: Hebrew Publishing Co., n.d.), pt. 3, p. 99.

[2] Lewis Hanke, *The Spanish Struggle for Justice in the Conquest of America* (Boston: Little, Brown & Co., 1965), p. 7.

[3] Rudolf Vrba and Alan Bestic, *I Cannot Forgive* (London: Sidgwick & Jackson, 1964), p. 12.

[4] Frederick Douglass, *Life and Times of Frederick Douglass* (New York: Collier Books, 1962), p. 395.

[5] H. Gollwitzer, Käthe Kuhn, and Reinhold Schneider, eds., *Dying We Live* (London: Fontana Books, 1965), p. 13.

# Violence and the Retreat
# from Reason

M. LIONEL RUBINOFF has taught at Trent University, York University, and the University of Toronto. He studied at the Academy of Radio Arts (Toronto), Queen's University, and the University of Toronto, where he received the Ph.D. in 1964. Professor Rubinoff is the author and editor of more than thirty-five books, articles, and reviews in philosophy and related disciplines. His books include *The Pornography of Power: A Study in the Phenomenology of Evil* (1968) and *Collingwood and the Reform of Metaphysics* (1970); and edited volumes such as *The Presuppositions of Critical History* by F. H. Bradley (1968), *Faith and Reason: Essays in the Philosophy of Religion* by R. G. Collingwood (1968), and *Tradition and Revolution* (1971). Professor Rubinoff is very active in programs of Jewish studies, was an elected member of the North York Board of Education, and has presented numerous television, radio, and special lectures.

# Violence and the Retreat
# from Reason

## by M. Lionel Rubinoff

## I. INTRODUCTION: THE CRISIS OF MODERNITY

The twentieth century comes to its testing time in a moment of great crisis. We live and breathe and have our being in an age of apocalyptic uncertainty. Our generation bears witness to the desperate plight of men who have grown powerful beyond their dreams but who yet suffer a poverty of spirit for which there appears to be no discernible remedy. We have shared the pain of watching generations after generations led to the slaughter bench of history. We have borne witness to, and have learned to suffer the scandal of, what can only be described as an assassination of innocence.

Perhaps the chief source of apocalypse in our time is the terror that comes from the realization that neither nature nor history seems any longer to be guided by a vision of the good, and that whatever men may have believed about that vision in the past was simply an illusion to be explained by ignorance of true causes. For modern secular consciousness, nature appears as an *immensely* powerful but soulless machine and man as one of the things it has made,[1] a chance deposit on the surface of the earth, carelessly thrown up between two ice ages by the same forces that rust iron and ripen corn.[2] Unlike nature proper, man is gifted with sentience and intellect. And from this intellect he has spun, over the centuries, illusions of hope founded on the prospect of achieving, with the aid of Providence, some measure of happiness and relief from the conditions of adversity. How disappointing, then, to discover, as Bertrand Russell once put it:

> that man is the product of causes which had no prevision of the end they were achieving; that his origin, his growth, his hopes and fears, his loves and beliefs, are but the outcome of accidental collocations of atoms; that no fire, no heroism, no intensity of thought and feeling, can preserve an individual life beyond the grave; that all the labors of the ages, all the devotion, all the inspiration, all the noonday brightness of human genius, are destined to extinction in the vast death of the solar system, and that the whole temple of man's achievements must inevitably be buried beneath the debris of a universe in ruins.[3]

Nor has history been any kinder with respect to our illusions. Just as modern man suffers the unhappiness and despair of realizing that he has never really had control over the forces of nature, so he also suffers the despair of having lost control over the machinery of history. Our favorite nightmare in the twentieth century is about our powerlessness in the giant grip of economic, social, and political structures;[4] the nightmare that Arnold Toynbee calls "the intractableness of institutions." The founders of our political, social, and economic institutions supported by modern science, technology, and the social sciences promised that these Leviathans were simply artificial creatures formed by the art of man, for whose protection and defense they were intended.[5] Yet rather than protecting us from adversity, the machinery of culture seems bent on our destruction. Oppression and exploitation, persecution and war, the torturing to death of human beings in vast, helpless masses are not new things on the face of the earth. What disturbs us is the fact that the founders of our culture made a covenant with man that there would be protection and defense against these things. But that promise has been betrayed by the record of history, and when we find it to be precisely the agents of this longed-for safety that are the chief authors of the evils for whose ending we have made them, hope turns to despair, and we are tormented by another Frankenstein nightmare, like Samuel Butler's nightmare of humanity enslaved by its own machines, only worse.

Our despair is made all the more difficult to bear to the extent that we once lived by hope. We are of a generation and a tradition that has been brought up to believe that culture is the basis of salvation. We believed that if people read good books, went to museums, subscribed to the opera, and loved symphonies, certain decencies would follow. As George Steiner has been quick to remind us throughout his writings, there has been at the basis of the Western tradition a deep-seated belief that human savagery and hatred and killing are caused by lack of education. People who read and understand philosophy won't believe in stupid, murderous slogans. People who love Bach, Mozart, and Beethoven are not going to do certain things to other people. People who spend their lives reading Virgil or Goethe or Shakespeare will understand each other across disagreements. But, above all, we have believed that people who have served God might expect some relief from the evils that are the lot of godless, and hence god-forsaken, peoples. To believe in God does not of course mean that one has somehow earned divine protection for adversity; it means rather that through believing in God man transforms his existence, makes himself into the kind of person who is capable of resisting the temptation to do evil. Even pragmatists and sociologists could see the sense of this. Like culture, religion is man's challenge to improve himself as man.

And yet, rather than having been purified and humbled by the combined forces of religion and culture, man still remains in essence a barbarian. Consider the absurdities and incongruities of recent history. Auschwitz, Hiroshima, and My Lai have taught us that murder and culture do not exclude each other. If these events prove anything, it is that it is possible for a person both to love poems and kill children. This barbarism is implicit even in the most revered and taken-for-granted aspects of our culture. George Steiner draws our attention to our fascination for the pornography of violence that masquerades as art and literature. We live in a world in which art not only flirts with but pays homage to the genius of cruelty and brutality. This kind of art prepares the imagination to believe that certain things could be tried or might be fun to look at, so that very subtly it undermines its own overt moral values. The concentration camp is one symbol for this kind of obscenity. The destruction of the environment is another. Something in man has made him murder thousands of species, not simply for food, but in gratuitous waste. Something in man makes him ravage landscapes and demolish the last places of beauty. Some suicidal demon in our civilization sees the evil that it does, yet continues to do it.[6] Man's capacity for evil, rather than having been transmuted, has, if anything, been intensified. Thus R. D. Laing reminds us, in a statement which sums up the accomplishments of the modern era, that:

> In the last fifty years, we human beings have slaughtered by our own hands something like seventy million of our own species. We all live under constant threat of our total annihilation. We seem to seek death and destruction as much as life and happiness. We are as driven, it seems, to kill and be killed as we are to live and let live. Only by the most outrageous violation of ourselves have we achieved our capacity to live in relative adjustment to a civilization apparently driven to its own destruction.[7]

What is most astonishing about the modern era, however, is the sophistication with which the performance of godless and violent acts of evil has become institutionalized and integrated into the normal routines of everyday living and working. The very same language and the very same reasoning that produces philosophy, science, technology, and culture produces as well the ideologies and alibis by means of which our energies have been employed toward the corruption of rationality and the support of evil. The chief scandal of our age is the assassination of innocence in the name of justice. "Peace with honor," "I was only doing my duty," "the national interest," "the manifest destiny." We believe that the rationale of our society serves the interests of justice. The fact is, however, that our society has been rationalized *in nomine diaboli*. The rationality of our time is, if anything, a disguised form of unreason, a propaganda of irrationalism, which, as Lewis Mumford complains, feeds "the forces of anti-life now swarming through our inner world, proclaiming that mechanical automation is superior to personal autonomy, that empty confusion is authentic design, that garbage is nourishing food, that bestiality and hate are the only honest expressions of the human spirit."[8] But nowhere is the propaganda of irrationalism more evident than in our current worship of the deities of apocalyptic destruction. What kind of logic is it which equates security with the capacity to destroy others? It is, I suggest, nothing less than a "logic of madness,"[9] a logic which, to the extent that it infects every aspect of culture and society, gradually achieves, through uncritical consensual validation, the status of normalcy.

Thus does the phenomenology of contemporary social existence confront us with the sinewy specter of apocalypse, the eclipse of God as well as the eclipse of reason. In the words of the poet W. B. Yeats:

Things fall apart; the cer
Mere anarchy is loosed
The blood-dimmed tide
   ceremony of innoce
   best lack all convic
   ull of passionate i
. . . . . . . . . . . . . .
   vhat rough beast,
   hes towards Beth

*if we can affirm no*
*ble and nothing h*
*murderer is nei*
*crematory fir*
*and virtue*
*accordin*
*good*
*we*
*w*

78

The crisis of modernit
Auschwitz, and My Lai, together with the failure of
to salvage the natural resources of the earth for the good of
mankind, seem to have destroyed the possibility of belief in any
kind of vision of the good, whether of the immanent or of the
transcendental variety. Add to this the increasingly anarchic
consequences of pluralism, and the situation becomes even
more serious. After these dread events occurring in the heart of
the modern enlightened, technological world, can one still believe in the idea of a transcendental good as the basis of necessary progress any more than one can believe in a good that
manifests itself in the form of a superintending Providence? If,
in the face of Auschwitz and the spreading polarization of
thought and purpose, one still wished to seek the transcendent
good, then, it would seem, one must turn one's back on history
in favor of either an eternity beyond history or else an individ-
ualistic inwardness divorced from it.

But this is to confess nihilism with respect to the relations
between history, belief, and action. It is to live by the belief that
whether or not the good exists makes no difference to the course
of history, and that my personal historical actions make no
difference to the transcendent good. Man and the good, in other
words, are simply indifferent to each other. If the good exists,
anything is possible, and if God does not exist, everything is
permissible. But since God's existence (even though it abstractly forbids much that is possible) makes no difference to
history, the distinction between what is possible and what is
permissible dissolves into desire. Everything is permissible
which is simply desired, and in a world in which there are
conflicting desires the only standard of justice is power. As the
Greek Sophist Thrasymachus once put it: "Might is right." This
position is summed up by Camus in *The Rebel*. If, writes
Camus, we believe in nothing, if nothing has any meaning, and

values whatsoever, then everything is possi-
s any importance. There is no pro or con: the
ther right nor wrong. We are free to stoke the
s or to devote ourselves to the care of lepers. Evil
are mere chance or caprice. From which it follows,
g to Camus, that since nothing is either true or false,
r bad, our guiding principle will be to demonstrate that
re the most efficient, in other words, the strongest. Then the
orld will no longer be divided into the just and the unjust, but
into masters and slaves.[11]  •

The poet Kenneth Rexroth once wrote that "against the ruin
of the world, there is only one defense—the creative act."[12]
But how does one create in a world in which murder and high
culture have learned to walk hand in hand? Faced with the
absurdity of a world in which "the worst are full of passionate
intensity while the best lack all conviction," many have chosen
the path of retreat: retreat into madness, into violence, and into
apathy. But this of course only further aggravates the problem
by removing from our midst the very persons from whom leadership might have been expected. Indeed, another scandal of
our age is the retreat from reason and the betrayal of their
professional calling by large numbers of intellectuals. That calling is summed up in the command of the Delphic Oracle to
"know thyself." This means, as it did for Socrates and Plato,
that we must let no day pass by without subjecting ourselves
to self-examination, and a life without this sort of examination
is not worth living. Through self-examination or diagnosis, critical consciousness seeks the sources of disorder. But all knowledge is for the sake of action, and it is for the purpose of acting
so as to repair the ruin of the world that the diagnosis of the
human condition is undertaken. In the midst of despair, reason
reaches into its Orphic depths and responds creatively.

One of the major sources of disorder in our time is the tendency to depart from the Platonic concept of rationality, which
stresses the unity of the virtues and the integration of man's
psychic powers: reason, appetite, and spirit. For Plato, only
that is desirable which is likely to contribute to justice, and all
human conduct is to be guided by a vision of the "Good." But
in our society we not only set man's psychic powers in opposition to each other by allowing them to compete, we also encourage a competition of Goods. Thus, for example, politics
competes with morality to the point where the word "politics"
has become synonomous with "immorality." In the world of

design, function competes with beauty; while everywhere Yeats's "ceremony of innocence" is drowned in the competition between reason and violence. It is with the hope of contributing to a deeper understanding of the sources of this disorder that the following diagnosis is offered for consideration.

## II.  THE PARADOX OF REASON: REFLECTIONS ON THE MYTH OF SATAN

One of the perennial tasks of philosophy derives from the observation that the very same reason that is the source of man's dignity and freedom is the source also of his perversity and servitude to passion. As Goethe's Mephistopheles exclaims, concerning man's miserable record on earth:

> His life might be better
> Had you not given him that spark of Heaven's sun
> He calls it reason and employs it resolute
> To be more brutish than any brute.[13]

Confronted by the paradox of reason, philosophy thus finds itself face-to-face with the prospect of a melancholy truth with which we have only barely begun to wrestle. It is the truth, namely, that perversity and barbarism are to be traced not so much to imperfections in the environment but rather to the very constitution of man qua man, and that civilization consists, therefore, not simply in advancements in technology but more essentially in the understanding and transcendence of man's primordial constitution. Or, as the poet Charles Baudelaire once put it, "The true theory of civilization is to be found not in the advent of gas or steam but in the diminution of the traces of original sin."[14]

Here the wisdom of tradition confronts philosophy with an even more provoking paradox. On the one hand, as the product of divine creation, man seeks a destiny commensurate with his divine origins. Man is in the first instance subject to the authority of the moral law. At the same time, however, he is fated by virtue of his original constitution to undergo that painful odyssey which has in fact characterized his history. Thus Darwin implores us to indulge with caution in our utopian dreams until the laws of our inheritance are better understood. For, writes Darwin, with all his exalted powers, and with all his noble qualities, "Man still bears in his bodily frame the indelible

stamp of his lowly origin."[15] Freud, too, warns that the path to
utopia, even though it is followed with the best of intentions, is
nevertheless fated to end in misery because of man's original
nature. "The truth," writes Freud, "which people are so eager
to disavow, is that men are not gentle beings who want to be
loved. . . . They are, on the contrary, creatures among whose
instinctual endowments are to be reckoned a powerful measure
of aggressiveness."[16] By aggressiveness Freud means nothing
less than the capacity—and, indeed, urge—to exploit others
without compensation, to use them sexually without their consent, to seize their possessions, to humiliate them and to cause
them pain, and finally, to torture and to kill them. Evil here
means very simply the violation of respect for person. *Homo
homini lupus* ("man is a wolf to man"): this is Freud's portrait
of man in the state of nature. And, says Freud, it is this very
same man who lurks beneath the veneer of civilization, waiting
for some provocation or opportunity to take over, and posing,
therefore, a perennial threat to the stability of civilization.[17] It
is for this reason that Freud urges respect for the new science of
man, which may yet play some role in the process whereby man
can recover ownership of his own destiny. Psychoanalysis
teaches that although man is "lived by his unconscious," the
task of therapy is to bring man into dialogue with his unconscious, thus liberating himself from bondage to it. It is by reliv-
ing and rethinking the drama of the unconscious that man
comes to transcend it.

The most dramatic representation of the paradox of reason is
the myth of Satan, which expresses in a vivid and insightful
manner the intuitive wisdom of Western man's self-understanding. According to David Bakan, who has written extensively on
the psychological implications of the myth, the chief analytic
component of the myth is suggested by the observation that for
those who believe in him, the Devil is experienced as an embodiment of external reality. He is, in fact, experienced as a
reality that is totally separated and alienated from the consciousness of the perceiver. Satan is also typically represented
as the tempter who calls forth the beast in man. It is he who
manipulates our inner drives, so that the pleasures and pains
that the individual experiences with respect to the committing of
violent and evil acts are experienced as having been evoked
from without, from some point in external reality called Hell.[18]
It is thus that the individual projects the inner felt reality asso-

ciated with the committing of violent acts onto some external source, which must now bear full responsibility for the impulses, drives, and experiences of pleasure that make up the contents of that inner reality. The individual experiences pleasure whenever he commits an act of violence but refuses to accept responsibility for having initiated such acts.

The mechanism whereby the individual projects the inner felt reality associated with evil onto an external source may be designated as the mechanism of externalization, or the mechanism of the projection of internal necessity. This mechanism can be seen to operate most effectively in a society that has been overly rationalized in the direction of bureaucracy. We must, however, distinguish between bureaucracy as an *ingredient* in society and bureaucracy as the *form* of society. It is when bureaucratic functional authoritarianism becomes the Procrustean bed to which the whole of society is compelled to conform that consciousness faces the temptation to transform the world into the kind of place in which it is now possible to act irresponsibly and without compunction.

In a society that instead of encouraging an innovative, creative, and reflective consciousness encourages a consciousness of submissive conformity ruled by the virtues of order and obedience, the performance of evil acts can easily become normalized and routinized. Bureaucratic authoritarianism, in other words, encourages individuals to resort to the mechanism of externalization as a way of engaging in evil without compunction. In addition to "counterfeiting" his experience of himself—in the sense that he experiences his behavior not as an expression of something internal to himself, but simply as a response to an external command—the individual further indulges in self-deception by regarding the imperatives of the "commanding" authority as compulsory, as something over which he has no control.

Such behavior bears the characteristic of banality. The banality of evil, as Hannah Arendt has pointed out, is expressed in the capacity for *engaging* in evil without *experiencing* it as evil. It is the performance of evil acts as part of one's job description. As such, the appeal to one's job description may be interpreted as a consequence of the mechanism of externalization. Although I am a being capable of temptation and capable of deriving pleasure by indulging in evil acts, and although I am a being whose very character and self-identity are themselves the product of a curious dialectic through which I must do battle with inclination and temptation, I am nevertheless unwilling to assume responsibility for myself, preferring instead to have my essence and my identity provided in advance of my existence—as part of my job description, or as part of my role. I therefore allow myself to be compelled. Officially, I act because I am *compelled*. I am simply doing my job. From the standpoint of intentional consciousness, however, I allow myself to be compelled *in order* to do my job. This is an experience that is phenomenologically equivalent to the experience of being possessed by the Devil; the two experiences share a common structure.

Let us pause for a moment to compare this analysis with the one given by Sartre in his important, but too often overlooked, *Sketch for a Theory of the Emotions*.[19] In this work, Sartre introduces the notion of "magic" as a mechanism whereby the world is transformed into the kind of place in which man is now able to act irresponsibly without compunction. In *Being and Nothingness* this mechanism is referred to as "bad-faith." In actuality, I desire to derive pleasure from the infliction of pain and suffering on others, and to enjoy the effects of asserting total mastery over other beings. But I do not wish to bear responsibility for so acting—in the sense that I do not wish to experience my actions as the result of choice. I therefore allow myself to be "possessed" by external compulsion; if I act it is only because I am either possessed by natural law or else compelled by authority to do so. And in a society that has by its consensual validation turned the image of man as "determined by natural law" into a self-fulfilling prophecy, it is easy to see how such acts of "magic" become normalized into what Erich Fromm calls "socially patterned defects."[20] Thus, while I may pretend that I act *because* I am possessed, the truth is that I am possessed *in order* to act. Through what Sartre calls the magical manipulation of the emotions, the individual frees himself from the painful feeling that the act was in his power, that he was free to do it or not. Such a flight is easily facilitated in a society that is mystified by the ideology of determinism; and this is in turn supported by a reverence for bureaucratic authoritarianism.

In his famous paper on demoniacal possession, Sigmund Freud identifies this condition as neurotic. The chief characteristic of the neurotic is that his behavior appears to be determined by external forces, when in point of fact we know that the origin is internal:

> Cases of demoniacal possession correspond to the neuroses of the present day; in order to understand these latter we have once more had recourse to the conception of psychic forces. What in those days were thought to be evil spirits to us are base and evil wishes, the derivatives of impulses which have been rejected and repressed. In one respect only we do not subscribe to the explanation of these phenomena current in Mediaeval times; we have abandoned the projection of them into the outer world, attributing their origin instead to the inner life of the patient in whom they manifest themselves.[21]

When the agent himself is in possession of the truth (which according to Freud has been repressed into the unconscious) and yet chooses to pretend ignorance with respect to it, then he may be said to be acting in bad-faith.

Notwithstanding the well-known dispute between Freud and existentialists like Sartre respecting the mechanisms through which a neurosis is acquired, there is yet a significant degree of agreement concerning the analysis of the structure and function of this particular neurosis. For Sartre, the ontological structure of consciousness is characterized by the conscious effort both *to-be-what-it-is-not* and *not-to-be-what-it-is*. Consciousness *is* freedom, and freedom is anguish. In order to escape the anguish of freedom, consciousness therefore choses to counterfeit reality so as to relieve itself of the burden of responsibility. Consciousness is freedom, yet it choses not to be free; preferring the security of inauthentic existence to the anguish of authenticity.

At the ontological level, this counterfeit takes the form of assigning to reality an unalterable essence that is believed to precede all existence. Time becomes nothing more than the moving image of eternity, and consciousness is now able to sustain the illusion of immortality. Translated into more existential terms, the formula "essence precedes existence" means everything from believing in the existence of God to believing in demoniacal possession. Indeed, for Sartre there is no difference in structure between acting through divine inspiration and acting from demoniacal possession. In either case we have a demonstration of bad-faith.

Freud argues that demoniacal possession could be regarded as an unconscious attempt to relieve oneself of the burden of insecurity by providing a father-substitute in the form of the Devil. The train of thought motivating the decision to negotiate a pact with the Devil may, according to Freud, be represented as follows: "Owing to my father's death I am despondent and can no longer work; If I can but get a father-substitute I shall be able to regain all that I have lost."[22] What is more, argues Freud, the Devil is a father-substitute in the same sense that God is a father-substitute:

> The evil spirit of the Christian faith, the Devil of Mediaeval times, was, according to Christian mythology, himself a fallen angel of godlike nature. It requires no great analytic insight to divine that God and the Devil were originally one and the same, a single figure which was later split into two bearing opposed characteristics.
>
> It is an example of the process so familiar to us, by which an idea with an opposed-ambivalent-content is split into two opposites contrasting sharply. The antithesis contained in the original idea of the nature of God is but a reflection of the ambivalence governing the relation of an individual to his personal father. If the benevolent and righteous God is a father-substitute, it is not to be wondered at that the hostile attitude, which leads to hate, fear and accusations against him, comes to expression in the figure of Satan. The father is thus the individual prototype of both God and the Devil. The fact that the figure of the primal father was that of a being with unlimited potentialities of evil, bearing much more resemblance to the Devil than to God, must have left an indelible stamp on all religions.[23]

In the particular case of a seventeenth-century painter, Christoph Haitzmann, whose case Freud diagnosed on the basis of historical documents, the painter pledges himself to the Devil "because after his father's death he feels depressed, incapable of work and is apprehensive about his livelihood."[24] Relief from the neurosis of demoniacal possession comes only after the painter invokes the aid of the Mother of God. Exorcism comes only when the painter renounces the sinful world and enters a holy order. Through dedication to the service of God he finally accomplishes what he was unable to achieve through having made a pact with the Devil; namely, a mode of life in which there are no cares about sustenance:

> All he wanted was security in life, at first with the help of Satan but at the cost of eternal bliss; then when this failed and had to be abandoned, with the Church's help but at the cost of his freedom and most of the pleasures in life. Perhaps Christoph Haitzmann was . . . one of those who . . . are unable to tear themselves away from the joyous haven at the mother's breast, who hold fast all through their lives to their claim to be nour-

ished by someone else. And so in his illness our painter followed the path from his own father by way of the Devil as a father-substitute to the pious father of the Church.[25]

The mechanism of externalization which on some occasions manifests itself as demoniacal possession is reflected also in our attitude toward "heroes" and "leadership." Hero worship is quite often nothing less than a disguised form of Devil worship. It is the demonic, Dionysian qualities of the hero rather than the Apollonian that are more often the source of fascination. Gangsters and outlaws have long been heroes of the folklore of Western man. Likewise the choice of a political leader is often determined by an unconscious perception of his demonic potentialities, sometimes legitimized under the concept of "charisma." In a society that has repressed opportunities for facing up to the demonic, people will find underground avenues of expression. One such avenue is prepared for by perverting the function of legitimate institutions in order to make them serve darker purposes: evil is thus legitimized under the cover of respectability. The choice of a political leader, for example, becomes a substitute form of gratification; the support of certain political ideologies becomes another. In such times, powerful political leaders with demonic qualities have a far greater chance of success than they would have within societies that have found more open ways of re-enacting and celebrating the drama of evil. Repressed societies are more likely to support demonic policies than are unrepressed ones.

One of the chief mechanisms through which repressed societies are unhinged by demonic political policies is the mechanism of eschatology: the belief that the events of one's life are the playing-out of some grand cosmic drama. This introduces yet another of the archetypal structures of evil as suggested by our hermeneutic of the myth of Satan. Just as in the myth Satan is represented as playing out a role in the cosmic drama of good and evil, so the enactment of violence is often legitimized by being presented as the fulfillment of a cosmic destiny. Thus Gert Kalow declares, with respect to the rise of the Third Reich:

Would Hitler have been able to rouse the masses . . . to such delirious enthusiasm, if there had not existed in Germany the idea or expectation that something in the nature of collective redemption was possible: a "messianic expectation among the common people". . . . combined with a superstitious belief in a world history which, by evolution and impelled by a higher automatic power, was moving forward to fulfilment?[26]

Here, too, language plays an important role, the language of *in nomine diaboli*. Just as the language of "I was only obeying orders" facilitates the mechanisms of projection, so the language of ideology—"it is our destiny," "it is our mission," "it is our national purpose"—introduces an external compelling force that is made to bear full responsibility for one's acts.

The most fundamental feature of the myth is the idea of locating evil in a source external to oneself. On the one hand, the image of Satan represents the idea of acting in accordance with what is experienced as an "external demand," whether that demand be interpreted as the demand of "reality" or the demand of a cosmic plan according to which reality itself is constructed. Thus, if I am inclined to commit acts of violence, it is only because I am compelled to it by the laws of reality. On the other hand, Satan represents the idea of evil as a foreign intrusion into what is otherwise a world of pure virtue. Evil here is always something done by unaccountable foreigners, and if I am now inclined to commit acts of violence it is only because I am forced by the circumstances to protect myself from such intrusions. In either case, the burden of responsibility is shifted away from the self to the other, and in both cases there is a repression of insight into the demonic sources of one's own nature.

The myth of Satan is the symbolic representation of the human tendency to protect one's illusions of virtue by creating an external source of evil. This is also likely to initiate a tendency to indulge oneself in acts of violence while at the same time either pretending to be ignorant of what one is doing or else justifying what one is doing on the grounds that it has been provoked. Such themes have been the subject of literary expression throughout the centuries. In Euripides' play *The Bacchae,* the king, Pentheus, refuses, as it were, to grant a permit to the Dionysian religious cult that has recently invaded Hellas. Pentheus is the archetypal rationalist who refuses to recognize the legitimacy of the presence of the irrational. The central theme of *The Bacchae* is the conflict between *sophia* and its opposite, *amathia*.[27] *Sophia* implies a firm awareness of one's own nature and therefore of one's place in the scheme of things. It presupposes, in other words, self-knowledge and self-acceptance, that is, acceptance of those necessities that define the limits of human fate. By contrast with the man of *sophia,* the man of *amathia* acts out of a kind of unteachable, ungovernable ignorance of himself and of the necessities that define the human condition. Puritan and pretender to virtue though he is, Pentheus, through his lack of self-understanding, is prone to far greater violence, harshness, and brutality than any of the evils to which he has dedicated his life to repressing. Pentheus forfeits his claim to *sophia* because he wantonly and violently refuses to accept the necessity that Dionysus incarnates. Pentheus is the embodiment of *amathia*.

Yet, like most puritans, Pentheus has a fascination with pornography and is prone to voyeurism. While not giving official recognition to the cult, he is prepared to eavesdrop on its rituals until he is caught and offered as a sacrifice by his own mother, Agave, the high priestess of the cult. This is the ultimate ironical fate of the puritan: that he is eventually consumed by the very evil against which he does battle, and for no other reason than that he refuses to confront and to understand his enemy. It is only by playing upon Pentheus's vulnerability, his deep ignorance of his own nature, that the god Dionysus (or the Devil) is able to possess him, humiliate him, and, finally, destroy him.

The *hubris* of Pentheus is exhibited also in the character of Oedipus. Like Pentheus, Oedipus is the personification of repressed necessity. Like that of Pentheus, Oedipus's tragic flaw is his wrath against his own reality. The whole drama is a progressive revelation of Oedipus to himself. Oedipus begins, however, with the posture of bad-faith, resorting to such tactics as "resistance" and "projection"—for example, accusing Tiresias of planning to betray the city and of having conspired with Creon against him, and so on. Oedipus's bad-faith is clearly a device for escaping the burden of responsibility for knowing himself. Yet in the end Oedipus learns that he is after all "only a man," that is to say, that he is, qua man, a creature of passion and a bearer of the demonic.

The issue is not simply recognizing it, but accepting responsibility for it as well. It is the failure and refusal to locate the sources of evil within the structure of one's own being, in order to avoid assuming responsibility for the evil that one does, which tends to perpetuate the corruption and brings on the Furies and the plagues. In short, the net result of this failure to integrate the demonic and Apollonian, in order to produce *sophia*, is the ultimate destruction of rationality. The fate of Pentheus is the fate of all men and of mankind itself. The consequence of man's pretended detachment from evil will be a reign of terror led by men like Thrasymachus and Callicles, the characters in Plato's *Dialogues* who represent the embodiment of the irrationalist "ethic of power." Thus Callicles declares, in a fit of pseudo-prophetic rage:

> There will come a day when the heroic individual will achieve his vengeance against the society of weaklings; there shall arise men sufficiently endowed by nature to shake off and break through and escape from the chains of mediocrity; men who will tread underfoot your text and your spells, your incantations and unnatural laws, and by an act of revolt reveal themselves, in the full blaze of the light of natural justice, masters instead of slaves.[28]

As Plato sees it, the influence of men like Callicles and Thrasymachus is directly proportional to the extent to which men pretend to be angels, on the one hand, while exhibiting in their behavior the advice that the thing to do is to "sin first and sacrifice afterwards from the proceeds."[29] It is bad enough that men pretend to be angels, but to do so while at the same time making pacts with the Devil is unpardonable. A society in which individuals indulge in this hypocrisy, while at the same time refusing to locate and experience the origins of this "moral schizophrenia" in the ambivalent duality of their own beings, is indeed a society in which men like Thrasymachus and Callicles will thrive and prevail: for they are the pornographers of evil who facilitate the transformation of the fantasies of repression into concrete reality.

Precisely the same point is made in novels like Rex Warner's *The Professor* and George Orwell's *1984*. In Warner's novel, Callicles is represented by Julius Vander, the brilliant protégé of a classics professor who represents the tradition of rational humanism. "I believe," says the professor, "that the world and human nature are fundamentally good, and that it is interference that is the cause of distortion."[30] The professor learns from Julius Vander, however, that in the effort to rule society by this maxim, humanists (as much because they are hypocrites as because they are humanists) have succeeded only in repressing man's demonic instincts. The result has been that once man is offered a political and social system that appeals to the dark, unsatisfied, and raging impulses that still lie within, centuries of enforced respect and complacency are turned overnight toward the vast relief of the practical enjoyment of hatred. Or, as O'Brien puts it even more forcefully at the end of *1984*: "We are different from all the oligarchies of the past in that we know what we are doing. . . . They pretended, perhaps they even believed, that they had seized power unwillingly and for a limited time, and that just round the corner there lay a paradise where human beings would be free and equal." But, says O'Brien, "We are not like that. We know that no one ever seizes power with the intention of relinquishing it. Power is not a means; it is an end. One does not establish a dictatorship in order to safeguard a revolution; one makes the revolution in order to establish the dictatorship. The object of persecution is persecution. The object of torture is torture. The object of power is power." And power, says O'Brien, real power, "is power over human beings." "How does one man assert his power over another? . . . By making him suffer. . . . Power is inflicting pain and humiliation. Power is in tearing human minds to pieces and putting them together again in new shapes of your own choosing. . . . If you want a picture of the future," says O'Brien, "imagine a boot stamping on a human face—forever."[31]

The repressed desires seeking counterfeit forms of expression include both those that have been acquired through socialization and learning, and those that have their origin in the libidinal constitution of man's primordial nature. The fact that consciousness is embodied as well as subject to social influences is a fact to which we have given far too little attention. It should thus be a primary task of contemporary philosophy to explore the implications for social consciousness and culture of the post-Cartesian view of primordial consciousness as embodied (as opposed to the Cartesian view of consciousness as a substance that qua consciousness transcends the fact of its embodiment). The phenomenological view of consciousness rests on the principle that embodiment is not accidental to, but is rather essential to, the constitution of consciousness qua consciousness.

The problem of the pathology of humanism, which derives from the facticity of embodied consciousness, is particularly well stated in *The Professor*. Toward the end of the novel an old cobbler lectures the professor on the inherent limitations of classical humanism. "What I accuse you of is your indifference to the fact of the damnation of the soul," he says, in a statement that may be treated as an affirmation of the embodiment of consciousness. The professor, who believes in the inherent rationality and goodness of natural man, replies that he has spent much of his time during the past years developing a plan, an economic plan that would do away entirely with poverty and would go a long way toward preventing war. "Would you not agree with me," he asks the cobbler, "that poverty and war are the chief scourges of this generation?" But the cobbler replies: "On the contrary. I believe that you and your philosophy are in the long run more dangerous and devastating than either war or poverty. . . . What makes our lives wretched is not so much poverty and hunger as the desire to escape from them. You and those like you gave us this desire. You urged us to be ambitious, to make good, to rise in the world, sometimes encouraging the most blatant and outrageous motives of greed and self-indulgence, sometimes pointing us towards the pleasures of the soul, culture, poetry, beauty of manners. Did you ever observe that if we were to follow your advice we should have to fight and kill our brothers? For there can be no culture and no self-expression without power, and power must always corrupt the soul."[32]

It is because of the libidinal context in which consciousness is embodied that power corrupts. Power is a very libidinal experience. "I have learned," says the cobbler, that "pain was not invented by the governing class. Evil and disappointment may be alleviated in some cases . . . but they spring from the soul of man. . . . Damnation . . . my friend . . . is the pretended detachment from evil, pain and death. . . . It is the attempt to gloss over the truth that man's life is infinitely wretched. . . . [It is] the incapacity to feel compassion for the infinite suffering of the living, the illusion that something complete may be made of a man's life. And that is why I said that neither war nor poverty is as dangerous to mankind as is your liberalism. For you in your detachment, endeavour to legislate for the abstract man. What a terrible insult to real living and tortured men and women. . . . You would abolish poverty in the name of science [and progress]. But in your scientific world, evil, under the most specious names, would come to be an accepted morality. For the aim of your science would be a brutal and mechanic efficiency, not the salvation of the soul through love. Your scientists would eliminate the weak, not see in them their own faces."[33]

The seeds of Callicles's revolt, leading to the Orwellian holocaust, grow well in the soil of a repressed pseudo-humanistic society, fertilized by the propaganda of irrationalism and cultivated by the irrationality of "functional rationality." In such a society, men are socialized to conform to standards that the society nevertheless openly violates in its very practice. The result of the cognitive and emotional dissonance created by what, following Plato, we have previously described as the hypocrisy of "sinning first and sacrificing afterwards from the proceeds" is the creation of frustrated aggression which, as Freud points out, seeks every possible avenue of expression, if not openly, then by subterfuge.

One such avenue is through the mechanism of what I have been calling the projection of internal necessity, as expressed by the image of Satan: the magical conversion of internal into external necessity. The mechanism of the projection of internal necessity that prevented Pentheus from recognizing the true significance of the god Dionysus, from recognizing that he himself is Dionysus, operates in all situations where men justify their acts by an appeal to authority—as in the case of Adolph Eichmann, who argued that he was merely a cog in the machinery of due process, that he was simply "doing his job," "obeying orders." It is thus that language itself becomes an instrument for the counterfeit legitimization of evil. Ordinary routine and respectable, time-honored phrases like "in the name of authority," "in the name of progress, truth, and freedom," "in the national interest," and "peace with honor" are simply facades for "*in nomine diaboli.*" The deliberate infliction of pain and death on others is only too easily facilitated by the linguistic magic enacted through the invocation, "I was forced to it by the circumstances, I was merely obeying orders." Such language, I suggest, is nothing less than a celebration in black magic.

## III. THE HERMENEUTICS OF THE MYTH OF SATAN:

### TOWARD A PHILOSOPHICAL ANTHROPOLOGY

### OF EVIL AND VIOLENCE

We have considered the hypothesis that certain forms of violence—including such violence as results in a violation of respect for person, property, and nature—arise not simply as a result of man's inherent capacity for aggressiveness but also as a result of a conscious desire to facilitate a flight from freedom and reality. The fact that the self-experience of the expression of violence is accompanied by a dimension of sensuality that is self-reinforcing makes it all the more attractive as a device through which the conversion of freedom into "thing-hood" may be facilitated. The flight from reality expresses itself not only in a renunciation of responsibility and a cancellation of freedom, but on some occasions it takes the form of an irresponsible satisfaction of desire. And, indeed, is there any greater satisfaction of desire than the achievement of mastery over the consciousness of others? For, as Bertrand de Jouvenel puts it,

> In every condition of life and social position a man feels himself more of a man when he is imposing himself and making others the instruments of his will, the means to the great ends of which he has an intoxicating vision. To rule a people, what an extension of the ego is there![34]

As represented by this hypothesis, violence appears as a species of evil. This does not account for all violence, but only that violence which seeks the domination of other beings as a condition for relieving oneself of the burden of responsibility for treating others under the category of freedom—that is to say, as subjects of "care."[35] To treat beings that are meant to be cared for as means for the satisfaction of the narcissistic will-to-power is evil. One of the major sources of insight into the structure of evil so defined is the already referred-to myth of Satan—according to which, as we have already noted, evil originates in the conscious submission to an external compulsion; an act which is undertaken by consciousness in order to facilitate a flight from the primordial reality of one's own nature. In order to appreciate better its possible relevance to the elaboration of a philosophical anthropology of violence, let us now take a more detailed look at the symbolism of the myth.

## A. The Myth of Satan

The first characteristic of the myth is that it places evil at the center of a cosmic drama. Indeed, evil is represented as the very yeast of creation. The paradox of the cosmos, as portrayed by the myth, is that in its state of perfect existence—let us call this, in the language of mythology, the *yin* state—the cosmos is unable to continue the process of creation. This applies as much to the creator as to the object of creation, the cosmos. The limitation of perfection—the perfection of God, the cosmic perfection of the Garden of Eden, and the perfect innocence of its inhabitants—is derived from the ontological fact that to the extent to which that perfection has been reached there is virtually no opportunity for further improvement. Before process and creation can be reintroduced into the cosmos, *yin* must pass over into *yang*. But before this can happen, *yin* must be seduced, as it were, by the intrusion of a foreign adversary.[36]

In almost all versions of the myth, the pattern is repeated. The story opens with a perfect state of *yin* (the context of the pre-historical cosmos) which passes over into *yang* (the context or form of the historically developing cosmos) as a result of the mediation of a foreign adversary. Adam and Eve are in a perfect state of innocence in the pre-utopian perfection of the Garden of Eden; Job is perfect in goodness and prosperity; Faust is near perfection in knowledge, to the point of boredom at being unable to conceive of any further challenges. The foreign adversary in the cosmic drama depicted by these stories is, of course, none other than the Devil. And it is to the symbolism of the Devil, therefore, that we must turn if we are to understand clearly the genesis of evil in the cosmos, the plot of the cosmic drama.

According to at least one version of the myth, the Devil was an archangel who was cast out of the heavenly paradise into the fiery desert of Hell for having betrayed his covenant with God. His name was Lucifer, which means "the bearer of light" (Isaiah 14:12). Like that of the hero of Greek mythology, Prometheus, who was expelled from the company of the gods for disobedience, Lucifer's crime consisted of his refusal to serve. Like Prometheus, Lucifer was driven by a craving for originality. He wanted to be the author of his own destiny, the bearer of his own light. He thus fell from heaven, where God's will remains absolute. But, if we may resort to the language of metaphysics for the moment, to be cast out of heaven constitutes a passage from one mode of existence to another, namely, from Being to Nothingness—a transition that is mediated by time. The Fall from Being is thus synonymous with the Fall into time.

The Devil may thus be regarded as a messenger and spokesman of nothing. Yet, as I have already indicated, it is only through the temporal encounter with nothingness that *yin* passes over into *yang* and being passes from a state of potential creativity into a state of actuality. Or, as Hegel was to put it finally, the rational becomes actual and the actual becomes rational only through a dialectic of self-negation.

The first act of the cosmic drama, which features the encounter between two superhuman personalities, is the Devil's expulsion from heaven. In the second act—according to some versions of the myth—the Devil reappears to make a wager with God to the effect that he, the Devil, will tempt man away from

God toward disobedience.[37] God accepts the wager and thus begins the third act of the drama, which witnesses the temptation of man and his subsequent fall. Or, as Milton was to put it in *Paradise Lost*, the Devil, having seduced God into accepting the wager

> Came furious down to be reveng'd on men,
> *Wo to the inhabitants on Earth!* . . .
> . . . . . . . . . . . . . . . . . . . . . . . . . . . . . . . . . .
> The Tempter ere th' Accuser of man-kind,
> To wreck on innocent frail man his loss
> Of that first Battel, and his flight to Hell.[38]

The fourth and final act has to do with man's redemption. It is through the redemption of man that the final transition from *yin* to *yang* is accomplished. This study is concerned primarily with the dialectic of *yin* and *yang* as it pertains to the temptation and the fall and only incidentally with the drama of redemption.

## B. The Drama of Temptation and the Fall

The drama of temptation and the fall is the central plot of what might be described as the second act of the cosmic drama of evil, the plot of the first act having had to do with disobedience. As Satan was himself cast out from heaven as a result of his disobedience, so did he engineer man's expulsion from the Garden of Eden. As the Devil fell from divinity so Adam and Eve fell from perfect humanity. Satan was banished to hell because he tried to take a short cut to divinity. And it was for having followed the same urge that Adam and Eve were likewise cast out into a fiery desert whose soil was cursed. This event was synonymous with the entry into time: with Adam and Eve begins the history of mankind.

Let us look more carefully at the symbolism of Eve's flirtation with the Devil and the consequences of her transgression. We note, to begin with, that what tempted Eve was not anything evil in itself, but merely the prospect of reaching divinity and immortality by a shorter route than had been assigned by divine law. As Denis de Rougemont puts it in his book *The Devil's Share*:

At the root of every temptation lies the glimpse of the possibility of reaching divinity by a shorter route than that of reality; by a road that one should oneself invent, in spite of the prohibitions imposed by the laws of creation, the divine order and the order of man.[39]

Thus, in the case of Christ, who did not succumb to the temptation, Satan proposed various ways of gaining power by a route other than that laid down by divine law—by the route of materialism and the achievement of a universal state through the use of the sword. To follow God's way is to surrender to a reality which exists prior to man's effort to bear witness to it. The virtue of this posture is innocent fidelity to God's preordained authority—as expressed in uncritical acceptance of the prearranged harmony of the cosmos. The metaphysical formula for this relationship to the cosmos is expressed in the statement "essence precedes existence." But to follow the path of human inclination, of one's own daemon, as it were, is to unleash the appetite for re-creating reality according to man's own image of himself. As God created man and the cosmos, so man bears witness to God by re-creating himself as well as the cosmos. The metaphysical formula for this posture, whose virtue is unending creativity, is "existence precedes essence."

The essence of the temptation, then, is the prospect of man's making himself more powerful than it was in his nature to be. It is in the assumption of power that we find the real source of impiety and corruption. In the case of Eve, the eating of the apple opens the eyes of man to the power of imagination and to the prospect of turning his fantasies into reality. In that act, man experiences his freedom as a capacity for directing his choice either toward obedience to God's way or else toward the challenges of his own imagination or daemon, the way of human pride. In the case of Faust, the prize is escape from the boredom of self-complacent tranquillity, the thrill of ascending the ladder of progress and of achieving even greater heights of glory than anything hitherto dreamt of by man.

We notice also that before the temptation Eve believed that it was simply not possible to disobey God's command, because to do so would lead to death. Eve did not even think of eating the apple until the serpent had first created doubt as to the reality of God's ordinance. The first device of Satan, then, implicit in the symbolism of the myth, was to cast doubt on the reality of the divine law. Thus it is written in Genesis:

And the serpent said unto the woman, Ye shall not surely die:

For God doth know that in the day ye eat thereof, then your eyes shall be opened, and ye shall be as gods, knowing good and evil. [3:4–5]

It is only when uncertainty is cast upon the authority of God's cosmic order that the possibility of temptation is opened up. Man is now tempted to re-create reality according to his own image of himself. Whichever of man's desires it is possible to realize becomes desirable, in which case, one is prepared to take whatever steps are necessary to realize that desire. Indeed, the very recognition of the possibility endows the object of temptation with even greater desirability and attractiveness—to the point where we experience its realization as an obligation. Kant pointed out that "ought" implies "can," or, whatever is obligatory must be possible. And with this, reason cannot take issue. It is the Devil's task, however, to confuse the relationship between obligation and possibility by making us believe the completely false claims that whatever is possible becomes thereby not only desirable but obligatory, and that all desires are equally valid expressions of one's daemon. It is with this logic that man begins his descent into hell as if it were in fact a pursuit of the good.

This lead to the second stage in the dialectic of temptation:

And when the woman saw that the tree was good for food, and that it was pleasant to the eyes, and a tree to be desired to make one wise, she took of the fruit thereof, and did eat. [Gen. 3:6]

It is thus never evil in itself which tempts but always a good that one imagines to be more desirable than what God or tradition offers—a good more suited to man's own conception of himself. Eve was not tempted by the desire to harm anyone. She was tempted rather by the idea of achieving divinity, of achieving what God had excluded from *His* conception of reality. To so deify oneself was contrary to the comprehensive plan of the cosmos. Temptation, in other words, is the utopian vision, the desire to re-create reality through revolution and revolt.

The Devil's tactic, then, according to the symbolism of the religious and cultural tradition as expressed in the myth, is to incite us to abuse our liberty and the goods of the earth. Evil is but a bad use of good. Man alone is endowed with freedom and with the power of speaking. The paradox is that the very same freedom with which he embraces God's law out of love and choice is the source also of disobedience and impiety; the very same language with which man sings hymns to God and through which he is able to tell the truth is also the language of contradiction, deception, and lying. The duplicity of man's being is the source both of his glory as well as of his fall. It is only because man is free that he has the power to sin. Sin is cheating with, or falsifying, the order of the cosmos.

It is by provoking the abuse of our freedom, then, that the Devil acts within us and blinds us. Man was given freedom in order that his obedience to God could have some meaning—for unless men are free to disobey, what value is there to obedience? Man was given speech in order to answer to the truth and to bear witness to it. But in order to give authenticity to his freedom and speech, he was also given the capacity to suffer and to resist temptation. Yet to suffer temptation at all is to run the risk of submitting to it. But because man is who he is—the being who seeks both *to-be-what-he-is-not* and *not-to-be-what-he-is*—he cannot suffer and surrender to temptation without at the same time being inclined to counterfeit his actions. It is thus that whatever man does is always perceived by him to be in the service of some good. As Pascal remarks, "never is evil committed with such ferocity than when it is done in the name of good. He who would act the angel, acts the brute."[40] Evil lies as much in the pretense of innocence and the impunity with which one counterfeits one's acts as in the acts themselves.

It is thus clear, as de Rougemont says, that the great satanic ambition must be to seize our speech in our mouths, in order to distort the witness we bear from the very outset. And this is why, according to de Rougemont, the Bible energetically affirms that when we lie "it is the Devil himself who pulls his tongue in our tongue."[41]

Now there are at least two ways of lying. A person can tell a lie about what he knows to be the truth—in which case his lie remains relative to an invariable measure of the truth. To so lie gives rise to the evil of deliberate deception. But one can also tamper with the very *criterion of truth itself*, so that one's *cheating* is now conceived under the guise of *creation*. "Man is the measure"; "all truth is relative"—that is pure lying. The moment you falsify the scale of truth itself, all of your virtues are at the service of evil and are accomplices in the work of the Evil One. There are, after all, no errors in truth where no truth exists, as there is no crime where no law exists. There is no longer any distinction between what is *desired* and what is *de-*

*sirable*, between what is *possible* and what is *permissible* and *obligatory*. It is here, according to de Rougemont, that we find the final reason for lying. It is always the desire for utopian innocence:

> The ordinary lie was but the omission or the contradiction of a truth, which still subsisted elsewhere and still judged us. But the diabolical lie denies the judge. It proceeds only from itself and proliferates autarchically, like a cancerous cell, introducing into the universe that sophism of pure anguish: the lie of the no truth.[42]

Thus is born the diabolical lie of pure nihilism.

## C. The Myth as a Clue to the Interpretation of History

A possible hermeneutic of evil has now been suggested. Evil derives from submitting to the temptation to be as gods, which leads to challenging and contradicting the order of the cosmos. Yet even this, even revolt, according to the myth, is part of the plot of the cosmic drama. As a consequence of the encounter between God and the Devil, the Devil sets out to tempt man away from God, and because the Devil succeeds, man is banished from paradise. The demonic disrupts the homeostatic relationship between man and the cosmos and brings down the wrath of God upon the disrupter. But in the fall is the beginning. For, as I have already suggested, the paradox implicit in the creation is the fact that it is only by being cast out in the first place that man can fulfill the divine aspiration which, in accordance with the plot of the cosmic drama, defines his destiny. The result of Adam's sin is the creation of history and civilization, in the course of which, man's understanding of himself and his relation to the cosmos far exceeds anything achieved during the period of innocence in paradise. The passion of Christ, the result of Judas's betrayal, is the redemption of man. And man redeemed, as Sophocles reminds us through his portrait of Oedipus, is much more of a man than was man in the state of innocence.

We have thus reached the following conclusions with respect to what is implied by the symbolism of the myth. Since God is a being for whom essence and existence coincide completely, whatever He creates must be as perfect as the creator. But having already given birth to perfection, it is logically impossible to improve upon or add anything to what has already been created. This is the source of a fundamental limitation of God's power: He has the power of *creating* perfection, but not of *transcending* it. How indeed, can perfection be transcended or superseded? It is for this reason that God or being (in so far as He exists in a state of perfect *yin*) can pass over into *yang* (the state of continuous creation) only when provoked by the intervention of a foreign intruder. The latter brings corruption into the state of being—thus introducing the need for further acts of creativity on God's part. It is for this reason that God is compelled to accept the Devil's wager, for the wager provides the only opportunity for fresh creation. At the same time, since God is a being for whom essence and existence coincide he can be neither the agent of evil nor the subject of tragedy. For it is only with respect to a being for whom essence and existence do not coincide that evil and tragedy are possible. Evil is a result of an attempt to force a coincidence between essence and existence, which is what the desire to be God amounts to. Finally, we must bear in mind the point already made, that in metaphysical terms the Devil's fall from being symbolizes a surrender to non-being or nothingness—in which case the Devil may be conceived of as the messenger of nothing.

If, then, the expulsion of Satan from the realm of being and the subsequent expulsion of man from paradise is part of a cosmic drama in which, as a result of having been expelled, man is given the opportunity of using his freedom as a source of creativity, then the *risk* of nihilism is also part of a cosmic drama. But the terrible thing about this is that nihilism, like the Devil himself, lives incognito. The *danger* of nihilism is that it *pretends* to be rational and succeeds in this deception. The pretense of rationality is enhanced by the fact that, although fallen from being, the Devil has not lost his technique, his knowledge, his skills. He is like a lover who no longer believes in love but still retains his power of seduction. Satan still has the knack, as it were, but no longer the vision. He has lost the sense of the end, and the glory to which the application of knowledge is destined. And what is done skillfully but without regard to the ends or purposes served, and without regard to the moral consequences of pursuing such ends, whatever is done for "no reason" or for reasons that are in reality nothing more than disguised excuses or alibis, bears the imprimatur of the Devil. And, to repeat, the language that justifies this conduct, language such as "I was only following orders," "only doing my job," "serving the national interest," is in reality *in nomine diaboli.*

Examples of such behavior may be found in a wide variety of contexts. Thus, for example, the distinguished psychologist Herbert C. Kelman complains about the intellectual mercenaries who make their skills available to meet demands without regard to the moral implications of the assignments they have accepted. "On the one hand," writes Kelman,

> there is the involvement of those social scientists who . . . are concerned with social issues. Their primary orientation is toward social change or toward the resolution of social problems in accordance with humane values. . . . On the other hand, there is the involvement of those social scientists who possess special skills relevant to the execution of certain policies and who have, therefore, been drawn into the process by officials in charge of it. Unlike the social scientists oriented toward social issues, they are not trying to change the system but rather are responding to the demands of the system by making their technical skills available to it.[43]

One of the most dramatic examples of what Kelman is complaining about is provided by the circumstances associated with the scandal known as Project Camelot. Project Camelot was a research project conceived by the United States Army as a means of quantifying the conditions of social unrest, riots, and insurrection in the Latin American countries. It would, in the words of one of the generals, "help us to predict potential use of the American Army in any number of cases where the situation might break out." It would also have provided data whereby crises could be provoked which might then justify United States military intervention. The project was never actually undertaken, but the mere fact that it was both conceived and organized at all is sufficient to present it as one of the most significant phenomena of our time. As the American sociologist Robert Nisbet puts it in his penetrating appraisal of the incident:

> what cannot be overlooked is the fact that a group of American social scientists, acting as social scientists, allowed the American military to believe that there was nothing scientifically wrong in the American social science project, under American Army sponsorship, entering the historically sensitive areas of Latin America

for the express purpose of discovering through every possible penetration of culture and mind, the conditions of social unrest, conflict, and insurgency. . . . Was there no one to say . . . "Your objective is your business and no doubt admirable from the point of view of the Army; as behavioral scientists we desire to be of such help as we can; but everything we know as behavioral scientists suggests the monumental, possibly catastrophic, unwisdom of such a project." . . . Does any sociologist believe that [he] can properly take refuge in the implicit statement: I am a behavioral scientist and if my sponsor orders it, it is not mine to reason why?[44]

But this is precisely what happens to all professionals who are educated in a culture dominated by a logic of functional rationality according to which the skills of researchers and the products of their research are available to whomever is interested in purchasing and consuming them. The professionals who made their skills available to Project Camelot did so not because they perceived the inherent justice of it but because they were obsessed with the thrill of applying their skills for the mere sake of doing so.

Further examples may be found in the various disclosures of the Senate committee investigating the Watergate scandal. On repeated occasions throughout their testimony, men like Mitchell, Ehrlichman, and Haldeman—not to speak of the many others involved—resorted to such excuses as "the national interest" and "national security." Ehrlichman kept referring to himself as "on assignment," never prepared to act without "marching orders" from above. He believed that morality and virtue are defined by whatever is in the interest of national security and order. Haldeman began his statement by emphasizing the high moral standards of the White House staff and then admitted having approved of plans to discredit the opposition Democratic party because he *believed*, but did not *know* for a fact, that its campaign was being financed by Communist funds. Meanwhile, the President, after expressing regret for the actions of some of his colleagues "whose zeal exceeded their judgment" and who "may have done wrong for a cause they deeply believed to be right," kept reminding us that while others wallowed in Watergate he intended to meet his responsibilities by doing the job he was elected to do.

The corrupt rationality inherent in the behavior of those who plead the excuse that "I was only doing my job" or "serving the national interest" may be further elucidated in terms of Karl

Mannheim's well-known analysis of "functional rationality" in *Man and Society in an Age of Reconstruction*.[45] In this work, Mannheim introduces a distinction between "substantial" and "functional" rationality, a distinction that resembles both Plato's distinction between *arete* and *techne* and Heidegger's distinction between meditative and calculative thinking.

As Mannheim uses the term, "substantial rationality" may be understood to refer to an act of thought that reveals intelligent insight into the moral and practical relationship between actions and the plan or purpose that that action serves. It would thus seem to be informed by what the Greek philosophers called *nous* and it is therefore grounded in *arete*. To act in accordance with *nous* or substantial rationality is to act on the basis of one's understanding of what is best. It is to address oneself to the question, "which of the various courses of action that are within the range of possibility *should* I pursue in order to bring about the greatest amount of good?" As Plato put it in the famous passage of the *Phaedo* in which Socrates addresses his friends on the eve of his death: the only thing a man should ever think about, whether in regard to himself or anything else, is what is best, what is the highest good—though of course he would have to know what is bad, since knowledge of good involves knowledge of bad.[46]

Functional rationality, although it is often confused with substantial rationality, is quite another matter. By "functional rationality" is meant something closer to what Plato meant by *techne*: the way something—a given industry, administration, problem, or activity—has been "rationalized." In such cases, the term "rational" refers to the fact that a series of actions is *organized* in such a way that it leads to the successful implementation of a previously defined goal. Consciousness is no longer subject to *cogito ergo sum*. It is rather a *facto ergo sum*. Every element or stage in this series or repertoire of actions receives a functional position or role. The value placed on such an organization will depend, moreover, on the extent to which the coordination of means has been achieved by the most efficient techniques. Such rationality, according to Mannheim, is in reality a disguised form of "irrationality." The irrationality of "functional rationality" derives not only from the kinds of goals pursued—although not all goals pursued are evil in themselves —but from the fact that the agent becomes so obsessed with *means* and *techniques* that he is virtually anesthetized by this into adopting an attitude of passive indifference to, or acceptance of, the goals. What gives the enterprise the pretense of rationality is the fact that it is *organized*. Thus Eichmann, for example, in his pursuit of "the final solution," regarded his actions as rational. He had organized a repertoire of technologically functional means toward the solution of a specific goal, and any action that is experienced as having a functional role to play in achieving the ultimate goal is, by virtue of this fact alone, regarded as rational. Indeed, as I have already indicated, so preoccupied is the agent with the organizational aspect of the enterprise, that his attention is concentrated almost exclusively on the efficiency of the means, rather than on the moral implications of achieving the goal. The agent sets out to solve a problem and achieve a goal for the sake of solving a problem and achieving a goal. As an example of how this works in practice, I cite the following passage from a recent book that is presented as an on-the-spot story of the Vietnam War:

> Dixie Station had a reason. It was simple. A pilot going into combat for the first time is a bit like a swimmer about to dive into an icy lake. He likes to get his big toe wet and then wade around a little before leaping off the high board into the numbing depths. So it was fortunate that young pilots could get their first taste of combat under the direction of a forward air controller over a flat country in bright sunshine where nobody was shooting back with high-powered ack-ack. He learns how it feels to drop bombs on human beings and watch huts go up in a boil of orange flame when his aluminum napalm tanks tumble into them. He gets hardened to pressing the firing button and cutting people down like cloth dummies, as they sprint frantically under him. He gets his sword bloodied for the rougher things to come.[47]

Not only is the nature and content of the goal secondary to the satisfaction of achieving it, but the agent's perception of the rationality of the goal itself is determined primarily by the success and efficiency with which it is achieved. If it is possible to achieve a given goal, then the goal itself must be rational.

It is thus that one acquires a completely false sense of rationality. Just as Hume in his famous analysis of causation pointed out that we confuse the psychological experience of "fulfilled expectancy" with the perception of "necessary connection" or "force," so the bureaucrat and technocrat confuse the psychological experience of the means bringing about the end with the reason or rationality for the sake of which the end exists. The confusion of the "means," which merely produces the ends in question, with the rationale, according to which the realization of those ends can be *justified*, is one of the major sources of the crisis of reason, which crisis consists of the loss of the capacity to reason in accordance with the Socratic injunction.

It is thus, also, that human action becomes a source of what we have earlier referred to as "the banality of evil," the capacity of engaging in evil without experiencing it as evil, of performing evil acts as part of one's job description. Such behavior, as Hannah Arendt and others have so ably pointed out, is not the expression of innate aggressiveness or sadism, but is the result, rather, of the agent's inability to challenge whatever discrepancies he might perceive between what he does and his moral beliefs. This is especially true of the way in which acts of violence, such as the events disclosed by the Watergate hearings, become assimilated to the agent's perception of what is rationally appropriate. For the Watergate conspirators it was more rational to obey the commands of their superiors than to disobey in the name of conscience. The same attitude received widespread exemplification during the late sixties and early seventies among those who condemned as treasonable and unpatriotic the actions of those who protested against the war in Vietnam. It is precisely this attitude of respect for authority at all costs which underlies the following editorial from the *Wall Street Journal* respecting United States support of the fascist military junta in Greece:

> We do not . . . deny that the junta is, on the record, repressive. It has squashed press freedom and other liberties associated with a free society. It relentlessly punishes political dissent. On these scores it is presumably repugnant to most Americans, including U.S. policy-makers.
>
> *Yet to make such repugnance the criterion of policy would be to indulge in diplomacy by emotionalism*—never a wise exercise. *Diplomatic recognition, or its recision, should not depend on emotional reactions but on considerations of the national interest.*
>
> If Washington can use whatever influence it has to induce more democratic conditions in Greece, that is worth doing. But the Administration has evidently decided, so far, that for strategic and international political reasons, the present basic policy is in the nation's interest. For that evaluation, it seems to us, it does not deserve chastisement.[48]

Such attitudes result from the learned habit of identifying the structure of rationality per se with the structure of functional rationality. At the same time, we must recognize the psychological context in which such habits are acquired. Freud suggests that some habits provide outlets for the expression of libido. It is thus easy to see how the habits associated with the exercise of functional rationality may become outlets for the expression of the libido of what Freud called the instinct for aggression, the instinct that, in the context of the hermeneutic of the myth of Satan, we have identified as the Faustian urge, or the mechanism of the expression of internal necessity, and which, in the context of Sartre's analysis, provides the impetus for the flight into magic.

When viewed from the standpoint of Freud, as exemplified in his previously-referred-to paper on demoniacal possession, the behavior associated with functional rationality may provide an outlet for the expression of aggression, which under normal circumstances the ego must repress under pressure from the superego. For while the ego will not permit the expression of self-initiated acts of violence, it can permit the expression of violence through acts that are perceived as legitimate responses to the command of authority. Just as Freud's neurotic rationalizes his violence by believing himself to have been "possessed" by an external reality, so the bureaucrats of evil believe themselves to have been compelled to their acts by the command of an external authority.

Precisely the same considerations apply to contexts in which individuals are compelled not so much by specific commands as by the generalized or universalized imperative of what Herbert Marcuse has called the technological a priori. Thus, individuals who are accustomed to manipulate and engineer variables in contexts where it might seem appropriate to do so gradually extend this attitude toward the perception of the entire field of human action. For, as both Freud and Sartre would be quick to point out, there is something compellingly sensuous and erotic about the experience of engineering and manipulating things, and this enticing quality begs the application of such engineering to all possible contexts—including contexts in which it is totally inappropriate.

It is thus from the temptation to universalize the craving for mastery and manipulating that we find ourselves developing the Faustian urge to apply our *techne* to the implementation of goals irrespective of their desirability, irrespective of their consequences, and irrespective of whether they will, in fact, contribute to the good.

## D.  The Paradox of Evil and the Problem of Theodicy

In addition to revealing a clue to the understanding of history as a process of "challenge and response," the myth may also be read as a projection or personification of the pattern of growth of the individual human psyche. The characteristics attributed to Satan are universal in man, and the role of Satan in the cosmic drama parallels the role of the demonic in the drama of individual consciousness.

According to David Bakan, the myth is built around various analytic notions that characterize the psychological growth of the individual psyche.[49] The three basic notions that account for the genesis of evil are: (1) separation, the experience through which consciousness is born; (2) mastery or the quest for power, the experience through which the ego emerges and acquires an identity; and (3) denial or repression, the experience through which the ego protects itself from pain and suffering.

In the myth, separation occurs when the Devil is "dethroned" and cast out of heaven, "put on his own," as it were. It is in much the same way that historical man is born when Adam and Eve are dethroned and cast out of the Garden of Eden, and that individual consciousness per se is born through the womb-fetus separation that gives rise to the birth trauma. There is also the experience of the child being put on his own, as symbolized by the various puberty rites characterizing all human societies.

In the case of the Devil, his fall is a fall into pure nothingness. For the Devil there is no possibility of atonement and redemption. In the case of man, however, there is the possibility of redemption. The Devil is totally determined by his satanic impulses; like God, his existence and his essence coincide completely. But whereas the essence of God is pure good, the Devil's essence is pure evil. Now, one of the consequences of being human is the fact that essence and existence do not coincide and man's essence is to some extent a product of his existence. Thus, whereas *separation* is an indispensable precondition of the possibility of ego growth, and is the very source of the incentive to creativity, man is yet free to overcome his primordial alienation from being, and to re-create or restore paradise on earth through historical action. At the political, cultural, and economic levels, separation appears in the form of tribalism, nationalism, and competitive free enterprise.

But separation is not without anxiety and despair. For separation gives birth to the second stage in the dialectic of self-growth, the need for mastery, as expressed in the will-to-power. Invariably, however, the individual person, state, nation, group, or tribe reaches the limits of its power potency and effectiveness without, of course, losing the appetites. As Faust exclaims:

> I shall not cease to feel in all attires,
> The pains of our narrow earthly day.
> I am too old to be content to play,
> Too young to be without desire.
> . . . . . . . . . . . . . . . . . . . . . . . . . . . . . . .
> The god that dwells within my heart
> Can stir my depths, I cannot hide—
> Rules all my powers with relentless art,
> But cannot move the world outside;
> And thus existence is for me a weight.
> Death is desirable, and life I hate.[50]

It is usually in the midst of such despair that the Devil reappears as an intruder from outer or cosmic reality with an offer of help. And it is in order to overcome his despair and thus satisfy his insatiable appetite for mastery and power that man makes a pact with the Devil—a pact which he readily represses, in order to relieve his guilt.[51] Instead of praising the Devil, he refers instead to "luck," "chance," "fate," "destiny," or, in more sophisticated terms, "the laws of the market," "the force of circumstance," and so on.

Thus, the Faustian urge is already implicit in the original act of separation. From the very moment the ego is separated off from its source, it is necessarily driven by the will-to-power. Such a will-to-power is intrinsic to the growth of the individual ego as well as to human development in general. At the political level, this is expressed in the equation of nationality with sovereignty. Just as the child discovers himself as a person by coming to desire dominion over himself, so the nation reaches its identity by wanting independence and dominion over its own affairs. Likewise, the enterprising employee wants to become an entrepreneur and go into business on his own. Unfortunately, the Faustian urge to strike out on one's own and to seek greater degrees of self-mastery often becomes confused with the desire for mastery over others. Thus nationalism leads to persecution, internationalism, colonialism, and imperialism. In business, the enterprising entrepreneur begins to swallow up less successful entrepreneurs, and there is born the corporate Leviathan and the exercise of corporate power.

But how is such power exercised? We must remember that one of the outstanding characteristics of the Devil is his mastery of knowledge. Indeed, as Augustine points out in *The City of God*, one of the root meanings of "demon" is knowledge.[52] Demons are those beings who have great knowledge—but it is knowledge without charity and without wisdom.

The association of great knowledge with the Devil is common in all forms of the myth. In *Paradise Lost*, for example, we find the point stressed with particular emphasis. In the course of tempting Eve, the serpent refers to the tree of knowledge as the "Mother of Science":

> O Sacred, Wise, and Wisdom-giving Plant,
> Mother of Science, Now I feel thy Power
> Within me cleere, not onely to discerne
> Things in thir Causes, but to trace the wayes
> Of highest Agents, deemd however wise.[53]

In Milton's version of the myth, the notions of separation and mastery are discussed in such a way as to suggest that they are mutually interdependent. Thus, for example, we notice that the Devil's temptation is offered immediately after a discussion of separation—i.e., after Eve has persuaded Adam that it would be better if they divided their labor and worked separately. Adam objects that there is not much purpose to labor pursued for its own sake. This makes no impression on Eve. Her sole objective is mastery per se, or as some contemporary psychologists would prefer to put it, "achievement"—an experience that is purely "irrational."

Thus Eve's desire to separate from Adam, and indeed her willingness to be separated from paradise itself, is already preceded by the primitive demonic desire for mastery, which is in turn reinforced by separation. The relationship between separation and mastery is dialectical.

Now the reason why separation reinforces the need for mastery is that separation makes it possible for the Devil to approach the individual alone and to capitalize on the competitiveness that characterizes the individual's behavior. It is much easier to tempt a person when he is competing with others, and it is much easier to give in to temptation when you are alone than when you are in the presence of others.

Thus, when Satan tempts her, Eve has already given in to the Faustian urge. If she is so easily tempted, it is because she wants to be. Her very being qua human is already rooted in the demonic, and because the demonic is intrinsic to the nature of man qua man, to be human at all is to exist in the mode of temptation.

The association of knowledge with ego-enhancement and power over the world and people comes out just as clearly in Goethe's *Faust*. Faust begins in despair. In spite of a life dedicated to the pursuit of knowledge, he says:

> Do not fancy that I know anything right,
> Do not fancy that I could teach or assert
> What would better mankind or what might convert.
> I also have neither money nor treasures
> Nor worldly honors or earthly pleasures.[54]

It is in the context of such despair that Mephistopheles enters with his temptation. To begin with, he offers Faust pleasure. But Faust rejects that:

> If ever I recline, calmed, on a bed of sloth,
> You may destroy me then and there.
> If ever flattering you should wile me
> That in myself I find delight,
> If with enjoyment you beguile me,
> Then break on me, eternal night!
> This bet I offer.[55]

The bargain with the Devil, then, is not for the purpose of winning pleasure, but for power: "For restless activity proves a man."[56] It goes, as Freud put it, beyond the pleasure principle to the reality principle, which promises more certainty and greater success.

Mastery is the fundamental goal of man's satanic impulse. Mastery over the secular world is the first object—and this is characteristically attributed throughout history and mythology to Satan. In the New Testament, John refers to Satan several times as "the prince of this world" (12:31, 14:30, 16:11). Paul even calls Satan "the god of this world" (2 Cor. 4:4). According to Matthew, when the Devil is trying to tempt Jesus, he takes him to a high mountain, shows him "all the kingdoms of the world, and the glory of them; And saith unto him, All these things will I give thee, if thou wilt fall down and worship me" (4:8–9). In the same story in Luke, the Devil puts it even more strongly, saying, "All this *power* will I give thee" (4:5–7; italics mine).

The third stage in the natural history of satanism is denial. The victim or sinner never admits that he has in fact made a pact with the Devil. Nor does he admit that what he does has its origin in his own will. Man denies the presence of the demonic within him, experiencing it rather as a compulsion initiated from some point in external reality. This in turn is counter-feited, as I have already indicated, by being represented as if it were something rational, such as "progress," "destiny," and "the force of circumstances." It is in this way that the Devil maintains his incognito, his disguise. For the Devil's cleverest wile is to convince us that he does not exist. God says, "I am what I will become." And according to God's ontology, this means that His existence is a perfect manifestation of the truth and goodness that characterize his essence. The Devil, however, since he has fallen from being, must declare: "If God is being, then I am non-being." He is "nothing" in the sense that he is "no body," a mere myth, and because of this, he can be "any body." And in order to protect himself from being recognized, he hides behind the camouflage of the grotesque—the "mythi-cal" image of the leering and horned demon with a long tail, which has the effect of making him inoffensive in the eyes of many people. "The Devil is a gent with red horns and a long tail; now I can't believe in a gent with red horns and a long tail: therefore, I don't believe in the Devil." Or, to put it another way: "The Devil is only a myth, hence he does not exist."

But there is a fundamental ambiguity that lies at the center of the Devil's non-being. For, while he is no-thing in the sense of being "no body," he is nothing also in the sense that he exists for "no-purpose" and for "no-reason." And for this reason he can serve any purpose and give the appearance of being reason-able when he is in fact destroying reason. And this, as we have already noted, is the source of the Devil's nihilism.

## E.  Toward a Theodicy of Evil

In the biblical story of man's fall, evil is represented as the voluntary act of disobedient man. Indeed, it has been a funda-

while relieving consciousness of the burden of responsibility. In the last analysis, the achievement of mastery over other beings is equivalent to an escape from freedom. For freedom involves self-mastery, arising within a context in which essence and existence can never coincide, and in which existence must always precede essence. Man is thus forced into a dilemma. On the one hand, he must act without the benefit of knowing in advance that the outcome of his acts is guaranteed by the existence of some pre-existing authority. On the other hand, he knows that whatever he does offers itself for judgment before the tribunal of justice. One way of avoiding this dilemma is to substitute the certainty of mastery over others for the uncertainty of self-mastery. Freedom thus comes to be identified with the exercise of power, pursued in accordance with external compulsion. Essence, in the form of authority, now precedes existence.

The latter possibility is emphasized in the myth by the symbolism of Satan as an embodiment of external reality; that is to say, as a foreign intruder into the psychic life of man in the state of pure innocence.

The myth also suggests that the flight from responsibility, undertaken at the command of external authority and offering satisfaction for the will-to-power, originates from the same source as man's creative powers. It is only because man is the being who is, as Sartre puts it, "condemned to be free" that he can seek to counterfeit the escape from freedom by presenting it to himself as a creative exercise of freedom. For, as the myth suggests, under the influence of Satan, evil is always pursued under the guise of creativity.

Man is qua man the creative rebel who seeks through rebellion to re-create reality. Sometimes the re-creation of reality leads to a Promethean revelation of truth, as in the case of art. Sometimes, however, rebellion is simply counterfeit creativity, seeking not to reveal truth, but to facilitate an escape from freedom.

But notwithstanding this characterization of the human condition, the self-conscious understanding of man's primordial nature constitutes an act of transcendence whereby consciousness prepares itself to resist the temptation to retreat from reason to violence. As Pascal puts it, "Man is a reed, the most feeble thing in nature; but he is a 'thinking reed'." There is, according to Pascal, no need for the entire universe to arm itself in order to annihilate him. A vapor, a drop of water, suffices to

mental teaching of the mythology of the West, as in contrast to Eastern mythology, that, while evil is anything that destroys life, it does not originate in some external cosmic force but is paradoxically a part of the will to life itself. For the Greeks, the traits of evil were peculiarly human ones. The divine purpose is eternally good. What disturbs the relationship between men and the gods and brings evil into the world (the kind of evil that is embodied in tragedy) has its origin entirely in the will of man. Greek mythology thus distinguishes carefully between, on the one hand, the cruelty of nature and the cruelty of necessity (as symbolized by the "cruel sea" and the ritual of sacrifice, e.g. the deeds of the Titans who cut the little god Dionysus to pieces) and, on the other, evil as "will."

The Greeks, like the Hebrews, while not discounting the cosmic sources of evil, place the overwhelming emphasis on man's responsibility for not only his fall but for his redemption as well. Nature before man was good but not moral. By partaking of the tree of knowledge both man and nature fall prey to the dialectic of good and evil; and man is condemned to eat bread in the sweat of his brow. And since God cursed not only man but the earth "for man's sake," the future redemption of fallen man applies not only to man but to nature as well, which was corrupted at the same time and through the same voluntary act of man. Thus the biblical myth contains the insight that even the origins of evil in man's natural constitution (the point stressed by Darwin and Freud) derive ultimately from his will and are therefore within the jurisdiction of his responsibility.

The history of evil began with Adam, who brought forth first Cain and then Abel; and with Cain's fratricide began the history of the human race as a history of sin.

The paradox of evil—that it originates in the will of one of God's own creations, and in a creation created in His own image—has thus for centuries been a source of consternation to philosophers. How, indeed, can the divine origins of evil be reconciled with the product? How, if God created the world, could He have permitted evil? This is the central problem for theodicy.

## IV. CONCLUSION: FROM FALLIBILITY TO FAULT

It has been suggested throughout the foregoing sections of this essay that the tendency of consciousness to flee from reality through a variety of forms of violence has its origins in the very structure of consciousness as such. Following Sartre, we have defined consciousness as the phenomenon that seeks both *to-be-what-it-is-not* and *not-to-be-what-it-is*. At the same time, we have suggested through our analysis of the myth of evil that consciousness is fated by its primordial, a priori constitution to suffer the paradox of having its very creativity depend upon the same forces that constitute the sources of violence and evil. The very same will-to-power that occasions the Promethean flight toward divinity is also the source of the Faustian descent into depravity.

Thus the metaphysical ambivalence that characterizes the Sartrean view of consciousness resembles the psychological ambivalence assigned by Freud. Both Sartre and Freud derive violence from a permanent disposition that is rooted in the human condition as such. Neither is prepared to encourage utopian expectations that violence can be eliminated through the mere rearrangement of the environment, though both recognize the role of the environment in facilitating the a priori disposition to violence. Finally, for both Freud and Sartre, the disposition to violence derives from the primordial disposition to escape the painful demands of reality as it presents itself to consciousness.

According to Freud, violence originates both in the universal tendency to parricide and in the unresolved conflict between eros and the death instinct, sometimes referred to by Freud's followers as *thanatos*.[57] Freud explains various types of neuroses, including demoniacal possession, in terms of the dynamics of the Oedipus and castration complexes, while war and other forms of aggression are explained in terms of the conflict between the biologically based instincts of life and death. Paradoxically, both sets of instincts are rooted in the same primordial narcissism that under some conditions leads the organism to creative survival and under other conditions leads to self-destruction and/or destruction of others.

Compare Freud's views with Sartre's position, according to which, consciousness is subject to an a priori ontological disposition to escape from freedom. Freud makes one's present behavior contingent upon one's biological nature interacting both with the environment and with one's past history. It is in this sense that we are lived by our unconscious and by our past; and our tendency to counterfeit reality through neurosis is thus a function either of past history or else of unresolved conflicts deriving from biologically based instincts.

But, whether we accept Freud's portrait or Sartre's, each case how the pathos and drama of man's trag derive from the ambivalence of the human condition. tan's fall from heaven, man's propensity toward violenc seem to be a precondition of the transformation of co ness into a source of freedom and creativity. Patholog lence is the risk of existing in the mode of freedom existence precedes essence.

There is in this drama—in addition to the already-men dramatis personae, God, Satan, eros and *thanatos*—the s in which the drama unfolds. Following Plato's observation society is the individual writ large, the sociology of evil attention to ways in which society organizes itself to faci the flight from freedom demanded by consciousness. The nological society—with its emphasis on bureaucracy and f tional rationality—thus seems a most appropriate one to fa tate the work of Satan. To the extent to which social design promote the rationality of *techne* over *arete*, society continu as it were, to honor its pact with the Devil. Driven by function rationality, the technological society is as demonically possesse as any individual neurotic.

The myth of Satan provides several clues to the understand ing of the structure of evil and provides a bridge between evi and violence. Evil is represented as the counterfeit of reality in the service of man's primordial need for mastery over the realm of being. At the psychological level, the satisfaction of this need takes the form of primitive narcissism. In itself, narcissism is not evil, for, as Freud argues, narcissism is a necessary element in the development of man's psyche. It is only when man's narcissistic tendencies come to dominate totally all of the other psychic processes that the possibility of evil makes its appearance on the scene. The source of fallibility, in other words, is man's nature qua man. But the origins of fault lie in the absolutization of what is normally only one aspect of man's nature— the elevation of man's narcissistic tendencies so as to make them the Procrustean bed to which all other urges, impulses, and desires are forced to conform. The Devil represents the symbolism of the process whereby the conversion from fallibility to fault takes place. When converted into a psychology of evil, then, the myth would seem to anticipate the Freudian doctrine of narcissism. When converted into a sociology of evil, the myth implicates all authoritarian and bureaucratic social structures that facilitate the psychological experience of mastery

kill him. But, were the universe to crush him, man would yet be more noble than that which slays him, because man knows that he dies and understands the advantage that the universe has over him. Of this the universe knows nothing.[58] The lot of man is misery, yet it is a sign of greatness to *know* that one is miserable, for in that knowledge man recognizes that he has fallen from a better state that once was his. His miseries, in other words, are the miseries of a great lord or a deposed king, and to know that one is miserable is therefore to yearn for transcendence.

And so, Pascal concludes, "let us not despair simply, but strive to think well. Therein lies the dignity of man. By thought he elevates himself and not by space and time."[59] In particular, it is through the purifying reflection of phenomenology, which seeks the essence of man qua man, and the conscious effort to relive the drama of inner consciousness, that the dignity of man is restored. For man, redemption through atonement is a consequence of self-knowledge. And this means coming to terms with the demonic dimensions of embodied consciousness. Through a phenomenology of embodied consciousness, we come to realize that, if simply driven out of existence by repression or projection, anger, rage, resentment, sexual passion, violence, and the lust for power and pleasure will only return to infect, to sicken, and to destroy. Western man has become so anesthetized by the bad-faith of pretending that he is an angel on the one hand, and of submitting to the tyranny of "functional rationality" on the other, that not only has he become a devil himself, but he is in grave danger of losing whatever immunity he has left to the infectious disease of irrationalism.

# Notes

[1] Robin George Collingwood, *The New Leviathan* (Oxford: Clarendon Press, 1942), p. 88.

[2] Carl Becker, *The Heavenly City of the Eighteenth Century Philosophers* (New Haven: Yale University Press, 1932), pp. 14–15.

[3] Bertrand Russell, "A Free Man's Worship," in *Mysticism and Logic* (Garden City, N.Y.: Doubleday & Co., Anchor Books, 1957), pp. 45–46.

[4] Collingwood, *New Leviathan*, p. 88.

[5] See Thomas Hobbes, *The Leviathan*. Hobbes writes, in his Introduction, "For by art is created that great LEVIATHAN called a COMMONWEALTH, or State, in Latin CIVITAS, which is but an artificial man; though of greater stature and strength than the natural, for whose protection and defence it was intended" (ed. Michael Oakeshott [Oxford: Basil Blackwell, n.d.], p. 5).

[6] George Steiner and Elizabeth Hall, "A Conversation with George Steiner," *Psychology Today,* February 1973, p. 57.

[7] Ronald D. Laing, "Violence and Love," *Humanitas* 2 (1966): 205–6. See also his *The Politics of Experience* (New York: Ballantine Books, 1968), p. 76.

[8] Lewis Mumford, Inaugural Lecture to the American Academy of Arts and Letters, Spring 1963. Cited in Samuel Hirsch, "Theatre of the Absurd," *Journal of Social Issues* 20 (1964): 59.

[9] Robert Lifton, *History and Human Survival* (New York: Random House, 1970), p. 376.

[10] William Butler Yeats, "The Second Coming," in *Collected Poems* (New York: Macmillan Co., 1950), pp. 184–85.

[11] Albert Camus, *The Rebel*, trans. Anthony Bower (New York: Random House, Vintage Books, 1954), p. 5.

[12] Kenneth Rexroth, "Disengagement and the Art of the Beat Generation," in *The Beat Generation and the Angry Young Men*, ed. Gene Feldman and Max Gartenberg (New York: Dell Publishing Co., 1958), p. 352.

[13] Goethe, *Faust*, trans. Walter Kaufmann (Garden City, N.Y.: Doubleday & Co., Anchor Books, 1962), pt. 1, prologue, lines 282ff.

[14] Charles Baudelaire, *Intimate Journals*, trans. Christopher Isherwood (Boston: Beacon Press, n.d.), p. 44.

[15] Charles Darwin, *The Descent of Man* (New York: Random House, Modern Library, n.d.), p. 920 (pt. 3, chap. 21).

[16] Sigmund Freud, *Civilization and Its Discontents*, trans. James Strachey (New York: W. W. Norton Co., 1962), p. 58.

[17] Ibid., pp. 59–60.

[18] David Bakan, "Psychological Characteristics of Man Projected in the Image of Satan," *Catholic Psychological Record* 5 (1967): 8–15; idem, *The Duality of Human Existence* (Chicago: Rand McNally & Co., 1966), chap. 4.

[19] Jean-Paul Sartre, *Sketch for a Theory of the Emotions*, trans. Philip Mairet (London: Methuen & Co., 1962).

20 Erich Fromm, *The Sane Society* (New York: Holt, Rinehart & Winston, 1955), p. 15. The deterministic position is well summed up in the following comment by the psychologist B. F. Skinner: "Every discovery of an event which has a part in shaping a man's behavior seems to leave so much the less to be credited to the man himself; and as such explanations become more and more comprehensive, the contribution which may be claimed by the individual himself appears to approach zero. Man's vaunted creative powers, his original accomplishments in art, science and morals, his capacity to choose and our right to hold him responsible for the consequences of his choice—none of these is conspicuous in this new self-portrait. Man, we once believed, was free to express himself in art, music and literature, to inquire into nature, to seek salvation in his own way. He could initiate action and make spontaneous and capricious changes of course. Under the most extreme duress some sort of choice remained to him. He could resist any effort to control him, though it might cost him his life. But science insists that action is initiated by forces impinging upon the individual, and that caprice is only another name for behavior for which we have not yet found a cause" (*The American Scholar* 25 [1955–56]: 52–53).

21 Sigmund Freud, "On Demoniacal Possession," in *Collected Papers*, ed. Ernest Jones, vol. 4, translation supervised by Joan Riviere (New York: Basic Books, 1959), pp. 436–37.

22 Ibid., p. 446.

23 Ibid., pp. 450–51.

24 Ibid., p. 468.

25 Ibid., pp. 470–71.

26 Gert Kalow, *The Shadow of Hitler: A Critique of Political Consciousness* (Chicago: Quadrangle Books, 1967), p. 31.

27 See William Arrowsmith, Introduction to "The Bacchae," in *The Complete Greek Tragedies*, ed. David Grene and Richard Lattimore, vol. 4, *Euripides* (Chicago: University of Chicago Press, 1958), pp. 530–41.

28 Plato, *Gorgias*, trans. W. Hamilton (Baltimore: Penguin Books, 1960), pp. 76–78 (Stephanus pag. 482–84).

29 Plato, *The Republic*, trans. H. D. P. Lee (Baltimore: Penguin Books, 1955), p. 97 (Stephanus pag. bk. 2, 365e).

30 Rex Warner, *The Professor* (London: The Bodley Head, 1936), p. 209.

31 George Orwell, *1984* (New York: Signet Books, 1950), pp. 200–3.

32 Warner, *The Professor*, pp. 209, 212, 213, 217–18.

33 Ibid., pp. 222, 224, 225, 227.

34 Bertrand de Jouvenel, *Power*, trans. J. F. Huntington (London: Batchworth Press, 1952), p. 110.

35 Other species of violence not accounted for are pathological expressions of violence, political violence, and crime.

For a definition of 'care', see Martin Mayeroff: "To care for another person, in the most significant sense, is to help him grow and actualize himself. Caring is the antithesis of simply using the other person to satisfy one's own needs. In the context of a man's life, caring has a way of ordering his other values and activities around it. Through caring for others, by serving them through caring, a man lives the meaning of his own life. In the sense in which a man can ever be said to be at home in the world, he is at home not through dominating, or explaining, or appreciating, but through caring, and being cared for" (*On Caring* [New York: Harper & Row, 1971], pp. 1–2).

[36] As employed in this discussion, the term *yin* refers to the pre-historical or eternal world of changeless, unactualized reality, while *yang* refers to the historical world of change, process, and time; and because it is a world of change in time, it involves error and fault, as well as creativity.

[37] Goethe, *Faust*, pt. 1, prologue, line 312.

[38] Milton, *Paradise Lost*, bk. 4, lines 4–12.

[39] Denis de Rougemont, *The Devil's Share*, trans. Haakon Chevalier (New York: Pantheon Books, 1945), p. 32.

[40] Pascal, *Pensées*, trans. W. F. Trotter (New York: Random House, Modern Library, 1941), p. 118 (sec. 358).

[41] De Rougemont, *Devil's Share*, p. 39.

[42] Ibid., p. 41.

[43] Herbert C. Kelman, "Presidential Address: The Social Consequences of Social Research: A New Social Issue," *Journal of Social Issues* 21 (1965): 22–23.

[44] Robert Nisbet, *Tradition and Revolt* (New York: Random House, 1970), pp. 257–58.

[45] Karl Mannheim, *Man and Society in an Age of Reconstruction* (London: Routledge & Kegan Paul, 1966), p. 52.

[46] Plato, *Phaedo*, in *The Last Days of Socrates*, trans. Hugh Tredennick (Baltimore: The Penguin Classics, 1954), p. 155 (Stephanus pag. 97c–98a). See also *Apology*, in ibid., pp. 59, 71–72 (Stephanus pag. 28b, 36c–38d).

[47] Frank Harvey, *Air War Vietnam* (New York: Bantam Books, 1967), p. 2.

[48] *Wall Street Journal*, "The Dilemma That Is Greece," editorial, 12 January 1970, p. 12; italics mine.

[49] Bakan, *Duality of Human Existence*, pp. 38ff.

[50] Goethe, *Faust*, pt. 1, lines 1547–70.

[51] Cf. Freud, "On Demoniacal Possession."

[52] Augustine, *The City of God*, trans. Marcus Dodds (New York: Random House, Modern Library, 1950), pp. 298ff. (bk. 9, sec. 20).

[53] Milton, *Paradise Lost*, bk. 9, lines 679–83.

[54] Goethe, *Faust*, pt. 1, lines 371–77.

[55] Ibid., lines 1692–98.

[56] Ibid., line 1759.

[57] For Freud's discussion of the death instinct see *Civilization and Its Discontents*, chap. 6.

[58] Pascal, *Pensées*, p. 116 (sec. 347).

[59] Ibid.

# PART TWO

## Violence, Persons, and Language

# Consensus and the Justification
of Force

TIMOTHY BINKLEY has taught at the University of Notre Dame and has held a post-doctoral fellowship from the National Endowment for the Humanities while studying aesthetics and art history at Temple University. He studied at the University of Colorado and the University of Texas, where he was awarded the Ph.D. in 1970. A member of Phi Beta Kappa, he has held numerous fellowships and awards, including an N.D.E.A. Fellowship at the University of Texas at Austin. He is the author of *Wittgenstein's Language* (1973) and several articles in the areas of aesthetics, ethics, and political philosophy.

# Consensus and the Justification of Force

## by Timothy Binkley

> . . . there is never a ruler of a city who would unjustly be ruined
> by the very city he ruled.
>
> *Gorgias* 519c

It is often held that moral justifications must be conducted
within a framework which is at least consistent with the paradigm of ideal consensus. However, such an account of justification cannot be given for most acts of force. I shall attempt to
demonstrate why this is so, and then discuss some of the theoretical and normative implications this result has for our discourse about force and violence, especially as it applies to
arguments for obedience to the authority of a state.

## I. TYPES OF FORCE

We shall first need to restrict our attention to a particular
type of force. Let us begin by limiting the following discussion
to acts of force which are perpetrated by human beings and
which have human victims, i.e. which produce some ill effect
upon a human being either directly or indirectly. Some of these
acts of force are utilized as deliberate means to a determinate
end, while other such acts have no clear goal beyond the immediate release of energy involved in the act itself. Calculated
political force, whether strengthening or deteriorating the hege-
mony of a state, generally falls into the first category; irrational,
"blind" force, as an outgrowth of frustration or anger, generally

falls into the second category. Let us call the former type of force *instrumental force*, and the latter *non-instrumental force*.

Within the first class we might wish to draw another distinction. Some instrumental force seems clearly directed against willful recalcitrance: it is designed to "force" someone (or some group) to accept or allow the end against his (or their) will. Its aim is to bring about a state of affairs which its victims do not want realized (at least at the time the force is applied); and the act of force is required precisely because of this aversion to the end. This is the sort of force which could be replaced by rational persuasion, and it is sometimes (though not always) used after attempts to change minds through argumentation have failed. On the other hand, there seem to be acts of instrumental force which are designed to accomplish a result having nothing to do with the willingness or unwillingness of the "victim." For example, most force which aims at humiliation or retribution has as its purpose something which is independent of the attitudes of the victims, and it cannot be replaced by attempts to convince the victims of the desirability of its end. In this class we would probably also place such acts as those designed for medical purposes.

For want of a better designation, let us call acts of the first variety *volitional-instrumental force*, and acts of the second variety *teleological-instrumental force*. In what follows, we shall restrict our discussion to acts of volitional-instrumental force (VIF) for reasons which will become apparent in the course of the discussion. It should be pointed out, however, that this class includes almost all acts of force which we might be interested in justifying (as opposed to excusing). More specifically, it includes the types of political force which capture much of our attention today. When a state uses force to preserve order, it is using force for an end which could be accomplished without force if the victims freely assented to the proposal for order. And when a revolutionary cadre uses force against a state, it also has an end in view which could be effected without force if those in power were to consent to the realization of the desired goals.

All acts of VIF are directed against intended victims, and any harm brought to an innocent bystander cannot strictly be considered a part of the VIF itself, but is rather an unintended by-product. The reason for this is that, since an act of VIF is a means to an end, any aspect of such an act which does not contribute to the realization of that end must be considered incidental and inessential to the act as VIF. This point is important because later on we shall bring up the matter of justifying VIF, and the justification of an act as a means must always refer to the end. Thus, we should keep clear the distinction between intentional force against a victim and unintentional force against a bystander. The former is open to attempts at justification; the latter is most typically not justified at all, but merely excused. In concentrating our attention on VIF we shall thus be concerned with the justification of force against intended victims.

## II. IDEAL CONSENSUS

William Frankena summarizes the paradigm of ideal consensus as follows:

> The fact that ethical and value judgements claim a consensus on the part of others does not mean that the individual thinker must bow to the judgement of the majority in his society. He is not claiming an *actual* consensus, he is claiming that in the end—which never comes or comes only on the Day of Judgement —his position will be concurred in by those who freely and clear-headedly review the relevant facts from the moral point of view. In other words, he is claiming an *ideal* consensus which transcends majorities and actual societies. One's society and its code and institutions may be wrong. Here enters the autonomy of the moral agent—he must take the moral point of view and must claim an eventual consensus with others who do so, but he must judge for himself. He may be mistaken, but, like Luther, he cannot do otherwise.[1]

Here we shall examine a much less restrictive paradigm which is more general inasmuch as it seems to attach to any sort of reason-giving activity and not just to the giving of moral reasons. This paradigm is entailed by Frankena's, so any weaknesses in the former will indicate corresponding weaknesses in the latter. Furthermore, since it is less restrictive, it will be less objectionable.

Now, what is this paradigm? It can be characterized as follows with respect to moral justification:

(i) The justification of an act conforms to the paradigm of ideal consensus only if it is possible that all men be reasonable with respect to the issues involved and accept the act as justified.

For the sake of convenience in the argument, let us formalize this principle as follows. Let

$V(y)$ = $y$ is an act of VIF.
$J(y)$ = $y$ is a justifiable act.
$H(x)$ = $x$ is a human being in the relevant societal context.
$R(x)$ = $x$ is a reasonable man with respect to the issues at hand.
$A(x,y)$ = $x$ accepts act $y$ as justified.

Then we can restate (i). Assuming $V(a)$, we get

(1) The justification of the act, $a$, conforms to the paradigm of ideal consensus only if
$\Diamond \; ( \; J(a) \; . \; (x)( \; H(x) \supset R(x).A(x,a) \; ) \; )$.

Before proceeding any further, it is necessary to elucidate briefly the import of the terms 'possible' and 'reasonable' as they are used here. Very generally, 'possible' can be interpreted to mean something like 'conceptually possible' and should not be read as strict logical possibility unless 'logic' is taken broadly enough to include general conceptual structures. Also, 'reasonable' should be understood somewhat more broadly than 'rational'. A man could be perfectly rational, i.e. self-consistent, yet hold quite unreasonable views or do unreasonable things. Being irrational is one way of being unreasonable, but one could also be unreasonable by failing to be "sensible" in word or deed, for example. This distinction is not hard and fast: the two terms are often used interchangeably in ordinary discourse. What is necessary here is just to recognize that a reasonable man is not merely a man who holds only to self-consistent propositions.

It should be noticed that (i) requires only that the consensus can be self-consistently imagined within our conceptual framework, and it makes no commitment to the desirability or the "practical possibility" of its attainment. It leaves room for someone who wants to hold that even in ideal circumstances reasonable men can disagree. All that is required is that agreement not be precluded.

Now does this paradigm follow from Frankena's? If we read

Frankena in the most literal way, we get the following statement of the paradigm:

(a) The justification of an act conforms to the paradigm of ideal consensus if and only if all men who freely and clear-headedly review the relevant facts from the moral point of view will ultimately accept the act as justified.

Presumably, freely and clear-headedly reviewing relevant facts from the moral point of view entails being reasonable with respect to relevant issues. But then the condition of reasonability would be placed in the antecedent, not in the consequent, as in (i). So to get (i) we will need to assume:

(b) It is possible that Frankena's paradigm still holds while all men freely and clear-headedly review the relevant facts from the moral point of view.

It might be objected that (b) is questionable on the grounds that universal agreement could change the nature of the act itself. This is indeed true, and in a moment we will see an example of just such a case. However, this problem is already present in (a): there is no guarantee that the agreement on the part of everyone who freely and clear-headedly reviews the facts from the moral point of view will not change the nature of the act. The prospects for rejecting (b) will be investigated later.

Whether (i) is a restriction we must place upon all moral justification is not an issue which will directly concern us here: we shall simply examine its applicability to the justification of VIF. However, it does seem that when abstractly considered it is difficult to deny the general validity of (i). We usually feel uneasy about a "justification" which in principle is somehow not open to universal assent: it would be at least as bad as an argument ad hominem. Moreover, (i) appears to be an assumption which pervades ordinary moral discourse in various forms. This is one reason why it is worth examining.

## III.  THE JUSTIFICATION OF FORCE

Someone may attempt to justify an act of force in one of two ways: by showing either that it is obligatory or that it is permissible. However, there are at least two senses of 'permissible', only one of which is relevant to the justification of VIF. In one sense, to say that an act is permissible is to say merely that it is not morally wrong. This gives the agent a right, or *liberty*, to engage in the act; but this liberty can often be contravened with impunity by another liberty which is no stronger than the first. Thus, it may be morally permissible for Jones to seek a profit, but this does not count against Smith's interfering with Jones' aspirations by seeking his own profit. Jones has thereby no moral grounds to complain against Smith: he has no "claim" against Smith. We do not normally seek moral resolutions to such conflicts, but rather let them work themselves out.

There is, however, a stronger sense of 'permissible' which means something more like 'allowable' or 'ought to be permitted'. In this sense, to say an act is permissible is to give someone a right, or *claim-right*, to act unimpeded by the interference of others. This right gives everyone a duty not to interfere with the agent, and it gives the agent himself moral grounds to complain against anyone who does. A claim-right cannot be infringed with impunity except under special circumstances, and then only by virtue of a stronger claim-right: One is always liable to answer for interfering with a claim-right. To say Jones is permitted to plant trees in his yard is to give Jones a claim-right to unimpeded action which cannot be transgressed except in special cases when a stronger claim-right prevails (for example, Jones may live on a corner and his trees may be a traffic hazard). An act is thus 'permissible' in this second sense only if both (1) it is not morally wrong, and (2) interfering with the act is morally wrong.

It is important to notice that a liberty can rarely, if ever, supersede a claim-right. The lumberjack cannot use his liberty to seek a profit as a justification for cutting down Jones' trees. The reason for this can be seen as follows. In order to justify violating a claim-right, one must be able to counter the "claim" or complaint which may be registered against any transgressor of the right. And this can be done only by matching that "claim" with another "claim" of the same general type which is stronger than the first. This requires reference to another claim-right.

Only the second sense of 'permissible' seems at all relevant to the justification of VIF for at least two reasons. First, the victim of an act of VIF always has a prima facie claim-right to avoid harm. This right can be superseded only in exceptional cases, and then only with the support of another, stronger, claim-right. But furthermore, the whole point of the justification of force is to show that what the agent is doing is not just "all right," but somehow "right." If there is no way to evaluate the relative ethical merits of conflicting acts of force, the justification of force hardly takes us beyond a "state of nature." This would be unfortunate, for the justification of force is thought to be crucial for the adjudication of certain types of conflicting claim-rights. For these reasons, 'permissible' will hereafter be used only in the second sense introduced above, and 'right' will mean 'claim-right'.

Now it can be shown that acts of VIF cannot be justified—as either obligatory or permissible—under the paradigm of ideal consensus given in the preceding section. In order to demonstrate this, we will need to assume the following principles:

(ii) If a person who is reasonable at the moment with respect to relevant issues accepts an act of VIF as justified, then he must also believe that the end of that act ought (or is permitted) to be brought about.

It is assumed here that the agreement comes at the end of a complete justification. Thus both 'ought' and 'permitted' need to be taken in an "ultimate" sense: to say that the end of an act of VIF ought to be brought about amounts to giving one or more persons a duty to act which is not overriden by another duty; and to say that the end of an act of VIF is permitted is to give one or more persons a right to act unimpeded which is not overriden by other rights. Keeping these senses of the two words in mind, we can proceed to state the other premises:

(iii) If a man is reasonable at the moment with respect to relevant issues, he cannot both agree that the end of an act of VIF ought (or is permitted) to be brought about and yet resist the exercise of the corresponding sanctioned duty (or right).

(iv) If y is an act of VIF with end z, and no one in the relevant societal context resists the exercise of the corresponding duty (or right), then y is unnecessary for the attainment of z in the sense that other means to z are available which involve less (or no) VIF.

(v) If z is the purported end of an act of VIF, y, and yet y is unnecessary for the achievement of z (unnecessary in the sense that other, less harmful, means are available), then $y$ is unjustifiable (assuming that $y$ has no other purposes than to bring about $z$).

Once again, formalization will be of some assistance. Let

$E(y,z)$ = $z$ is the end of act $y$.

$O(x,z)$ = $x$ believes that $z$ is a state of affairs which ought (or is permitted) to be brought about.

$W(x,y)$ = $x$ is willing to allow the exercise of the right or duty connected with the justified act of VIF, $y$.

$I(y,z)$ = $y$ is unnecessary to the achievement of $z$.

$U(y)$ = $y$ is unjustifiable.

Suppose again that $V(a)$ and also $E(a,b)$. Then we can write

(2) $\square$ $\quad (x)( H(x).R(x).A(x,a) \supset O(x,b) )$.

(3) $\square$ $\quad (x)( H(x).R(x).O(x,b) \supset W(x,a) )$.

(4) $\square$ $\quad ( (x)(H(x) \supset W(x,a)) \supset I(a,b) )$.

(5) $\square$ $\quad ( I(a,b) \supset U(a) )$.

In addition to these five principles, it will also be useful to make explicit a sixth:

(6) $\square$ $\quad ( U(a) \supset \sim J(a) )$.

Once again, the modality is conceptual.

The primary concern here shall not be over whether these principles do in fact embody true claims. Our purpose shall be to explore the applicability of these principles, along with (i), to the case of VIF. However, since the main question has to do with the paradigm of ideal consensus given by (i), (ii)–(v) will be recognized as conceptual truths which are more fundamental and less questionable than (i). Even more than (i), these four principles would seem to be operative presuppositions for a great deal of normal moral discourse. Although a detailed argument for each one of them shall not be given, it would be in order to offer a rationale for each before proceeding:

(ii) If a reasonable man accepts an act of VIF as justifiable (either obligatory or permissible), then he must accept its goal as an end which it is justifiable (obligatory or permissible) to pursue. For, the justification of means is subordinate to the justification of ends; indeed, special care is required if the means are acts which, considered by themselves, produce only harm.

(iii) A man may dispute means, but if he agrees that something ought (or is permitted) to be achieved, he will be considered unreasonable if he also claims or acts as though he believes that it ought not to be achieved.

(iv) Since an act of VIF is designed to force someone to do or accept something against his will, it will be unnecessary if no one resists what was supposed to be forced upon someone.

(v) Whatever unnecessary force is, it seems clear that once we deem an act of force unnecessary, we pronounce it unjustifiable since it will involve unnecessary harm.

The argument that justifications of VIF cannot fit (i) can now be given as follows. If, with reference to (i), we suppose that all men are reasonable and accept an act of VIF as justifiable, then they must accept the end of that act as at least allowable (ii), (iii). But then there will be no man who could be the victim of a justifiable act of VIF because all men are willing to permit what was supposed to be forced upon some of them. Thus the act will be unnecessary and unjustifiable (iv), (v). In other words, any act of VIF which we try to justify within the framework given by (i) will turn out not to be justifiable. The formalized argument proceeds as follows:

(7) $\square$ $\quad (x) \, ( \, (H(x) \supset R(x).A(x,a)) \supset (H(x) \supset O(x,b)) \, )$, from (2).

(8) $\square$ $\quad (x) \, ( \, (H(x) \supset R(x).A(x,a)) \supset$
$\qquad\qquad\qquad\qquad (H(x) \supset R(x).O(x,b)) \, )$, from (7).

(9) $\square$ $\quad (x) \, ( \, (H(x) \supset R(x).O(x,b)) \supset (H(x) \supset W(x,a)) \, )$, from (3).

(10) $\square$ $\quad (x) \, ( \, (H(x) \supset R(x).A(x,a)) \supset$
$\qquad\qquad\qquad\qquad (H(x) \supset W(x,a)) \, )$, from (8), (9).

(11) $\square$ $\quad ( \, (x) \quad (H(x) \supset R(x).A(x,a)) \supset I(a,b) \, )$, from (4), (10).

(12) $\square$ $\quad ( \, (x) \quad (H(x) \supset R(x).A(x,a)) \supset U(a) \, )$, from (5), (11).

(13) $\square$ $\quad ( \, (x) \quad (H(x) \supset R(x).A(x,a)) \supset \sim J(a) \, )$, from (6), (12).

Needless to say, this argument assumes that the justification in question is prospective, not retrospective. This assumption seems unobjectionable since most retrospective justification gains meaningfulness by reference to its implications for forethought and deliberation. In any case, the conclusion that VIF cannot be prospectively justified within the paradigm is sufficiently unsettling. It should also be noticed that in order for the argument to go through we need only assume that the *victims* are reasonable. The act may in fact still be committed, and then the reasonability of the perpetrators is called into question.

We can conclude from this argument either (a) that there is no such thing as justifiable VIF; or (b) that VIF is justifiable only within a modified, but still valid, paradigm of ideal consensus; or (c) that the notion of an ideal consensus ought itself to be rejected as an unsound justificatory principle. Robert Paul Wolff has defended (a), arguing that violence (which for him means 'illegitimate force') is a fundamentally confused notion precisely because the distinction between legitimate and illegitimate uses of force is specious. His argument proceeds from the autonomy of the will and follows a somewhat more political treatment of force than the one given here (as indicated by his use of the term 'legitimate' instead of 'justified'). However, insofar as he descries a conflict between 'right' or 'just' and 'force', his basic conclusion is the same.[2]

Yet before accepting either (a) or (c), we ought to explore the prospects for (b) since it seems, at least initially, to be the most attractive of the three.

## IV. MODIFICATION OF IDEAL CONSENSUS

We generally feel that we can distinguish at least clear cases of justified force from clear cases of wanton violence. The question that poses itself now is how we are to account for this distinction in light of the above discussion. The most obvious place to begin is with the assumption that the victims are reasonable (or "possibly reasonable") men; for we usually do think of victims of justified force as in some sense unreasonable, and if they are unreasonable the reductive argument fails. So the conceptual account of justified force can be rectified by adding the stipulation that the victims must be excluded from the class of reasonable men, other things being equal. Accordingly, one step in the justification of force (assuming other things are equal) will be to demonstrate that the proposed victims are unreasonable at least in the relevant context and with respect to the relevant issues. The above argument then indicates that a justification of VIF differs from other moral justifications insofar as it commences with a jump beyond the level at which universal agreement is (conceptually) possible. And this is no small difference, as we shall soon see.

A full development of the notion of justified force from this point of view will not be undertaken here; instead, it will be shown how the proposed new account represents something of a false victory which often portends in practical matters a struggle after Pyrrhic victories. 'Justified force' turns out to be a more tenuous concept that we might at first expect; for even if the conceptual ground has been set straight, reality remains intractable.

Before proceeding with this, however, it is worth pointing out that traditional defenses of the immorality of disobedience to law usually accept essentially this approach to the justification of institutionalized force. The contract theory, for example, relies upon the notion that it is immoral and unreasonable to violate a contract, other things being equal. And any theory which argues from the inherent justice of a particular form of government seems eventually to try to show that it would be unreasonable for a man not to consent to such a government. John Rawls, for example, tries to determine which form of government the rational man (our "reasonable man") would choose.[3] According to such accounts, institutionalized force against law violators can be justified within the paradigm of ideal consensus simply by excluding the victim from the class of reasonable men on the grounds that he knowingly and willingly violated a contract or else he "irrationally" did not consent to a particular form of government. Let us now examine the implications of this way of accounting for the justifiability of VIF.

We normally suppose the case of society against the criminal to be a clear instance in which violence and justified force can be understood and adequately handled without moral qualm (more on this later). But what of the revolutionary or semi-revolutionary situation in which large groups (or, for that matter, small groups) of seemingly rational men on both the side of authority and the side of resistance find themselves potential victims of what is claimed by other seemingly rational men to be justified force? If both contending factions are in fact reasonable to the (relatively superficial, but nevertheless important) extent that they talk calmly and coherently about their respective positions, each will probably "reasonably" reach the conclusion that the other faction is "unreasonable" in some respect. And now, if we wish to adjudicate the dispute and try to decide whether in fact some force is justified, we will have to come to a decision about who (if anyone) really is reasonable. But this task carries with it almost insurmountable difficulties for a rather simple reason: the notion of 'reasonability' and, more particularly, assumptions about what properties "define"

reasonability and unreasonability lie at the foundation of discourse as the pre-rational and pre-discursive criteria of reasonability. Accordingly, the ultimate assessment of the meaning
and denotation of these labels, 'reasonability' and 'unreasonability', is typically a matter of attitude or outlook or life style.
Some people consider it prima facie reasonable to accumulate
wealth, repel Communist aggression, spend vast sums on defense, etc., while others take it to be prima facie unreasonable.
Although we do not usually disagree about what the general
characteristics and the most basic criteria of reasonability are,
whether it is instantiated in a particular case is the subject of
disparate opinion. There are, of course, limits within which such
issues can be discussed; but when we reach the limit what we
generally find is a criterion of reasonability which is placed
beyond question, beyond argument, at least for the time being.
At the point where we begin to reach the indicators of reasonability, trying to come to a uniform assessment will be more a
matter of "perception" or sensitivity than of reason; and dis-
agreement becomes correspondingly more a matter of insensitiv-
ity than of irrationality. At this level, discourse is designed to
sensitize, not to demonstrate; and the moral agent, like Luther,
must "judge for himself."

We are now in a better position to assess the proposed modification of the justification of VIF. According to the altered
paradigm of ideal consensus, the situation in which VIF is used
and justified is a kind of non-ideal situation whose non-ideality
cannot be interpreted as a mere non-realization of a possible
ideal: it is "ideal" non-ideality. This troublesome aspect of the
proposal is revealed also in the odd second-level specification by
which we are required to adjust the justificatory framework for
each new instance of justification. It must be determined not
only how a normative system applies to a particular case, but
also who will be considered qualified to assess this evaluation.
In most justification, the appeal to reasonability is perfunctory if
it is made at all; but with the justification of VIF, that appeal
needs to be on a par with the substantive normative claim itself.
To what extent the issue of reasonability is significant will depend upon circumstances; but it is nevertheless always present
and ready to overshadow the putative issue over force.

Because of its relation to the criteria of reasonability, the
justification of force seems to call forth a justification of the attitudes which support an entire practice. This is because the

real issue will not be force, but rather whether the victim's outlook, his "system," is worthwhile—and, by apposition, whether that of the perpetrators of force is worthwhile. For example, the question whether violence or civil disobedience are justified is usually not a real issue when the government in question is considered one of the disputants. This is because it would be unreasonable for a government genuinely to admit it was wrong and yet refuse to change. In other words, a government would not find itself in the position of encouraging civil disobedience or violence against itself. So the real issue between the government and its detractors is whether in fact the governmental policy in question—and even the form of government itself—is morally defensible. The same sort of comments would apply to any situation in which VIF is being urged: the victim simply cannot reasonably hold that he is wrong and yet refuse to change; so the real issue is whether he is in fact wrong. Thus force is not primarily an act justified within a system but, more importantly, an act which institutes, supports, or perpetuates the justificatory system itself along with a whole "vision" of the world. A set of attitudes provides justification for force, but the same acts of force grant the attitudinal system its efficacy. So the justification of force within this system forms something of a degenerate case. Justification comes to an end, and then we act . . . often with force.

This argument shows, I believe, that the justification of VIF is sound only to the extent that a society possesses, as a matter of fact, a genuinely shared sense of what is reasonable. But this means that truly justifiable VIF is nonexistent for the same reason that in the ideal state obedience to law would never be a problem. Accordingly, the justification of VIF, like the justification of a state or a society itself, can never be perfunctory or peremptory but can at best only be tentatively secured in shared attitudes. The real issue will not be whether force is justifiable in this system or that, but whether the system itself is justified. In other words, the parameters for justification must themselves be "justified," which is to say they must be grounded in a common sensibility.

Bernard Harrison makes a similar point in his paper, "Violence and the Rule of Law." He focuses more on the concept of injury rather than the more general concept of reasonability, but it is clear that an understanding of the content of both concepts rests upon general attitudes that will be flexible. Harrison begins by setting out what he takes to be essential constituents of "the rule of law" and then proceeds to show on the basis of these that it is illegitimate

> to suppose that one can erect a *general justification for obedience to the laws of an actual society* on the basis of the claim that the legal and constitutional arrangements of that society definitively embody the rule of law, since if we are correct, the rule of law can never be *definitively* embodied by the institutions of any actual society although the institutions of one society may constitute a more adequate embodiment than those of another.
>
> The reason why no set of constitutional arrangements can definitively embody the rule of law is, as we have seen, that our everyday concept of injury proved to be a fairly elastic and extensible one.[4]

The structure of his argument is similar in some ways to the one used here to show how attitudes and force reciprocally support one another. The general point is that one can never argue that a person is obligated to refrain from VIF on the grounds that any reasonable man can see that the act is against certain general "principles of reason"; for he may counter with another sense of 'reasonable' or, as in Harrison's analysis, with another sense of 'injury' which gives him reason to claim his act is justified. A justification of VIF—or of any "volitional-instrumental" injury for that matter—can only rest upon an interpretation of 'reasonable' (or 'injury') which excludes the prospective victims,

> for a just society is precisely one to which all reasonable citizens can consent, that is, one by the operation of whose institutions no reasonable citizen can consider himself injured. Any justification of inequality must therefore be an *ad hominem* directed at the poor.[5]

They are "unreasonable" for being discontent, for considering their plight an injury.

What is noteworthy about this way of looking at force is that it seems to account for a great many of the situations in which force is actually being used or considered today. For example, many contemporary political problems having to do with imperialism, defense, environment, self-determination, repression, etc., involve confrontations of attitudes that often seem to embody something very much like different criteria of reasonability, or at least differing perspectives, differing visions of the world which imply different criteria of reasonability. Many violent confrontations today result from conflicting attitudes or systems of thought, and the justification of force is eclipsed by the forceful encounter between vying systems and criteria of reasonability. The adversaries can only dismiss one another as immoral, selfish, deceitful, misguided, or otherwise displaying characteristics of unreasonability. There is no "common ground."

Thus force and violence—even when they are "justified" go deeper than reason. They are typically appealing in circumstances where one attitude or set of attitudes confronts another. At this level even seemingly rational expressions can become elucidations and assertions of one attitude against another, and the most salient distinction between adversaries will determine only their relation to power. The non-negotiable demands of dissidents and the vituperative epithets of authorities differ primarily on which side of the police line they originate from. This is, of course, a very significant difference, since we usually attach a special responsibility to the caretakers of our government. But what is important to notice is that both sorts of expression are more assertions of attitude than rational asseverations. Insofar as they deal with reason, they deal with the criteria of reasonability.[6]

## V. SOME NORMATIVE RESULTS

On the basis of the foregoing discussion, we can now draw outlines of several more practical suggestions. These results are based upon the conclusion that a paradigm of ideal consensus is at best highly problematic and at worst specious when applied to certain difficult moral issues. More specifically, justifications of VIF cannot be "institutionalized" since they are endemically tentative, always resting upon shared attitudes: to justify VIF is to justify the "institutions" utilizing it.

1. The preceding discussion of the notion of consensus helps explain why violence breeds violence. Since the victim of an act of VIF cannot both be a victim of justified force and also accept the justification, he always has at least a prima facie justification for counter-force. It is thus propitious to encourage a fuller understanding of the vicious circle of violence, which recom-

mends to anyone trying to lower the level of violence that he should begin at home. In particular, it is incumbent upon a government concerned about violence to scrutinize its own acts of force at least as carefully and as deliberately as it does the acts it condemns and punishes. We cannot encourage reasonable discourse by eschewing it and engaging in the kind of activity most inimical to it. This is perhaps the extent to which pacifism is eminently reasonable.

2. One required step on the way to the justification of VIF within the modified paradigm is the assessment of the prospective victims as unreasonable; but since this step tends ineluctably toward strife, we should be cautious in committing ourselves to it—and a fortiori to the whole program of justifying force. It ought to be with reluctance that a society classifies some of its citizens as unreasonable, because this can be the first step toward an irrevocable bifurcation of the community beyond the point of rational discourse. Moreover, even when a political community finds itself "forced" to judge some men to be unreasonable and to treat them as criminals, it is advisable that it nevertheless take them to be basically rational human beings who have suffered only a temporary and deleterious lapse from reason (except in obvious cases of insanity, where we don't quite treat the violator as a full-fledged criminal anyway). This guide provides for the possibility that the "criminal" can be reached and rehabilitated through reason so that at least the insidious effects of his unreasonability can be controlled and eliminated. (Unreasonability is not by itself pernicious. The real problem is to reduce suffering, not nonsequiturs. One might even say that there is a need to be less preoccupied with rationality, at least, and to better understand the attitudinal character of reasonability.) With this in mind, some serious questions can be posed about the nature of imprisonment and other forms of punishment and correction in modern culture.

3. Because the kind of confrontation which results in the application of force is typically an opposition of attitudes or— less congenially—of prejudices, it would seem vital for a society to actively cultivate the greatest toleration over the widest range of attitudinal disagreements possible, and to provide as much an open forum for varied opinion as it can. It is most dangerous for a government to play the game of attitude assertion when harmony requires that we understand other views to the extent that we agree to differ. We might wish to view in this light the tradition reflected in the following remark by Rudolf Carnap:

Once I referred in a talk with Einstein to the strong conformism in the United States, the insistence that the individual adjust his behaviour to the generally accepted standards. He agreed emphatically and mentioned as an example that a complete stranger had written him that he ought to have his hair cut: "Don't forget that you now live in America."[7]

4. The nature of violent conflicts makes it imperative for there to be a court of appeals with a truly impartial judge to adjudicate the situation and try to meliorate the problems. In a political community this judge is ultimately the state through one of its officials, so the responsibility for ensuring impartiality rests with the government. In cases where it is itself deeply involved, special care is fitting, since there is no official higher authority by which it can in turn be evaluated. The business of government would seem to be primarily the reduction, not the application of force; and this it cannot do if it identifies itself with some special interest, thereby alienating itself from other interests. The autonomy of government makes its own justifications too facile unless it is a disinterested party.

Moreover, a citizen must have the feeling that he has access to those institutions which possess power. He will be immediately alienated from the "attitudes" in power unless he has a clearly formulated and relatively easy means of questioning and criticizing those attitudes and receiving some responsible reply to his objections. (Attitudes can, after all, be debated, though the form of argument will often be more aesthetic than deductive.) As Hannah Arendt points out, this is an especially difficult goal in a modern bureaucracy where hardly anyone feels he has any access to power.[8] But it is a challenge that cannot be neglected. A government is supposed to serve the people. Its success can only be measured by those it serves. So part of its service must certainly be to provide open channels of communication.

5. Finally, we need to recognize that premature judgment confuses more than it helps when what is needed is a common ground for understanding and not blame, denigration, and separation. We might be suspicious of officials who are more often excited about the issue of appeasement than that of responsive representation. Since the victim is always at the disadvantage of having to justify or disavow his basic outlook in order to avoid possible harm, a government needs to treat the potential victims of its force with a certain amount of consideration. And when it

finds itself a prospective victim, it needs to defend its policy before defending its power. Or, in Arendt's terms, a government ought to govern by "power" instead of by "force" or "violence"; i.e., it should win consent by trying to persuade with reasoned argumentation instead of forcing consent by threats of harm.

> Power and violence are opposites; where the one rules absolutely, the other is absent. Violence appears where power is in jeopardy, but left to its own course it ends in power's disappearance. This implies that it is not correct to think of the opposite of violence as nonviolence; to speak of nonviolent power is actually redundant.[9]

Those who possess political power assume the risks and responsibilities of justifying their exercise of that power beyond showing merely that it is legal, that it is justifiable within its own rules. A government can always find a plethora of "legitimate reasons" for its acts; what it needs, however, is a set of shared attitudes and a sense of community. Thus the "victim's disadvantage" is always part of the price of power. A ruler cannot rule long without engendering some sense of common purpose. This is why Plato says that a ruler is never unjustly overthrown by the people he rules.[10]

# Notes

1 William K. Frankena, *Ethics* (Englewood Cliffs, N.J.: Prentice-Hall, 1963), p. 96.

2 See Robert Paul Wolff, "On Violence," *Journal of Philosophy* 66 (1969), pp. 601–16, and *In Defense of Anarchism* (New York: Harper & Row, 1970).

3 See John Rawls, "Justice as Fairness," *Philosophical Review* 67 (1958): 164–94; "Distributive Justice," in *Philosophy, Politics and Society*, ed. Peter Laslett and W. G. Runciman, 3d series (Oxford: Basil Blackwell, 1967); and *A Theory of Justice* (Cambridge: Harvard University Press, 1971).

4 Bernard Harrison, "Violence and the Rule of Law," in *Violence*, ed. Jerome A. Shaffer (New York: David McKay Co., 1971), pp. 160–61.

5 Ibid., pp. 175–76.

6 Stuart Hampshire has an interesting discussion of contemporary disputes that revolve about criteria of reasonability in his article, "Russell, Radicalism, and Reason," *New York Review of Books* 15 (1970): 3–8.

7 Rudolf Carnap, "Intellectual Autobiography," in *The Philosophy of Rudolf Carnap*, ed. P. A. Schilpp (LaSalle, Ill.: Open Court, 1963), p. 25.

8 Hannah Arendt, *On Violence* (New York: Harcourt, Brace & World, 1970).

9 Ibid., p. 56.

10 An earlier version of this paper was read at a joint colloquium of the Departments of Philosophy of Calvin College and the University of Notre Dame. I am indebted to Ken Konyndyk of Calvin College, who read a comment on the paper, and to other members of both departments for helpful criticisms.

# Social Force, Social Power, and
# Social Violence

RUBIN GOTESKY has taught at Northern Illinois University and the University of Georgia and has also been a visiting professor at Rutgers University, Emory University, the University of Chicago, New York University, and Tulane University. He was awarded both the M.A. and the Ph.D. at New York University. He is the author of more than one hundred articles and reviews in philosophy, the social sciences, and related disciplines, and his books include *Liberalism in Crisis* (1948) and *Personality: The Need for Liberty and Rights* (1967). Professor Gotesky has been the editor of *Philosophy Forum*, co-editor of *Philosophica Mathematica*, contributing editor to the *Humanist*, and executive editor of both the *Journal of Ultimate Reality* and the *Encyclopedia of Ultimate Reality*. He is also general editor and editor of some of the volumes in the *Topics in Contemporary Philosophy* series.

# Social Force, Social Power, and
# Social Violence

## by Rubin Gotesky

## I. FORCE, POWER, AND VIOLENCE AS PHYSICAL

It is obvious, I think, even to those most opposed to force as a social instrumentality, that it is a physical fact; and it is from this physical base that I wish to begin my analysis of social force, social power, and social violence. I do not mean 'physical' in the sense in which the notions of force, power, and violence are analyzed to a subatomic level or to the level of the electrical, magnetic, or plasmic. It is sufficient that the physical is experienced at the human observational level—at the level of the billiard ball, or the push-pull, strain-stress human experience. Theoretically, the adequate interpretation of this physical experience may need all the formulae of Newton and Einstein, Maxwell and Planck, but nothing of what I shall say is, I believe, in conflict with anything most physicists say.

Of these notions, only one, 'violence', needs special interpretation, since it is not given a technical interpretation in physics or chemistry. Even so, despite this lack of technical interpretation, physicists and chemists use it to describe phenomena which occur in extremely short periods of time and which alter significantly the spatial relations, structures, and qualities of objects. Astronomers, for instance, speak of periods of "violent" activity on the sun when sunspots become numerous, or of the violent effects of novae. Physicists speak of the explosive effects of atomic fission, and chemists of the violent reactions of sodium dropped into water. Thus it is possible to give a normal—if not a technical—description of 'violence' in physical terms.

I shall use the word 'force' to mean something—whatever that is, whether present in all nature, like gravity, or peculiar to a given class of things or a thing—which is capable of producing or does produce a change in motion, in shape, in quality, or in all of these aspects. Obviously, this description conforms to the usual physical definition and even incorporates the distinction between potential and actual force, a distinction that is not, at this stage, important. Thus I say a 'force', visible or invisible, is at work when something—say a ball at rest—begins to move or when, in motion, it ceases to move; when a drop in temperature turns a fluid like water into ice; when a blow on the head of an animal kills it; or when the pressure of a hand on clay alters the shape of the clay from a "shapeless" lump into a female figure. In many cases what force or forces are actually at work may not be known; and it may be necessary to invent something that may not exist to "explain" the changes wrought; but, in either case, I shall mean by 'force' something producing or capable of producing the changes observed.[1]

I shall use the word 'power' to mean the amount or degree of force in operation.[2] Thus if the force that moves the wheels of a car is sufficient to make it move at a velocity, say, of eighty miles an hour, I shall say this force is of a *certain power*. Thus, forces vary in power; and I shall say power is lacking to lift a weight if the force available is not sufficient to lift it. Thus, in my way of describing 'power,' power is a function of force, not force a function of power.[3]

I shall use the word 'violence' to mean extensive and radical changes within a short interval of time produced by given forces in the qualities and structures of anything. It is important to note that if these extensive and radical changes occur over a great interval of time, there is no dislocation and disequilibration in the relations and interactions of the parts of the transformed thing or in its relation to other things in its neighborhood. In brief, there is no violence. It is the relative shortness of the interval of time in which given forces act that results in the making of judgments of profound disturbances, dislocations, and transformations in the thing or things acted upon. The use of the term 'relative' indicates that the context in which I speak of a "short interval of time" determines what is meant by 'short'. What is short in the life of persons may be long in the lifespan of a fly. What is short in the life of a planetary system may be an eternity to human beings.

These descriptions or definitions of 'force', 'power', and 'violence' have certain advantages theoretically and, I believe, practically. One theoretical advantage is that human beings are recognized as moving about in space and time. Thus, human beings are recognized as possessing force and exerting it in a certain amount or degree and within a longer or shorter period of time. It also follows, as in physics, that the effect or effects intended may not occur because the force or forces exerted, i.e., the power, may not be sufficient to produce the effect or effects. Another theoretical advantage is that these notions of 'force', 'power', and 'violence', without doing "violence" to them, can be legitimately supplemented by special restrictions to make them applicable to society.

Practical advantages also follow. One recognizes that physical force, power, and violence are ultimately the sine qua non not merely of physical but also of *social* change. In other words, if human beings desire certain kinds of social change, they must learn what social conditions are necessary, what social means are to be used, and what skills must be available and usable to make them. It is not enough to phantasize about the ultimate force of reason or the pen. Such forces are effective, i.e., have adequate power, to make social or other changes only under given conditions; and these conditions must be known and, above all, usable. By themselves, they are as effective as a wish to live forever.

## II. NON-SOCIAL HUMAN FORCE, HUMAN POWER, AND HUMAN VIOLENCE

Force, power, and violence, as so far described, cannot be specifically distinguished from social force, social power, and social violence. As a step toward distinguishing them, I shall begin by describing some obvious instances of *human* force, *human* power, and *human* violence that are not instances of *social* force, *social* power, and *social* violence.

Robinson Crusoe, sole survivor of a wreck, finds himself on an island unoccupied by any other human being. He is hungry and goes seeking food. He finds a tree laden with fruit. He grasps a branch and pulls it down so that he can reach for the fruit with his other hand. He is obviously exerting a *force* of sufficient *power* to bring the fruit within the grasp of his hand, but neither the *force* nor its *power* is a *social* force or power. Further, the fruit is so hard, he cannot break its shell with his teeth. Consequently, he uses a stone to crack the shell. The force with which he hits the fruit breaks it into edible bits. The sudden, radical change in the fruit or the radical means used is not *social* violence.

Now why is this human force, manifested as power and violence, not 'social'? The answer is obvious. It involves no other persons, no social interactions between them, no institutional setup or structure. Nevertheless, though this force is not social, there is something importantly different about it. It is not ordinary physical force. First, it is exerted for a *purpose*: it is intended to produce anticipated effects or outcomes. Second, it is *economic* in the sense that it is a *selected* force—at least, in terms of that through which it is exerted: the stone, the grasping hand, the pulling arm. Finally, it is an evaluated force in that it is considered in terms of its *effectiveness*: if it fails to achieve its effect, Crusoe will reconsider it, for example, in terms of the amount or degree of force (i.e., the power required in terms of the kinds of instrumentalities and conditions through and under which it was exerted).

On this planet, in the absence of living and human things, physical force as such is without purpose, intention, telicity. Given Crusoe, given his purpose, the force he exerts becomes purposive, but the force in itself is not. However, there is a case in which it makes sense to speak of force as purposive or *telic*: when it is wholly identified with an organism, as when one says, "Man is the *force* that has changed the balance of nature," or "That man caused the mood of the party to change," or "The forces of law and order must act now." But it does not follow that a force is *telic* simply because it is present in a living context. The force exerted by a human being on the earth as he walks is not telic.[4]

Even within a social context, there are cases of human force which are *not* social. These are the cases of *individual* force, power, or violence that affect no one but the individual involved; they are identified by the fact that no traceable side-effects upon other individuals and institutions follow from them. A simple example of this is a lonely bachelor taking aspirin before he goes to bed or writing a letter never sent and immediately destroyed.

## III.  NON-SOCIAL FORCES HAVING SOCIAL EFFECTS AND SOCIAL FORCE

The forces so far distinguished, whether human or non-human, are plainly not social forces. They have no social effects. But there are non-social forces which do have social effects; and they are important to the extent that they have such effects. Nevertheless, they need to be clearly distinguished, as far as this is possible, from *social forces*. An avalanche, an earthquake, a tidal wave, chromosomes and genes, and muta-tions in plants and animals often have significant social effects, both useful and catastrophic. Nevertheless, they are not social forces; they are *non-social* forces, environing and penetrating society. A *social force* is a force exerted by an individual or individuals living in a society, or by a social group or an institu-tion, which has social effects, i.e., affects other individuals, groups, institutions, etc. These social effects may be of different kinds or different according to the social force or forces used; they may be great or small, approved or condemned, enduring or temporary, disequilibrating or homeostatic, local or plane-tary; they may take a long time to appear or appear quickly and dramatically, or they may be any combination of these.

A few examples may serve to make my description of social force clear. A man enters a liquor store and presses a knife against the ribs of the proprietor, saying, "Open your register and safe and hand me all the money." The intruder occupies a well-recognized social position: he is a thief. He, his words, and his knife together compose a social force. Whether they produce the intended effect of getting him money is another matter, but together they produce a social effect of some kind. The social effects may not be those he intended. The proprietor may leap at him or scream for help or fall down in a dead faint or die of a heart attack. To give another example, a wife may say to her husband, "If you hit me again, I'll call the police." She and her words compose a social force, but they may not be effective. Her husband may hit her again. In both instances, the thief and the wife may have made an inadequate assessment of the force they used, but whether well-assessed or not, it produced some amount of social effect. The social effect in such cases is usually relatively small, but it may be enlarged as it stimulates new seriations of social forces such as police action.

In the case of group or institutional force, social effects are usually larger than the above, and often they may be very large. I mention one spectacular example of relatively recent origin. A group of Weathermen secretly placed bombs in various places and then informed authorities in various states that bombs would go off at stated intervals in certain public buildings. The verbal and non-verbal social effects of such force were tremendous. The public authorities mobilized the police, FBI, CIA, and National Guard. A thorough search was instituted in every public building. Plans were hurriedly made or activated to anticipate, intercept, and/or extirpate all such radical groups wherever they existed. Laws were formulated and passed to enlarge existing police and espionage agencies and centralize their activities, to give them the right to intercept and search suspicious-looking persons carrying suspicious-looking parcels, to restrict the movements and rights of individuals to organize, to examine mailed parcels and mail, and to bug telephones, offices, and homes. The so-called "alarmed public" began writing, telephoning, and telegraphing congressmen, state representatives, the President, and state governors to take drastic action against anyone who, even by a stare, threatened the solid foundations of respectable society. Important public personages in government, education, and business made "significant" speeches about the necessity of re-establishing "law and order" and a reverential respect for both. The thundering cry everywhere was, "Down with violence and anarchy."[5]

These illustrations will, I hope, help to distinguish a non-social force from a social force. Both have social effects; but a non-social force penetrates society without being a part of it, while a social force is a social element—a component of, or a process within, society.

## IV. NON-SOCIAL POWER AND SOCIAL POWER

The same distinction holds between non-social power and social power. The sun by its heat can destroy the crops of a nation and thereby bring about famine, revolution, and the collapse of a government. The sun is a *powerful force*, but its power is not *social*, even though it is plainly an absolutely necessary condition for both biological life and social life. Rather, we would define 'social power' as the measure, the amount or degree, of the social effects that a social force or forces—say, a man, a group, or an institution—produces or can produce in a given social context. Such power may be accidental, as when a man in a nuclear plant mistakenly pushes the wrong lever or button and starts an uncontrollable nuclear reaction.

The basis for such greater or lesser social power, whether or not accidental, obviously lies in the social organization and existing social instrumentalities. For example, a farmer in a small town in Iowa may say to the visiting President, "Stop that war in Vietnam on any terms," but the force of that farmer's words will have no effect upon the war. The President, on the other hand, saying these or similar words to Kissinger, his emissary in Paris, will have the result of radically altering the situation in Vietnam and the world. The plain reason is that the farmer is not related to a seriate constellation of social forces capable of producing the enormous effect of stopping the Vietnam War; it is obvious that the President is so related.

## V. NON-SOCIAL VIOLENCE AND SOCIAL VIOLENCE

The same distinction holds for non-social violence and social violence. A sudden rise in temperature over the earth to about 200° F would result in the sudden collapse and destruction of all modern civilization. Such a temperature change would be socially violent in its effects, because it would disrupt established social relations all over the earth, but this sudden change, violent though it is, would not be social violence. A war or a revolution, on the other hand, is a violent social force; each produces within a short period of time radical dislocations and disequilibrations in the lives of human beings and in the long-established institutional arrangements between them.

Consider one typical revolution, the French. Old, established institutions and relations were destroyed; new social institutions were born. Social production, which had been organized in terms of small producers protected by a feudality, was wrenched apart. The producers were made independent and thus were deprived of the established protections that the feudality provided. Legal institutions, such as special courts with special laws for the clergy and the feudality, were abolished. Suddenly, people who, like their ancestors, were in positions of great power lost these positions and were exiled, destroyed, or forced to survive by eating garbage thrown in the streets. On the other hand, others who, like *their* ancestors, had been hounded, thrown into prison for one reason or another, and prevented from making a livelihood, suddenly became persons of great power controlling large social domains, even to the determination of life and death for the inhabitants.

## VI. FURTHER ELABORATION ON THE ABOVE DISTINCTIONS

My use of the word 'force' for anything which produces or can produce, (or that which *in* anything produces or can produce) change or effects, I think, seems clear enough. In this sense, one can speak of gravity, a billiard ball, a person, or a word as a force. Depending upon circumstances, one may prefer to speak of gravity as a force; in other circumstances, of a person, a word, or an institution as a force. The preference lies, I think, in the effects with which one connects the force and from which one predicts or hopes to predict effects.

However, I am not sure I have made so clear as I would like what I mean by a *social force*. I mean by a *social force* any component of a human society or *anything in* such a component which is believed to produce or to be capable of producing a change, large or small, sudden or slow, catastrophic or happy, in that human society or any human part of it. In this respect, a person or persons, a machine or machines, a social process, or any combination of these is a social force or a constellation of social forces. These and their like are the only things I want to call 'social forces', even though there are forces such as the sun, an avalanche, or a tidal wave which can produce tremendous social effects—even to the point of destroying a human society.

## VII. SOCIAL POWER AND SOCIAL VIOLENCE AS MODES OF SOCIAL FORCE

Social power and social violence are not social forces but rather *modes of expression* of social force. 'Power', I say, is what a force or forces is normally able to effect. This is a different way of saying what I have said before. A force—whether it is large or small—often is said to be of great power when it produces large effects, and of small power when it produces small effects. In other words, 'power' is a measure, in amount or degree, of the effects that a force produces or can produce when it is exerted. 'Social power', therefore, is a normal measure of the effects that any individual, group, institution, or combination of them produces or can produce.

I want to supplement this by saying that social power as a

normal measure of social effects is not to be confused with social effects produced by *accident* by an individual, a group, or an institution. An individual who accidentally presses a button which results in the destruction of a city obviously possesses social power at the moment of pressing the button, but this social power belongs to him only accidentally. It does not belong to him as a *socially intrinsic and persistent characteristic*; it is not a normal constituent of his social position and function. In the sense in which I speak of social power, it is always a normal, persistent characteristic of some individual, group, or institution; and it derives from a persistent social relation of such individuals, groups, or institutions to other individuals, groups, or institutions.

'Social power' in relation to 'social force' is no different in essential respects from 'power' in relation to 'force'. Given certain circumstances—a natural or created constellation of interconnected forces—a small force may have enormous power, i.e., it may produce an enormous number of far-reaching effects. In other circumstances, an enormous amount of force may be so confined as to produce few or no effects. If a force exerted in such circumstances normally or frequently can produce an enormous number of effects, then it has enormous power; and whoever or whatever exerts that force or is that force possesses enormous power. Thus, given persons, groups, or institutions established in certain social contexts may have enormous social power which they can express through the utilization of a small force—for example, a spoken word, a telephone call, a letter, or a speech. The reverse can also be true. A force or constellation of forces that has *potentially* enormous power can be so confined as to be able to have little effect, i.e., little power. For example, the force of a voting populace is legally enormous, but the voting structure is usually so articulated as to make that force powerless to alter the total structure of any society in any significant sense.

Social power, as I have said before, follows from the existence of a structured constellation of social forces in which an individual, group, or institution occupies a definite, functional position. The President of the United States can start and perpetuate an undeclared war or stop it; he can refuse to release funds to serve some large, social purpose; he can order the destruction of cities or the opening of new markets to trade. His social power, as a normal function of his position, is measured by the wide and varied social effects that the social force or forces placed at his disposal produces or can produce. The man in the street, the peon in the field, or the soldier in battle do not possess such social power as a normal component of their social position and function.

## VIII. FOUR RESTRICTIVE CONDITIONS ON SOCIAL POWER

There are a number of restrictive conditions surrounding social power that I must emphasize. First and again, social power, as a *normal* function of any organized social situation, is not to be taken as something accidentally manifested.

Second, the possessors of great social power as well as those on whom this social power is exercised are not entirely ignorant of *how, within what limits, and for what social goals such social power is and can be used.* Nevertheless, it does not follow that this knowledge with either group is particularly large. Of course, those who possess great power usually know better than most others how it is used, what are its limits of effectiveness, and what kinds of effects it is likely to produce. However, this does not mean that they are able by so-called reasonable scientific standards to know too much about its uses, limits, and effects. The reason for this is that what they know is frequently distorted by prejudice, illusion, mythical presuppositions, bad theory, and self-interest.

This sort of knowledge is minimal for those on whom social power is exercised. What they know is generally limited to what they learn from their narrow experience. Consequently, they are usually terribly ill-informed, terribly prejudiced, and almost always the victims of oppression and deceit. Simple proof of this is their poverty, their existence at the near limits of boredom, starvation, disease, and death.

Third, social power is not a respecter of morality, legality or custom. It is both legal and illegal, moral and immoral, customary and iconoclastic, depending upon who exercises it, when it is exercised, and for what purpose. The Mafia, for example, has enormous power. This power is both legal and illegal, moral and immoral, customary and iconoclastic; and it is exercised to serve those who possess it and to reduce its opponents to impotence or to annihilate them if the former is impossible. Furthermore, this power is distributed in different measure to different individuals, groups, and institutions. How it is measured out depends upon social time, social place, and social organization or structure. What has been said about the Mafia *especially* applies to the national or multinational states, past and present.

Finally, social power is not necessarily *non-violent*. It is—so to speak—non-violent when the usual productive processes satisfy, more or less, the diverse customary needs and expectations of individuals, groups, and institutions. It turns violent when it is necessary to prevent the dislocation and disequilibration of the normal productive processes. All states use state power this way every day of their existence.

## IX. SOCIAL VIOLENCE

At this point, perhaps, I may be able to say something more to help clarify what I have already said about violence. Note that I have nowhere said that social violence is something different from social force or social power. It is simply a special mode of manifestation of one or the other. Just as social power has been described as the normal measure of *social force* available to a person, a group, or an institution, so *social violence* is again simply social force acting explosively or having explosive social effects. That is to say, social violence is simply a name for that normal social force or those normal social forces which dislocate and disequilibrate a social state of affairs, or, in other words, a given constellation of social arrangements.[6]

Violent social force may occur in all sorts of social situations. It may occur in a street or when police meet demonstrators or when the military might of nations engages in battle. I am not, however, interested in those cases of violent social force which are *accidental* or *non-institutionally based*, even though they may have serious effects. A man going berserk, shooting twenty people and terrorizing others has distinct social effects; but this is not a case of the *normal* exercise of institutionalized social violence. I am only concerned with institutionalized social violence, i.e., with the social violence that a person, a group, or an institution can release because each is normally in an institutional position to release it. In short, I am essentially concerned only with *institutions of violence*.

What I have just said is not as clear as I would like it to be. First, I want to narrow down what sorts of institutions of violence I am concerned about. I am not interested in such institutions of violence as street gangs; Murder, Inc.; or the Mafia. These are by-products of a given social system of production, and, as such, they deserve sociological study as to why they exist, how they are organized, and what they do. But they have no interest for me, simply because they are not institutions of violence *existing to maintain or subvert an established system of production*. The only institutions of violence I have an interest in are those which exist, or have been created, to maintain and perpetuate a productive system, or to transform it in some significant respect.

Even though I am not interested in criminal institutions of violence, to make my conception of social violence clearer, I shall include them, temporarily, in my classification of such institutions. In general, most complicated societies nurture four sorts of institutions of violence: the police, the military, the criminal, and the "subversive."[7] Each of these institutions may be composed of a multiplicity of institutions, as is the case today. There may also exist institutions relatively independent of them, such as the CIA, the FBI, the MKD, and "security" departments in business, crime, or universities, but these always have formal and informal connections with the police and the military.

Of these four basic types, the one—as I have already said— that I have no interest in is the criminal. I have already given my reasons: it is hardly ever concerned with maintaining or changing a productive system, although it may sometimes be called upon to help achieve one or the other. Generally, it accepts the productive system of which it is an essential part. Of the three I am interested in, the first two, the police and the military, are creations of and supported by the controllers of the productive system; they exist to maintain that system. The last, the subversive, is not a creation of the controllers of a productive system, even though it is a growth within it.

What identifies these institutions is that they exist to be violent, when necessary. The members of such institutions are trained to be violent; they learn how to use all the important weapons of violence according to function and occasion. In general, they are alike in these respects: First, when necessary, they dislocate persons and things and disequilibrate institutional arrangements. Second, they do this explosively, i.e., within a short period of time. Third, they do the first and second either to re-establish normal institutional arrangements that have been seriously disarranged or to create a radically different state of affairs. The police and the military are used to achieve the former; "subversive" institutions, the latter.

## X.  THREE CAUSAL POSITIONS OF SOCIAL VIOLENCE

Social violence is usually taken to be a cause which produces certain effects, but it is not always a cause. Consequently, it is essential to distinguish the three causal positions of social violence. To make it easier to talk about these social positions, I introduce linguistic abbreviations for fairly complicated expressions. Social forces that within a short interval of time are dislocative and disequilibrative of persons, groups, institutions, and established arrangements I shall call 'violent' or 'social forces of violence', according to grammatical need. The social effects that are dislocative and disequilibrative within a short interval of time I shall call 'violent effects' or the 'effects of violence'. Social forces that are locative and equilibrative, or usually considered such, I shall call 'non-violent', or, preferably, 'homeostatic' or 'forces of homeostasis'. I do not want to call such forces "forces of peace" because this is usually used as a term of laudation; and people differ strongly as to whether social forces that maintain a homeostatic state of affairs are necessarily to be lauded.

Logically, there are four kinds of relations between violent and homeostatic forces:

(1) *One in which violent forces produce a sequence of violent effects.*

(2) *One in which violent forces produce homeostatis, i.e. a return, more or less, to the social status quo, or a new social order.*

(3) *One in which homeostatic forces produce a sequence of violent effects.*

(4) *One in which homeostatic forces preserve homeostasis.*

These relations are not absolutely distinct; these forces relate to each other through a continuum of variations in amount or degree of violence or homeostasis. For the present, I am only concerned with the first three. (The fourth, which is not a relation between violence and homeostasis, is only mentioned here to complete the permutations. For many thinkers, it stands for the ideal social arrangement.)

The most obvious example of the first relation is a squadron of soldiers killing, burning, and destroying whatever they find that can be destroyed. As a result, inhabitants flee; production of goods and services ceases; enduring institutional arrangements collapse and are not restored.

An obvious example of the second is a political party or a vigilante group restoring what is usually called "law and order" or "justice and peace" by violently removing a looting and killing government "gang."

An obvious example of the third is the cultural revolution in China, which resulted in the complete collapse for several years of China's educational order. The evolution began smoothly enough, but it ended in internecine war.[8]

It is important to note that the violence in these three cases does not occupy the same causal position. In the first, the violence is both cause and effect, i.e., it is the total situation or state of affairs; in the second, it is the *effect*; and in the third, the *cause*.

## XI. REASONABLE GROUNDS FOR SOCIAL VIOLENCE NOT AVAILABLE

Failure to recognize these different positions has resulted in thinkers taking one of two theoretical attitudes: (a) violence is a moral and healthy condition of the social life, and homeostasis is a sick and destructive condition of the social life; or (b) homeostasis is the only proper and ultimate condition of the social life. This last, of course, describes the fourth permutation: homeostatic causes producing homeostatic effects.

The tendency to recognize only these two positions has resulted in obscuring one very important fact: *there is no universally acceptable method of establishing the rightness or wrongness of social violence.* Justifications are always met by counterjustifications; and any violent social action is valued and justified as right or wrong depending on the social groups, institutions, or societies involved. Perhaps more accurately, I ought to say that there is no universal basis for justifying either violence or homeostatis. Whatever defenses, justifications, or apologies are offered satisfy those who believe one way and dissatisfy those who believe another. In saying there is no universal basis for justifying violence or homeostatis, I mean there are no accepted procedures, logics, or verification processes that can be used to establish for all concerned the rightness or wrongness of one or the other. Furthermore, there are no accepted uniform principles of prudence or morality that can be satisfactorily used to justify or condemn the performance of any intention. This does not mean that recommendations have not been and are not being made about procedures, logics, and confirmation processes or universal principles of prudence and morality. There is a plethora of them. My point is that there is no widespread acceptance of any of them for the settlement of human affairs.

To provide plausible evidence for what I have just said, I shall describe the sort of attitudes and justifications found among those who are involved in one or another of the three permutations of social violence. What I want to show is that there is no *justification* of a so-called rational sort that is widely accepted as preferable by all or nearly all who live within the context of one or another of these permutations. I do not say that there' are *no* justifications. Admittedly and invariably, justifications are offered, each reasonably standing on its own ground and believed more than adequate by its supporters. Such justifications almost always contradict or deny each other, i.e., each justifies its own particular kind of violence, but rejects all others as *unreasonable* morally or prudentially.

Let me take in turn each of the permutations. In the first case, most inhabitants whose dwellings and means of livelihood have been destroyed; who have been wounded, beaten, or crippled; whose relatives have been killed or harmed; and who, from fear for their lives, have fled and hidden themselves would consider both the violent cause (the rioters and soldiers) and violent effects (the burnt and destroyed dwellings, the killed, crippled, and wounded, the fleeing and hiding) as horrible catastrophes. To them, this violence is likely to be considered absolutely immoral, evil, and depraved. They would ask, "Why should this be done to us? We are civilians, peaceably doing what we do."

To most of the soldiers, the violence would be, on the whole, justified. They would consider it part of an essential military operation: the reduction of the enemy to impotence and a preventive measure against possible retaliation. That the innocent suffer, that property essential to life is destroyed—these are simply regrettable but unavoidable incidents in the carrying out of an essentially just military operation. To the non-military who benefit from such violence, it means the removal of undesirable, long-obsolete social arrangements: the land, its people, new and old, and its resources can now be organized on a sound modern basis.

In the second case, in which the militarized political party or vigilante group violently removes from office a governmental "gang," the "respectable" people see this action as the only possible way of getting back "honest government," "law and order," "justice and peace." To those who have, as a result, lost everything, both the violence and the restoration are patently unjust and unjustifiable; the only rational course is to destroy the restorers and the restoration by whatever means are available. To those who have neither lost nor gained, the violence is not likely to be a matter of serious concern, especially if it brings a new stability.

In the third case, in which non-violent forces are considered responsible for bringing about a state of continued violence, all sufferers would tend to criticize the means employed in one of three ways, by saying (a) the wrong non-violent means were employed, (b) the leaders were too stupid to correct their mistakes in time, or (c) violence was obviously the only means that could have been effective.

Perhaps a less startling formulation of my thesis might be: there are always conflicting justifications of violence. Groups, institutions, and societies approve of violent means, effects, or combinations of both basically in terms of expectations and actual outcomes over the short or long run. Since such expectations differ and since outcomes rarely satisfy the expectations of all involved, it is hardly ever possible that consensual agreement, if it happens, will last very long. In the end, which justifications dominate or are suppressed depend upon who acquires social power and continues to occupy the seat of power. The justifications approved by those in power are the ones taught to most members of succeeding generations. All others are condemned as nonsensical or suppressed from sight.

The reason for this is plain. Those who survive and dominate a social order are not inclined to believe that their survival and domination are matters of plain good luck. They justify their domination on the grounds that they have created the best possible society and are the best possible rulers. Whatever social weaknesses and evils can be demonstrated are explained away as either necessities of nature or removable, in the course of time, by intelligence, patience, and good will.[9]

## XII. THE STATE AND INSTITUTIONS OF VIOLENCE

At great length I have been trying to say two things. The first is that force is present and operative everywhere. 'Power' and 'violence' are simply modes of manifesting force: the former expresses the measure of usable or efficient force; the latter, the compression and release of force within a short interval of time.

Typically, 'violence' refers to a quantitative and qualitative dislocation and disequilibration of relatively stable structures and their parts, occurring within a relatively short period of time. Such dislocations and disequilibrations are often described as transformatory, i.e., productive of something altogether new, or as annihilatory. Since no structure or situation on any scale is known to be indefinitely stable, violence is inevitable at some time or other. Social force, social power, and social violence are respectively special kinds of force, power, and violence, and they possess special characteristics.[10]

The second thing I have been attempting to say is that there is no moral or prudential justification in general for social violence in terms of some universal principle or procedure, although attempts have been made time and time again to find them. There are always, of course, *justifications* of particular cases of social violence, but these justifications are rarely in agreement. If consensual agreement occurs, it is not on the basis of any principle, but of expectations, i.e., anticipated outcomes. However, it is the outcomes over the long or short period that are the cementers or destroyers of agreement. In any case, the apparent universality of such agreement at any particular time does not last very long; and it is generally based on ignoring, suppressing, or screening out opposed opinion, achieved often by a variety of unpleasant techniques employed on those who have the courage or foolhardiness to act and speak in opposition.

Constantly, I have tried to make clear that I am not concerned with force, power, or violence as such, but only with their social formations; and further that I am not concerned with their socially *unorganized* expressions. I am only concerned with social force, social power, and social violence as socially organized, socially recognized, socially established, and belonging to individuals, groups, or institutions as integral parts of their role in maintaining or transforming a social order. This concern excludes organized violence that has no such role.

I want now to say something about those social institutions that have acquired in time and by the intentions of specially situated individuals and groups the established social right to be violent. This social right to be violent is usually so strongly entrenched and naturally associated with such institutions and their personnel that it seems to belong to them by divine right. In discussing such institutions, my purpose will be generally to identify these institutions and explain their social necessity

(Sections XIII and XIV); and to say something about the almost universal belief that such institutions, given certain conditions, can be made to disappear (Section XV).

## XIII. INSTITUTIONS OF VIOLENCE AND THEIR SOCIAL NECESSITY

First I shall begin by stating something about 'society'. By 'society', I mean any aggregation of human beings organized in some specific way so that it (the society) indefinitely continues the survival of generations of such aggregations in whole or in part in more or less the same formations. This definition requires a refined elaboration, which is not possible in this paper. However, I need to summarize two of the most important of these refinements.

(1) Nobody, in any society, survives indefinitely. It is the succession of surviving kinship descendants that is socially important.

(2) Not all or even most of the members of a society are concerned with the survival of all the members of any generation or even with that society's survival from generation to generation.

In general, societies are so organized as to favor the survival of some of their members over all others; and those members who are favored are usually so organized as to preserve the organizational structure that favors them and their descendants against all the others who are not so favored. Many members— and often a fairly large percentage—of a society may be born to be destroyed as quickly as possible in order to provide the favored few with all of their usual social advantages.

In order better to understand this process of social survival selection, it is necessary to distinguish the factors that make possible the survival of a society generation after generation. First, there are the *material resources*, which are usually further distinguished into (a) *raw materials*: the earth, seeds, metals, natural or produced objects, and human beings used in this process; (b) *instrumentalities*, usually man-made, which are involved in using material resources; and (c) *finished products*. Whether anything is raw material, instrumentality, or finished product depends upon its place in the productive process. Hard carbon may be a raw material if it is to end as a faceted diamond; it may be an instrumentality if used to cut hard material; or it may be a finished product if used as an ornament.

Second, there are the behavioral, spatial, and temporal relations between all human beings and such material resources. Respecting these, three are important: the productive, the distributive, and the controlling.

## A. The Productive Relation

Productively, human beings may be related directly to the material resources through acquired skills that enable them by means of instrumentalities (human beings, too, are instrumentalities) to produce whatever products the members of that society use.

Again, they may be related indirectly as administrators, planners, or organizers to the productive process, their function being to organize the flow of materials and the arrangement of instrumentalities so as to produce the products required for social survival. (Notice that I am not saying that administrators, planners, or organizers attempt to organize the productive process most efficiently in the best interests of all.)

Again, they may be related to the productive process as *protectors*. From the necessity of protecting the productive process arise states and governments with their various organs of violence: basically, the military and the police. Of course, states and governments are rarely so all-encompassing as to offer protection for all phases of the productive process. Consequently, administrators often establish their own protector agencies to prevent productive sabotage and destruction. In modern advanced societies, such protector agencies play, as a whole, very subordinate roles. The protector agencies provided by state and government are infinitely more important.

Lastly, human beings may be related as owners or as privileged enjoyers of the productive process and its products. Owners and privileged enjoyers usually have the remotest connection of all with the productive process. They may know of its existence only through their retainers and through the products that they make constant use of.

In so far as human beings or groups of human beings are involved as producers or as helping to protect and preserve the productive process, it is customary to speak of a *division* of productive labor. By some conceptions of this division of labor, administrators, owners, and protectors are all considered to be producers. By another conception, those involved directly or indirectly as producers are separated from those who own, administer, protect, or enjoy the usufructs of production. I adhere to the latter conception, even though it means in some few cases an overlapping of productive function.

## B. The Distributive Relation

Distributively, human beings are related to the productive process in terms of what they receive in goods, education, and other products. Distribution of this sort is simply a specialized case of the total distribution of materials, instrumentalities, and human beings required by the total productive process. Steel is brought by trucks or railroads to automobile factories; and particular kinds of workers are produced, trained, educated, and distributed to different production units according to function, time, and place.

But here I am not concerned with the total process of productive distribution. I want to deal only with what people receive for themselves through the productive process. In commodity societies this kind of distribution is usually expressed in money terms, but I prefer not to speak in such terms. Money tends to hide what it actually means as quantities and qualities of food, clothing, leisure, education, amusement, health, housing, etc. When distribution of goods is translated into concrete rather than money terms, there is never any difficulty in knowing *what* is distributed, to *whom*, in what amounts, in what quality, and why. In such concrete terms, it is relatively easy to observe that those who own, manage, or control large areas of production are the ones who receive the most, far beyond anything they can use, and who can guarantee the most for their heirs. In contrast, those who are owned, managed, and controlled receive least for themselves and their descendants. Admittedly, this is no new observation, but it is either forgotten or rationalized when expressed in purely monetary terms.

## C. The Controlling Relation

Distribution of goods and services immediately introduces the matter of control, not because distribution is more fundamental than the process by which things are produced, but because it is through distribution that most people learn who controls what and whom. Most people may not know who really controls what they receive, but they know at least this: that someone other than themselves controls what they get, because they do not. If they are persistent enough, they will discover which individuals, groups, or institutions control them, and how. This knowledge may not be as refined as scientifically minded persons might like, but it is adequate enough. In some societies, it is easier than in others to learn this. Who controls, for whom, and what may be so obscured by institutional complexity and ideological myth that those who are controlled may live out their lives, unthinkingly and uncomplainingly, in a Kafka Castle.

## XIV.  STATE AND GOVERNMENT

Most societies—certainly, modern ones—are so organized productively as to favor the few against the many. Because they are so organized, they need institutions the prime function of which is to protect and preserve this order of production against those who are not so favored. As I said earlier, the primary agencies for this purpose are the state and government. Let me say a word about how many thinkers relate the one to the other.

The state is made to appear as something invisible behind what is visible. Many jurists, political scientists, and philosophers have described it as an invisible, unchanging entity that somehow invisibly and intangibly exercises power over its subjects or citizens. Most jurists have named this invisible power 'sovereignty': the property of absolute, unlimited, amoral control over the subjects. Some have bound it with a moral constituent to limit this control, or have even identified it with the highest moral law. The latter identification has usually been the work of philosophers; most jurists have known better.[11]

This conception of the state creates an indefinite number of unsolvable problems. How can the state collapse or lose power? How can it take such Protean political forms as monarchy, oligarchy, plutocracy, limited democracy, etc.? Why, above all, does it seem always to favor certain individuals, groups, and social classes? Such problems are not solvable by the notion of the state as an invisible entity.

I shall not concern myself with these problems. I shall take it as a fact that the visible state is that institution which is granted and usually possesses the force to harm or destroy human beings; to take away, alter, or destroy their property; to distribute both human beings and property according to the needs and interests of those who directly or indirectly control the state. I shall take it as fact that its *primary* function is to defend the productive structure and those, in particular, who control and benefit most from its operation. I shall also take it as fact that the state's use of violent force and the instrumentalities that make such force violent is determined by the needs and requirements of the productive system. The government is not something different from the state, but simply the specific structure that the state assumes as the protector agency of a given productive order at any period in its history.

The institutions today that are essential parts of the state or government are the *legal* and the *protective*. The *legal* are those institutions that legislate and adjudicate; the *protective* basically are the *military* and the *police*. The state at one time did not possess or need so many distinct institutions to perform its basic function of preserving and protecting the total productive process. But the division into legislative, adjudicative, military, and police, with their respective subdivisions—agencies, departments, etc.—has followed from the continued growth in the complexity of the productive process.

This basic division into the legal and the protective has helped to give the state the appearance of moral legitimacy, but it has also served to obscure the formidable role of state institutions of violence—the military and the police—in preserving a productive system. Since no productive system is absolutely stable, and change within it dislocates and disequilibrates to a greater or lesser degree its operation, the legal institutions of the state function, more or less, to find and set up rules to keep the system of production in operation, and this means, of course, the system of distribution involved in it. Dislocation and disequilibration are invariably expressed in lesser or greater violence, in typical crimes and in actions of protest, strikes, demonstrations, etc. At such times, the legal institutions usually take on the appearance of rationally re-establishing homeostasis because they revise old rules or create new ones; and the supporting protector institutions of violence, acting in terms of such rules, take on the appearance of preventing and reducing social violence and of restoring order. All who refuse to accept or abide by the rules inevitably appear to be disturbers of the peace, fomenters of disorder. Consequently, it seems just and right that such institutions must act to prevent all actions that endanger existing social arrangements.

That state institutions of violence use violence in its various modes somewhere every day of their existence is generally overlooked or mistakenly viewed as non-violence by most people, who accept the productive system of which they are parts. The vast majority of such state acts of violence—i.e., acts done in the performance of duty—are against individuals or small groups committing typical acts normally defined as criminal. In these cases, the violence involved is not usually visible. However, the violence of state institutions of violence is clearly recognized when the military or the police or both appear in large numbers against others. At such moments, the violence or the threat of it is clearly visible, whatever the justification. When this is the situation, one thing is patently obvious: The forces of law and order are visibly there to preserve the productive system from attempts to alter or destroy it.

Mention was made above of typical crimes. These are usually handled by the police—whatever kinds of police may exist: uniformed, non-uniformed, etc. Many of the non-typical crimes —the political or the subversive, such as riots, strikes, uprisings, and demonstrations—are also generally handled by the police. However, if the situation is serious, the military is often called in to assist.

Wars and revolutions, whether internal or external to the state, are usually handled by the military. Unlike the police, the military is everywhere recognized as a state institution of violence. Whether used internally or externally, the role of the military is not merely to preserve the existing productive system —the usual role of the police—but also to extend, where necessary or desirable, the boundaries of the existing productive system.

Ordinary or typical crimes rarely destroy the established productive system. Those who commit such crimes are usually as supportive of the productive system as those who are most favored by it. Ordinary criminals are usually responsible for a mild redistribution of movable property; nothing more. This is also true for typical wars between similar productive systems. As a usual thing, those who own, administer, and control such systems simply wish to replace the old with themselves or with new owners, administrators, and controllers under their control. Sometimes, they may wish to update a less modern productive system. Nevertheless, such wars are always dangerous—even when inevitable—in two respects: they are often completely destructive of the embattled productive systems, or they create the conditions for a productive revolution, i.e., a radical change in the established system of distribution, production, and control.

Of course, when I say that the police and the military protect the existing system of production, I mean this to be understood not in any abstract economic sense—the sense in which many economists usually talk. I mean this in the concrete sense of protecting whatever is produced according to established social modes of production and distribution. Protective agencies—the police and the military—do not, in general, protect a productive system that allegedly serves the interests of all (this is the academic economist's dream of a productive system), but rather a specific productive system almost always organized to advantage the few against the many. To understand *what, who*, and *how* they protect, the *particular* productive system must be carefully studied. There is no other way of finding answers to the *what, who*, and *how*.

One other thing must be said. I assume that the police and the military would not be required if more than enough were produced to satisfy the cultural needs and desires of everyone. In other words, the police, as a special agency, exist to protect *property* that others need or desire. Crimes against persons are, in most cases, crimes to acquire property; people who need or desire property belonging to others will maim or kill to obtain it. The military, as a special agency, mainly exists (a) to protect *big* property and the modes of its ownership and control against the propertyless, and (b) to extend the sway of big property over its competitors. If this were not the case, there would be no need for the military. However, since this is the case, state "forces" of violence are a necessity for those who support and are advantaged by a given system of production.

No matter how anyone may try to justify one or another of the productive systems, past or present, this function of institutions of violence cannot be denied. If one defends the institutions of violence of the United States, England, or France, one cannot legitimately deny that their state "forces" of violence are used essentially to protect the rich and favored against the poor and disfavored. One cannot factually deny that any person or group who seeks to remove the privileges and advantages that accrue to the owners, administrators, and controllers is suspect, watched over, isolated, and sometimes imprisoned, hounded, or killed. The more extreme the doctrines and persistent the actions of such persons and groups, the more hostile and brutal become their surveillance and ultimate treatment. The English and American way of treating such persons or groups may be gentle in comparison with the Greek, the Russian, or the Chinese, but the difference between them is one of degree, not of kind.

The same holds for the Russian and Chinese productive systems. One may prefer their systems, which lack individual or corporate owners of the *means* of production, i.e., of the railroads, the factories, the mines, etc.; but one cannot deny that their state institutions of violence are used to protect *state* administrators and controllers and their modes of administering and controlling state property against all who desire to reorganize that system to the advantage of the controlled and the poor.

One significant consequence of this recognition of the role and necessity of state institutions of violence is the theory, diversely developed and documented by all sorts of thinkers, that a productive system cannot be reorganized without expropriating and removing the "rich," i.e., the owners, administrators, and controllers, from the seats of productive power. Furthermore, this expropriation and removal cannot be done without organizing counter-institutions of violence which have their base in the "people."[12]

This conclusion is not usually contested where productive systems lack some sort of electoral or advisory legal system for influencing ruler judgment or bringing about social change. It is widely recognized that counter-institutions of violence are the only means of changing such productive systems. However, this conclusion is widely contested in those cases where productive systems possess some sort of electoral or advisory legal system. Here one finds two well-known opinions: the reform or liberal, and the revolutionary—each, of course, having its own many varieties and divergences.

The liberals tend to hold that the state institutions of violence have lost their historic and habitual function of protecting a given productive system. They hold that these institutions have been transformed and now serve mainly to protect all humanity from the few who are immoral, evil-intentioned, greedy, and power-hungry. When present institutions of violence are used in their historic role, liberals tend to consider such uses temporary perversions or deviations caused by an evil and powerful few. Given time, such perversions and deviations, they believe, will become less and less frequent. Finally, they expect the voice of reason everywhere to prevail.

The revolutionaries tend to believe that even the "best" of such systems, the democratic, is a facade obscuring the traditional and inevitable functions of the state. They see state legal institutions as existing primarily to maintain the productive system in a state of relative equilibrium; and the protective institutions—the institutions of violence—as existing primarily to prevent the non-rulers, the ruled, from radically transforming it. Thus, revolutionaries tend to insist on the necessity of creating counter-institutions of violence having their base in the "people," and of developing "revolutionary" strategies for overthrowing the established productive order.

I have not mentioned one special theory which is connected with the preservation or maintenance of an established productive system. It is a theory that becomes especially popular whenever large owners, administrators, and controllers become fearful of revolutionary movements. Generally, it involves certain accommodations to revolutionary demands in order that tighter controls can be imposed on the operations of the existing productive system. It also involves a less restricting conception of the role of state institutions of violence. Notions are developed and implemented to create special agencies with enormous power to act both internally and externally, i.e., within the confines of the national or multinational productive systems or outside them. Examples of this theory are the Nazi and Fascist systems.

As societies today are productively organized, one conclusion seems inevitable: state institutions of violence will not vanish from the social scene or wither away. No matter what revolutionaries or idealists may hope for and promise, once they, too, attain the seats of power, they will find themselves irresistibly creating and perpetuating their own kinds of protector institutions in order to preserve the new productive system against its enemies and critics. However, the conclusion must not be drawn from this seeming certainty that revolutions cannot and may not make beneficial changes in the lives of the vast majority, despite the initial cost in destruction of life and property.

In any case, arguments about the futility of revolution and the preferability of slow, gradual reform never, in the long run, influence the poor, the exploited, and the dissatisfied. The vision and hope of a better world—in whatever sense this is understood—is a compelling force that produces protest, rebellion, and revolt. The social violence that usually or ultimately meets actions of protest strengthens the mass attitude that organized social counter-violence is the only successful way of creating the better world.

Several corollaries follow: (1) Given such institutions, any success in transforming a productive system and its modes of distribution depends upon the creation of counter-institutions of violence capable of defeating and destroying the enemy state institutions of violence. The amount or degree of social dislocation and disequilibration will, of course, depend on the weakness of the enemy state institutions of violence, the strength of the counter-institutions of violence, and the total strategic brilliance of those seeking to transform the established productive system.

(2) It is not likely that those who own, administer, and control a productive system will allow themselves to be ousted without a maximized struggle of violence. Depending on its severity, state violence against individuals, groups, and members of counter-institutions will increase in intensity, duration, and kind until they are either annihilated or reduced to total impotence.

(3) All groups and individuals opposed to each other will find their own kinds of justifications for what they do. These justifications will be accepted or rejected, changed or modified, according to changing circumstances and needs. The justification of those who triumph will dominate the social arena; all other justifications will tend to disappear or fade away, existing, if at all, in the minds of underground individuals and groups.

(4) If the revolutionaries attain power, they will statify their institutions of violence or create new, more effective ones. These will be justified at first as temporary institutions, required to destroy or render impotent all who endanger the new productive order. Later, as the new order stabilizes, they will become permanent, ineradicable parts of the new productive system, maintained to protect it against those who are ruled, and to extend, where possible, its domain. The irony of this re-creation of permanent state institutions of violence is its voiding of the original thesis of the makers of this revolution that their revolution will destroy the necessity for institutions of violence.

## XV. CAN STATE INSTITUTIONS OF VIOLENCE DISAPPEAR?

One theoretical basis today for the making of revolutions is that a society can be created on a world scale which will not require state institutions of violence to maintain and preserve it. Is there any reasonable basis for believing this? Are there reasonable grounds for believing that a productive system can be

created—whatever and however the social forces employed—
that will have no need for permanent institutions of violence?
This may be for many too strong a formulation. Perhaps this
more modest formulation is preferable: Are there plausible
grounds for believing that a productive system can be created
which would require at most, few, if any, permanent institutions
of violence? This question needs elucidation. The expression,
"few, if any, institutions of violence," should be interpreted as
meaning that if such institutions were needed, they would
hardly, if ever, use violence and this only in the most extreme
situations, when conditions clearly support its necessity. Implicit in saying this is the belief that social situations would
hardly ever occur in which violence would be necessary. Such
extreme situations would occur only in small locales. Implicit
also in saying this is the belief that matters of unjust distribution
of goods and of the dissatisfactions of individuals, groups, or
institutions would be settled nearly always by prompt consulta-
tion and objective evaluation.

In the late eighteenth, throughout the nineteenth, and during
the early twentieth century, writers like Fourier, Saint-Simon,
Proudhon, Bright, J. S. Mill, Marx, Engels, and Lenin—each in
his own way—provided imaginative (some of them even called
theirs scientific) answers to this question. It is impossible here
to state the variety of conditions each laid down for creating
such a society, but it is important to state two conditions about
which most of these writers agreed. The first was that private
and corporate property, i.e., private and corporate ownership
and control of those productive means by which social goods
and services are produced, must be replaced by communal or
state ownership and control. The second was that enough goods
must be produced to guarantee every human being whatever he
requires to make a self-satisfying life. Most of them believed
that the first condition must be achieved before the second.
Some,—for example, Fourier, Saint-Simon, and Proudhon—
believed that both could be achieved through the organization
of small, self-sufficient communes. Others like Marx, Engels,
and Lenin believed that these conditions could be achieved only
on a world scale.

Plainly, the experience of the nineteenth and twentieth centuries shows that the first condition—the establishment of
communes or of the state controlling the basic means of production—does not guarantee the second. The communes have
never succeeded in establishing themselves as permanent social

institutions despite thousands of attempts, nor have they influenced the majority of humankind to organize themselves in like structures. State control of the means of· production has been achieved in a number of countries, but not one has been able as yet to produce enough goods and services to guarantee most persons within their domains a self-satisfying life. Distinctions between rich and poor, between rulers and ruled, are as strong among them as they are in capitalist states.[13] The state institutions of violence play as large and as pervasive a role in the lives of Soviet people as in capitalist states. Indeed, it may with strong justification be said that in Soviet states they are even more powerful and pervasive.

Since the second condition has as yet not been fulfilled to any significant degree, it is not possible to say definitely whether these two conditions suffice to achieve the stateless society. Nevertheless, there are good reasons to believe that they are not sufficient. One reason is that any productive system—however organized—which gives power to one group of human beings to control the actions and determine the long-term goals of *all* others inevitably requires institutions of violence. If such a productive order consists of relatively separate productive systems, then there must exist institutions of violence for each system, serving external and internal protective needs to prevent revolution and to make war on each other. If it is a world system, then its institutions of violence must be wholly internal: to prevent revolution. Those who have promoted the idea of establishing a world government have recognized the necessity of such institutions even though they have deceptively described them as primarily performing police duties on a world scale. However, a world government—even if it were feasible—composed of antithetic productive systems would constantly face the specter of revolution. Its so-called police force would, therefore, need to be a huge military force.

Another reason is that producers must be controlled in any productive system that forms an interdependent whole of parts and functions, for they must be kept at their jobs whether they like it or not. For example, were farmers to refuse to produce agricultural products essential to the maintenance of human labor, they would need to be compelled to produce. Were producers of energy to refuse to produce energy, they would need to be compelled to produce energy. Consequently, institutions of violence are required.

These reasons show that two more conditions—at the very

least—must be satisfied if a stateless or nearly stateless society is to be created. The third condition is that no human being or group of human beings shall be in a normal functional position to control the actions or determine the goals of other human beings. The fourth condition is that no human being need be functionally identified and tied to any productive position. Whether most human beings do or do not produce or whether they perform this or that function at any given time must not affect the production of essential goods and services. To satisfy these conditions, social production must obviously achieve almost complete automation.

These four conditions are external or—I might say—environmental. However, there is one more condition to satisfy, which might be called internal or psychological: Human beings must be able to use constructively the social resources made available to them. I mean by the adverb "constructively" that (a) these resources produce self-satisfaction, and (b) human beings no longer need or desire to destroy each other and the productive system that provides these remarkable resources.

I do not believe that these five conditions are ever likely to be met. Even so, it does not inevitably follow that a society less organized to do violence and better able to satisfy the needs of nearly all living human beings cannot be created. However, I do not believe that humanity will ever have the opportunity to find out whether, to any satisfactory extent, such an objective can really be approached. I do not believe that modern civilization can survive. Its sojourn on this earth is, as reckoned by social time, too short.

These are my reasons, summarily stated: (1) In order to survive, the advanced productive systems are today forced desperately to compete with each other for essential material resources and markets. They are not only forced to compete with each other, but they are forced to seek absolute control over the poorer, non-mass-production societies that possess essential material resources. The result of this desperate struggle can only be nuclear war and the demise of modern civilization.

(2) The advanced productive systems cannot control the rate at which they are exhausting human and material resources. Their inability to control the utilization of resources is resulting in the pollution of the air, the ocean, and the earth and the destruction of the plant and animal life essential for human survival.

(3) There exist no social groups, élites, or social classes

capable of taking over world control of existing productive systems in order to prevent these consequences.

(4) Even if such social groups, élites, or social classes were available, the rapidity with which productive systems over the world are pushing toward nuclear war, ultimate pollution, and exhaustion of resources precludes the possibility of their taking over social power in time.[14]

# Notes

1 My remark about "inventing a force" should not be misunderstood. Newton used the words 'gravity' or 'gravitation' to name the force that attracts objects to each other. Some might well call whatever it is that Newton named 'gravity' an invention, yet the word serves to identify something at work between physical particles or things. Goethe used the expression 'elective affinity' to name whatever it is makes men and women truly love each other. This something may also be described as an invention. Moreover, even though these somethings, gravity and elective affinity, were felt by their inventors to exist, they are invisible entities. It is obviously a serious question whether either of them can be felt even as an attracting force. However, in Newton's case, his invention is a success, because he confined gravity within mathematical formulae that make possible the relatively accurate prediction of the movements of billiard balls, steam engines, and the tides. In Goethe's case, his invention is a failure, because he was unable to develop formulae by means of which predictions could be made as to which men and women would fall truly in love with each other (Goethe, *Elective Affinities,* trans. Elizabeth Mayer and Louise Bogan [Chicago: Henry Regnery Co., 1963]).

2 R. P. Feynman offers as a definition for force: "If a body is accelerating, then there is a force in it"—i.e., wherever a change in motion occurs, it is caused by a force. "Power," he says, "equals the work done per second" or "the work done by [a] force on [an] object"—i.e., the force producing effects on the object. These definitions of Professor Feynman are admittedly, as he himself says, not very exact, because they are non-mathematical. Mathematically, of course, force is loosely defined as mass times acceleration ($F = ma$) and power as force times distance ($P = fd$). For our purposes, the non-mathematical descriptions of physical force and power are preferable, since they are able to serve as a basis for more specialized descriptions of human, non-social, and social force and power (*The Feynman Lectures on Physics,* vol. 1 [Reading, Mass.: Addison-Wesley Publishing Co., 1963], secs. 12–1, 13–1).

3 Both Hobbes and Russell make power, not force, the determinant factor of change in society (Bertrand Russell, *Power: A New Social Analysis* [New York: W. W. Norton & Co., 1938], pp. 10, 35 ff.). Russell's reason is exactly that of Hobbes. Men desire both power and glory, but power comes first. Thus the relation of power to force, as defined by physicists, is converted. In physics, power is a mode or manifestation of force; for Hobbes and Russell, force—at least in society—is a mode or manifestation of power.

I object to this conversion on two grounds. First, it creates an unnecessary problem: that of reconciling the accepted concepts of physics with the reverse psychological concepts of Hobbes and Russell. What good reason is there for making force derivative from power in society, when in physics the reverse is the case? If only for the sake of intellectual economy, it seems preferable—if it can be done—to derive social power from social force as an analogue to physics. Of course, social force has properties that physical force does not have, but these differences do not justify making it a derivative of social power. After all, the social world is of the "substance" of the physical world; it is, of course, more than physical, but it is *still* physical. The physical world works in it and through it.

My second objection is that Russell defines power as "the production of intended effects" (*Power*, p. 35). Implied in his definition are (1) the presence of force, i.e., of something capable of producing effects; and (2) the measurement of effects produced, for power varies in the work it does, i.e., in the production of effects. Thus power is a *measure* of the amount or degree of force required to produce effects. By Russell's definition, the distinction between force and power disappears. Yet, as in physics, it seems essential to distinguish force from power, one being the source of power, the other the measure of effective force.

The human concern with power arises from the need to control effects, to be able to produce or prevent effects—greater or smaller in range, quality, and quantity—according to need. Human beings want to be able to use a small amount of force to produce as many effects as they desire. This explains the human interest in power. To have power means to have disposable force available in some structured arrangement in order to produce anticipated effects. However, the fact that human beings, in one respect or another, desire power does not make it any less a mode or manifestation of force.

[4] 'Force' as used here may seem ambiguous, since anything can be said, in given circumstances, to be a force. This, of course, is true. But there is one restrictive condition in applying the word to anything: This is that predictions of effects with some degree of probability of occurrence should be derivable from whatever is named a force. If this is not or cannot be done, then whatever is named as a force is not a force; it is a pseudo-force, a pretension of a force.

Striking examples of expressions frequently used without submission to this restriction are "economic force," "intellectual force" and "social force." Frequently, historians fail to identify the economic, intellectual or social forces, or to indicate what effects they are likely to produce. A proper use, for example, of the expression "economic force" would mean naming the force and indicating the effects that follow from it. For example, the cotton gin and the capital invested in South Asia have often been called "economic forces"; and many of the historians and economists who have called them such have also specified the effects, small and large, that they have produced. One may be seriously mistaken in calling something a force and asserting that it has had, or will have, certain effects, but in doing so, the mistake can be found out.

[5] The Weathermen probably expected the downtrodden and exploited American working class to rise up immediately to their support. After all, were they not acting in the working-class interest? Unfortunately, the Weathermen exist in the same dream-world as rational liberals, but at the opposite pole. The Weathermen believe in bombs and the rational liberals believe in reason as the essential means for bringing about the good society. Neither group will succeed. The Weathermen have already destroyed themselves; the liberals will be permitted to dream until the time comes to put away their dreams or spend the remainder of their lives in psychiatric institutions.

[6] The word 'normal' seems likely to produce misunderstanding. I do

not want it to be understood in the sense of "what *usually* takes place." This expression is usually understood in any one of the following senses: (1) What takes place is unusual in being a *rare* occurrence, as in the case of nuclear weapons being used in a local war. (2) What takes place is *different*, as in the case of a speaker who, though he almost never deviates from his prepared address, makes a few impromptu comments. (3) What takes place is totally unexpected, a surprise, as in the case of the late Lyndon B. Johnson refusing to run as a presidential candidate for a second term. Of course, the three senses may be combined.

For lack of a better adjective I use 'normal' to identify those social forces that are recognized as belonging to the functional role of a person, a group, or an institution. Social violence, for example, is not, in this sense, normal to a priest or Buddhist monk; it is not a characteristic of their patterns of behavior. This, of course, does not mean that a priest or Buddhist monk may not suddenly go berserk. However, social violence is normal to a policeman, a squad of policemen, or the army or navy, even though they may rarely use it or use it differently or surprisingly. It is a characteristic of their functional role, an accepted pattern in their patterns of behavior. It is a mode of behavior they have learned, and they are expected to behave violently if and when the proper circumstances require it.

[7] I do not like the word "subversive"; it has moral connotations that rise and fall with social circumstance. For example, organizations considered "subversive" today, if they attain their goals tomorrow, become eminently respectable and glow with the highest moral aura. But I do not (for now) know a better word. As describing groups, persons, or institutions, it means that they are ready, prepared, and able to be violent for the attainment of their goals: *the alteration of a productive system in some significant respect.* Thus the word applies to all persons, groups, or institutions—whether reactionary or revolutionary—organized for violence and willing, when necessary, to use it.

[8] William Hinton, *The Hundred Day War* (New York: Monthly Review Press, 1972).

[9] Obviously, I could have used far more effective examples such as the French or the Russian Revolutions. The diversity of justifications for making or not making these revolutions was enormous; and this diversity was represented or symbolized by the diversity of political parties, groups, and individuals, each of which gave different justifications for doing what each did every time there was occasion to do something. In one respect, it would have been easier to show what happened both to the justifiers and their justifications. As Socrates said, it is easier to show in the *large* what is happening than in the small. But using such examples would have lengthened this paper enormously and raised endless controversy, not about the diversity, but about whether any particular instance is interpreted correctly.

[10] In Section II, I mentioned that social force acquires new properties. It acquires the property of (a) being used to achieve a purpose, (b) being selected to produce anticipated effects, and (c) being evaluated as to its effectiveness in case it fails to produce the effects anticipated. But these properties, I also pointed out, were not enough to make it social. To be a social force, it has to operate in a social context where it is used to influence, change, modify, or destroy human beings, institutions, social processes, arrangements, or artifacts.

[11] See Robert M. MacIver, *The Modern State* (New York: Oxford University Press, 1947), pp. 8–16 et passim.

[12] The word "people" is used loosely here to cover all the ranges of its use by revolutionaries. Marxists use the expression "the people" when they mean a motley of social classes including the proletariat, farmers, peons, and lower middle classes, which they believe play an essential role in any given country in making a revolution possible. When they desire to be more exact, they speak only of the proletariat, or the alliance of the proletariat and the farmers. The French revolutionaries of the eighteenth and early nineteenth centuries meant by the "people" the farmers and serfs and the urban bourgeoisie, artisans, and workers. They did not include the aristocrats and the priesthood.

[13] Although this is admitted, defenders of Soviet society say that all— even criminals—are provided with the minimum essentials of life: each eats, has a place to live, a job, and an opportunity to realize his potentials through free education. Negatively stated, no one starves, is not employed, or lacks opportunity for education and self-advancement. This, in itself, say its defenders, makes the Soviet state, despite its serious defects, preferable to the capitalist state.

[14] See Rubin Gotesky, "Modern Civilization: Its Demise," *Philosophy Forum* 12 (1972): 67–111, for an extensive array of arguments justifying the reasons stated here.

# An Anatomy of Violence

HARRY GIRVETZ has taught for many years at the University of California at Santa Barbara. He studied at Stanford University and received the Ph.D. from the University of California at Berkeley in 1937. Professor Girvetz is the author of numerous books, articles, and reviews in the areas of moral theory, political and social philosophy, and nineteenth-century philosophy. His books include *From Wealth to Welfare* (1950), *Evolution of Liberalism* (1962), and *Beyond Right and Wrong* (1973); he has edited *Contemporary Moral Issues* (1963, 1968); and has edited and co-authored *Science, Folklore and Philosophy* (1965), *Democracy and Elitism* (1966), and *Literature and the Arts: The Moral Issues* (1971).

# An Anatomy of Violence

## by Harry Girvetz

## I. THE CATEGORIES OF VIOLENCE

John Herbes, in his "special introduction" to the report submitted to the National Commission on the Causes and Prevention of Violence, observes that the Commission, as it addressed itself to the problem of violence in America, was unable to find a significant work on the subject. H. D. Graham and T. R. Gurr, editors of the report, find that social scientists "have largely eschewed the study of violence in America,"[1] and they note the absence of an entry on "Violence" in the new edition of the *Encyclopedia of the Social Sciences*. A distinguished scholar, Hannah Arendt, also finds it surprising that violence "has been singled out so seldom for special consideration" and she goes on to find it "a rather sad reflection on the present state of political science that our terminology does not distinguish among such key words as 'power,' 'strength,' 'force,' 'authority,' and, finally, 'violence.' "[2] I am interested in only two of these terms—*force* and *violence*—and I will venture definitions somewhat at variance from those on which Dr. Arendt relies.

Force or violence is harm perpetrated on persons or property ranging, in the case of persons, from restraining their freedom of movement to torture and death, and, in the case of property, from simple fine or damage to complete expropriation or total destruction. Violence and force are not usually differentiated, but I find it useful to distinguish them and I think a distinction can be made out without too much defiance of usage.

I would distinguish force by its *legitimacy*. *Force*, as I here think of it, is authorized coercion, involving physical or economic sanctions, justified by reference to established principle and incorporated in a system of law or, in preliterate societies, simply taken for granted as a part of the accepted or traditional "scheme of things." J. M. Cameron in a recent article on violence rightly points out that "what is taken to be unalterable, a part of the natural order is not singled out as violence."[3] And, of course, what is called force in one culture or period may be regarded as violence in another. As Cameron notes, brutal floggings which today would be regarded as outrageous and intolerable violence were part of the routine discipline of Wellington's army. But Wellington used "force" to mold his army, not violence. To be sure, there may come a time when the prevailing and heretofore accepted notion of legitimacy is challenged by at least one of the groups in a society whose consent is necessary if there is not to be revolution or civil war. At that point the distinction between force and violence becomes confused until the issue is resolved, as in the case of our Civil War.

It is a distinctive feature of modern social organization that, in contrast to early periods, force is invoked only by the state which is, indeed, accorded a virtual monopoly in its use. If an individual might once have been permitted to punish an assailant, this is no longer the case, although he may, of course, take appropriate emergency measures to protect himself. And, if the church once enjoyed the right to punish heretics, it has long since been bereft of that right. If employers once used private armies to break labor unions (sometimes with appropriate pretense of legitimacy, i.e., government sanction) this could not easily happen in present-day America. Parents may still restrain or punish their children and here and there a teacher may be permitted to use corporal punishment, but such uses of force are peripheral and exercised solely at the discretion of the state.

A common error consists of identifying all exercises of power, particularly when the source is political, with the use or threatened use of force. However, the threat of or use of force is far from representing the only way in which the state exercises power. Indeed, the extent to which a government relies on force is a fair index of its weakness. It will rely as much on perquisites: patronage, handouts, and what Americans call "pork." Above all, it will rely on persuasion, using that term in the broadest sense to include conversion of the major factions or parties in a society to a belief in the fundamentals of the social order of which they are a part, a belief sufficient to provide the kind of basic consensus which assures that opposition is always loyal opposition.

But my theme is violence rather than force, and it is to violence—defined as illegitimate and unsanctioned acts of individuals or groups of individuals intended to inflict injury on others —that I wish to give my attention.

It may be said at the outset that the state sometimes uses violence as well as force, that is to say, the coercion it uses may be quite illegitimate, as when the police use coercion punitively and beyond what is needed to quiet a disturbance or restrain a culprit. In Isla Vista, the once troubled student community adjoining the campus of the University of California at Santa Barbara, police action was a mixture of force *and* violence. At Mississippi State it was a case of sheer violence. When the state uses its power to coerce for purposes which are extralegal and have no basis in consent or acknowledged principle, such coercion takes the form of violence. Surely it was violence that the Nazis inflicted on the Jews, violence that Stalin inflicted on his victims, violence that, at least until recently, some Southern leaders would inflict on the Negro who rejected their notion of a proper relationship between the races.

However, it does not get us very far to talk about violence in general. It is necessary to distinguish different categories of violence. I find four such categories, although I am not sure that they are exhaustive or mutually exclusive and there may well be a preferable classification.

## A. Economic Violence

I refer here to the large category in which individuals are driven to violence, that is, to do injury to others, from economic need. I do not include here those hardened criminals for whom satisfying their economic needs in this way has become a way of life that they prefer even though alternative ways of life might be open to them. Neither do I include those who, while their aggressions are directed to an economic reward, cannot be said by prevailing standards to need that reward. On the other hand, the need may not be as exigent as Jean Valjean's when he stole a loaf of bread to feed his starving family. I would include the embezzler who steals from his employer to repay gambling debts, the addict who mugs a victim to get money for another "fix," the recently arrested bank robber who embarked on his hazardous career because he was hopelessly in debt to loan sharks. Admittedly the robber's was the foolhardy recourse of what we would call a "weak" character. The point is that neither he, the addict, nor Jean Valjean would have engaged in violence if there had been some other way open to them. Such people would prefer not to be aggressive; the harm they do to persons is incidental and often accidental. They have moral standards and are aware of breaching them, even though some of them may be more prone to temptation than the rest of us.

I will not linger on this category, interesting though it may be to ask ourselves whether such crime is on the increase (which I doubt), and what social conditions and methods of correction would reduce such aggression to a minimum. Neither will I raise here the crucial question of whether theft is morally justifiable where there is a maldistribution of wealth *that has no functional justification* and the deprived have no other recourse, or where individuals are *arbitrarily* excluded from an opportunity to seek the goods of life. No doubt such arbitrary exclusion explains why blacks are not convinced that "the laws of theft are as important to Negroes as they are to anyone else," although it so happens that it was a Negro judge, James B. Parsons, the first of his race to be appointed to the Federal bench in the continental United States, who said that. I stress *arbitrary* exclusion. Often the worst disabilities will be tolerated if only a rationale is provided. The commonest rationale is that there isn't enough to go around. A better one is that deprivation endured now will lead to prosperity later. Still another, favored years ago by Calvinists, was that prosperity is a mark of God's favor and poverty of His disfavor. If there is indeed a contempt for law among blacks, manifest in a far greater incidence among them of economic violence, this will be mitigated only when it becomes evident that they are not gratuitously excluded from the benefits which the law is intended to protect.

## B. Anomic Violence

As though nagging poverty were not enough, the island of Sicily, as we all know, is the seat of an infamous society known as the Mafia. Since the families generally referred to by this name often wage relentless war on each other until the ranks of their male members are nearly decimated, the sense in which they may be called a "society" is not altogether unassailable. Nevertheless, the Mafia has its hierarchs and henchmen. Its rulers gather occasionally in formal conference, and it appears to conduct itself by a kind of code, albeit one that is as brutal as it is bizarre.

If we are to believe one of its chroniclers, there was a time when the leaders of the Mafia thought of themselves as social benefactors, although, given the nature of their activities, the claim strains credulity. But whatever the past may have contained, the recent crimes of the Mafia have been so heinous as completely to preclude the possibility that the perpetrators could really believe they were promoting the public good. This change, if it was one, resulted at least in part from the repatriation of gangsters, like the late Lucky Luciano, who imparted a certain American efficiency to the antique methods of his more provincial colleagues. Extortion and graft took on new and ingenious forms; traffic in drugs and assorted rackets became a major industry, and violent death a daily occurrence. We are told that the homicide rate of Palermo is the highest in the world, and, since not even the grief-stricken relatives of the victims will brave the vengeance of the Mafia by testifying against the murderers, the crimes go unpunished.

The Mafiosi correspond to the anomic men designated by Professor R. M. MacIver as those who have substituted disconnected urges for moral standards. They are a law unto themselves. They rule by terror. Their sole weapon is injury or the threat of injury. They do not pause for preachments, they seek no conversions. Suffering no pangs of conscience, oblivious of the rules by which most men are governed, impervious to considerations of justice, they have no need for those rationalizations—transparent or opaque—by which the normal man tries to conceal his baser motives. They would be the first to scorn ideologues and system-makers; their interests and energies are generally exhausted in the act of pillage itself and the immediate conditions that make it possible. Except as objects of plunder their victims are of only marginal interest to them. It seems appropriate, therefore, to coin the term "mafianism" for all exercises of power that seek no extenuation and have no objective other than plunder, no means other than violence or the threat of violence, and no limit other than the satiation of the oppressor and the impoverishment of his victim.

Happily, mafianism is a rare phenomenon, partly because it is a highly inefficient method of exploitation, partly because even the most brutal men generally need some formula for legitimizing their activities. The absence of such a felt need may indeed be taken as pathological and as a hallmark of the truly criminal mind. Thus, mafianism is simply organized criminality—almost institutionalized and in complete control of a society, as under a Duvalier or Trujillo in such blighted Caribbean countries as Haiti and the Dominican Republic, and hardly structured and lurking in the interstices of a society, as the case of our own Cosa Nostra.

Social scientists have taken over Durkheim's term "anomic" (or "anomy") to designate such a state of normlessness. According to R. M. MacIver, "Anomy signifies the state of mind of one who has been pulled up by his moral roots, who no longer has any standards but only disconnected urges, who has no longer any sense of continuity, of folk, of obligation. The anomic man has become spiritually sterile, responsive only to himself, responsible to no one."[4] I would not identify anomic man as thus described with the so-called "psychopathic personality" to be referred to shortly under the title of "psychogenic" violence. Anomic men exhibit what the American Psychiatric Association in its *Manual* on mental disorders calls "dyssocial reaction." The *Manual* says:

> This term applies to individuals who manifest disregard for the usual social codes, and often come in conflict with them, as a result of having lived all their lives in an abnormal moral environment. They may be capable of strong loyalties. These individuals typically do not show significant personality deviations other than those implied by adherence to the values or code of their own predatory, criminal or other social group.[5]

Harvey Cleckley observes that those showing dyssocial reaction are nonetheless "capable of loyalties and seem in their rebellion against society to have some standards of their own, even though these may be immoral and condemned by law."[6] Tough gangs such as our Hell's Angels or England's Teddy Boys of the 1960's and its present-day Skinheads, may well fall under this rubric.

## C. Psychogenic Violence

Under this head I include all violence resulting from or associated with mental or personality disorders ranging from psychoneurosis to those major psychiatric disorders which are called psychosis. Included under this rubric is aggression relished or enjoyed for its own sake, which in its more pronounced form is called sadism. Included, also, is the antisocial behavior of psychopaths, a familiar, if baffling, clinical entity. As Cleckley notes, most fully developed psychopaths, in addition to perversely inviting failure in whatever they undertake, "also commit aggressive anti-social acts. They forge checks, swindle, steal repeatedly, lightly indulge in bigamy. . . . Some [commit] murder or other shocking felonies, usually with little or no provocation, often without comprehensible motivation." And yet the psychopath often exhibits outstanding intellectual ability and, as Cleckley goes on to say, is so free from "the manifestations of ordinary psychiatric disorder" that it is difficult to believe that "deep within him may be concealed a deficiency that leads not to conflict or unconscious guilt, but instead makes him incapable of feeling normal remorse or of appreciating adequately the major emotional experiences of human life." Indeed, the psychopath "expresses normal reactions [of love, loyalty, gratitude] with a most impressive appearance of sincerity and depth."[7]

If psychopaths are at any given moment difficult to identify, we must not forget that even in the case of psychotics most clinicians do not distinguish qualitatively between a person suffering from psychosis and so-called normal people. The difference is regarded by them as a quantitative one.[8] The seemingly most civilized country in Europe taught us in the years preceding and during World War II of the brutal indignities that so-called normal men can inflict upon defenseless victims. We are reminded of this again as we read about the My Lai massacre.

I stress this—as I have stressed the psychiatrists' view that the psychotic and the normal individual are not different in kind, and as I have stressed also the deceptive normality under most circumstances of individuals who are actually psychopaths —for special reasons which will become apparent when I turn to my final category of violence, the category that interests me most.

## D. Ideological Violence

I use this term to embrace all violence in behalf of a political or social objective. Here the essential factor is that the individual does not directly promote his own interest or advantage, i.e., that his use of violence serve a "cause."

I find it useful to distinguish three forms of ideological violence: terrorism, insurrection, and revolution.

1. *Terrorism.* This is a technical term in the lexicon of the political scientist. As the term is used here, terrorism refers to a technique for bringing about social change which relies on the action of heroic, if romantically messianic, individuals, rather than on mass action, and therefore it takes the form of sabotage and assassination. Terrorism is never a frontal attack on the police or armed forces but is intended to demoralize the government by destroying strategic targets or striking down specific individuals. Such terrorism is not to be confused with governmental terror, which masquerades as law enforcement and is the desperate recourse of rulers so fearful of their tenure that they are bent upon exterminating all real or imagined opponents.

The methods of terrorists are necessarily conspiratorial, and recourse to terrorism occurs among those who have either abandoned or never entertained the hope of achieving change by working within the system. Thus the terrorist scorns reform —with its reliance on legal means for effecting social change— as a snare and delusion, even in a democracy. Typical of terrorist groups were the Irish Sinn Feiners, the Russian Socialist Revolutionaries, and the anarchist followers of Bakunin and of Kropotkin with his "propaganda of the deed." Terrorism was rejected by the Bolsheviks, who based their strategy on mass movements and, like Lenin, were hostile to the romantic messianism of the anarchists.

Some of the recent rhetoric of the American New Left could have been taken verbatim from the 1879 program of the Russian Narodnaya Volya (People's Will):

> Terroristic activity, consisting in destroying the most harmful person in the government, in defending the party against espionage, in punishing the perpetrators of the notable cases of violence and arbitrariness on the part of the government and the administration, aims to undermine the prestige of the government's power, to demonstrate steadily the possibility of struggle against the government, to arouse in this manner the revolutionary spirit of the people and their confidence in the success of the cause, and finally, to give shape and direction to the forces fit and trained to carry on the fight.[9]

Terrorists are revolutionists in a hurry, impatient not only with the slow pace of legal reform, even when such reform is available, but with the inertia of the masses whose torch they believe they carry.

Historically, as G. D. H. Cole points out in his *History of Socialist Thought*, terrorism has tended to retard rather than advance the cause of social reform. The victims of the assassins are easily replaced; a regime that might have tolerated dissent or failed out of sheer inefficiency to root out dissent is galvanized into action; and all reformers are more plausibly stigmatized as wild-eyed bomb-throwers.

2. *Insurrection.* Like terrorism, insurrection is a frontal attack on government, but distinguished from revolution in that it is local in scope, usually limited in aim, and usually deficient in positive program. Generally, the objective in insurrection is modification of government policy. Insurrection would be more appropriately described as rebellion if the objective were territorial secession. Insurrection is common to loosely organized states with a weak national tradition, a weak central government and primitive transportation facilities that reduce the mobility of the government's armed forces. However, insurrection and its potentialities may require re-evaluation in circumstances such as those which prevail in the United States, where government can deploy overwhelming force but is reluctant for various reasons to do so. Thus, violent protest may take on an insurrectionary character that it does not actually have, as in the case of the ghetto riots and the recent riots on our campuses, where militants were able to capitalize on the government's reluctance to spread the conflict or on the government's sheer inability to dispense even-handed justice and provide incarceration for small armies of dissidents.

3. *Revolution.* Revolutions are of various kinds, and I shall not linger here on an anatomy of revolution. I am concerned with social revolutions rather than with palace revolutions or political revolutions, although a brief description of the latter is perhaps in order.

A palace revolution simply rotates the "ins" and "outs" without significant modification of government policy or disturbance to the underlying system of class relationships. This has been revolution Latin American–style, although one suspects that countries like Brazil and Argentina are due shortly for another kind of revolution. A political revolution may involve a change in the form of government, for example from monarchy to republic, or it may be an attempt at territorial secession, in which case it would more accurately be termed a rebellion. The revolution of the American colonies is more aptly called a rebellion. In all such revolutions the basically prevailing system of privileges and rewards remains intact. It is when these are fundamentally modified that we have a social revolution such as the French Revolution of 1789 or the Bolshevik Revolution of 1917.

It would be tempting at this point to explore in detail the sense in which the right of revolution is part of our American tradition. I have done this in my *Evolution of Liberalism* and will not linger on the topic here. I would rather concentrate on those necessary conditions without which a social revolution cannot occur. There has been so much loose talk about revolution in our country that we would do well to give these conditions at least brief attention.

First, a social revolution cannot occur unless there is a fundamental disparity between the power of an ascendant class and the rights and privileges its members actually enjoy. In the eighteenth and nineteenth centuries the middle class came increasingly to possess power. But it lacked the rights and privileges— even the suffrage—that go along with power. To the question that formed the title of his celebrated pamphlet *What Is the Third Estate?* The French Abbé Sieyès answered, "Everything." "What has it been hitherto in the political order?" he asked next. "Nothing." "What does it desire?" "To be something." A revolution was therefore inevitable.

Second, a social revolution cannot occur unless there is a fundamental disparity between the productive potentialities of a given social system and the extent to which it realizes its potentialities. In eighteenth-century France the prevailing system of class relationships served to retard rather than release the productive capacity of that country. In Marx's terms, which are applicable to the experience of eighteenth-century France, as they are to Czarist Russia, there was a contradiction between the "forces of production" and the "relations of production." That is to say, human and physical and technical resources were available for the expansion of production. But the prevailing socioeconomic system prevented their use. In the 1930's the prevailing system of class relationships that we call capitalism was similarly inhibiting, producing a stagnant condition of mass unemployment and mass deprivation which, had it continued, would surely have led to a revolution.

Even so, it would not have led to a successful revolution in the absence of two more conditions. There must be adequate leadership, and there must be the vision of a way out.

## II. VIOLENCE AND THE NEW LEFT

Such are the varieties of violence: economic, anomic, psychogenic, ideological. It is against this background that I would like to discuss the preoccupation—ranging from flirtation to infatuation—of the New Left with violence.

Commenting, before his untimely death, on what he called the rising mystique of violence on the Left, Richard Hofstadter observed: "Those who lived through the rise of European fascism, or who have watched the development of right-wing groups in this country over the last generation, or have fully recognized the amount of violence leveled at civil-rights workers in the South, are never surprised at violence cults on the Right." More arresting, he found, is the decline of commitment to nonviolence on the Left, and the growth of a disposition to indulge in or to exalt acts of force or violence.[10]

Let me deal first with the rhetoric.

The far Right, says Irving Howe, "shrewder than its symbiotic opposite on the far left, has never articulated an ideology of the rope and the bomb; it has done its dirty business and kept its mouth shut."[11] This is not quite true, to be sure. The Nazi and Fascist glorification of violence for its own sake is too well known to require documentation here. And the philosopher who dreamed that in some other age than this "rotting and introspective present" we may once again have spirits of "sublime malice, spirits rendered potent by wars and victories, to whom conquest, adventure, danger, even pain, have become a need" was hardly a leftist. Thus spoke Nietzsche.[12] He is echoed by Heidegger, who interprets human existence as a "thunderstorm of steel," and was preceded by Hegel, who found in war the deeper meaning that "by it the ethical health of a nation is preserved."[13] No leftist they.

But Howe is correct about right-wing terrorism in the United States. Our racists and vigilantes, having no intellectual spokesman, have gone about their business in silence. Not so the New Left and such guiding spirits of the New Left as Frantz Fanon. Nor Jean-Paul Sartre, who writes in his preface to Fanon's *The Wretched of the Earth* that "irrepressible violence . . . is man recreating himself" and that it is through "mad fury" that "the wretched of the Earth" can "become men." Sartre adds that "to shoot down a European is to kill two birds with one stone . . . there remains a dead man and a free man."[14]

However, the rhetoric of violence embraced by the New Left involves more than the elegant articulations of a Sartre or the mystique of a Fanon. It includes the curious use of obscenity, the use of obscenity in contexts where it has never before been used. To be sure, the Left has never been known for its civility. A tradition of verbal abuse goes back at least as far as Marx, who is notorious for his acerbity. Leftists are incorrigible schismatics, and the language they use in dealing with each other can hardly be called endearing and affectionate. But the vogue of obscenity among leftist militants is something new and different.

Obscenity is not new, of course. It has been part of the common man's language of abuse since there have been common men. No doubt it is his compensation for lacking the vocabulary of the literate and educated. What is *new* is the injection of obscenity into the discourse and debate of literate people in contexts where obscenity has never before been used. This is no longer a continuation of the Marxist tradition of acerbity in debate. Neither should it be understood as an attempt to identify with the common man. It is something else. It is, I contend, an integral part of the New Left's recent preoccupation with violence.

Liberals and libertarians have muted their criticism of the obscenity vogue. No liberal wants to be charged with prudery, nor with being a slave to conventional morality, nor with arbitrarily imposing his standards on others, nor with inhibiting free speech. Criticism of obscenity seems to put one in one or another of these postures. Even worse, no aging liberal wants to be reminded of the generation gap. In consequence, the real point has been obscured and is rarely, if ever, made. I object to the use of obscenity as a polemical weapon, not because it offends my sensibilities—which it does—but because it halts dialogue and discussion so that no other encounter is possible except a violent one. Beyond this, to characterize an adversary with one or another of the obscenities now in popular use among dissidents is in effect to deprive him of his humanity, to degrade him, to exclude him from the company of decent men. The import of what one says is that he is beneath contempt; therefore any injury that may be done him is justified. Joe McCarthy's use of the word "Communist" served the same pur-

pose: Communists are disloyal and one does not parley with
traitors, one destroys them. Use of "pig" to designate policeman
paves the way for the same consequence; after all, pigs are for
slaughter. Contrary to the chant we learn as children, words, as
well as sticks and stones, *can* break our bones. Obscenity is not
innocuous verbal expletive. It is the attempt to inflict pain in
circumstances where one lacks the physical means of inflicting
injury. The time may have come for us to see that we have been
conned: that the obscenity kick is not, and surely not *merely*, an
exercise in libertarianism, nor is it merely a device for mocking
authority by saying what is forbidden, nor merely a reflection of
our sexual emancipation, nor merely a way of declaring war
against middle-class values—it is also an index of our involve-
ment in violence. In the beginning, we might remember, there
was the *word*.

Let us now turn from the word to the act. What is the case
for violence as we have heard it made by the New Left?

We are first reminded of the horrors of the Vietnam War. We
are confronted with our failure to dispense social justice to our
black and brown minorities. We are told of the impoverished
one-fifth whose standard of living should indeed affront the conscience of any affluent society. We are reminded of the disgrace-
ful condition of our cities and the neglect of our basic services,
of our warped order of priorities, of the enormous gap between
our preachment and practice. In my judgment, we are justly
faulted, although I must add that there is a failure to achieve
historical perspective among solipsists who have come to regard
the reading of history as irrelevant. To point, for example, to
the brutal use of women and children in mines, mills, and
sweatshops at the turn of this century and to note that such
exploitation is nearly banished today; to call attention to the
reduction of the sixty- to sixty-five hour work-week to forty
hours is often to evoke wide-eyed surprise from young New
Leftists, or the charge that one is whitewashing the system.
Even so, much of the indictment is deserved. It has, of course,
long been voiced by non-violent liberals and leftists.

The conclusion drawn by the militants is that the whole system is hopelessly corrupt. We must tear it down and start over
again. It is argued—often, it may be added, with some measure
of plausibility—that those in power will reject substantive reform (or pay only lip service to it) unless confronted by violence or the threat of violence. This is the only language they
understand. Violence is, after all, very much a part of the Amer-

ican tradition, as American, Rap Brown has told us, as cherry pie. We won our freedom as a nation by recourse to violence, and history shows that the great advances of mankind have been made possible by violent revolutions. Anyhow, everything else has been tried and we have no other recourse. Why, indeed, complain about violence; look at what we were doing in Vietnam and what we have done to the black man and the Indian.

I will be brief with those who hope for revolution. None of the conditions for revolution discussed earlier is even remotely present in the United States. On the contrary, majorities and all politically significant minorities in this country oppose each other within the framework of a *basic consensus*. Either implicitly or explicitly, they recognize, underlying their differences, a basic *community of interest* which not only assures a "loyal opposition," but a tolerant majority prepared to contemplate the possibility of its defeat. Deplorable though it may be, it is a fact that neither the "massed, angered forces of common humanity" nor an ascendant, but as yet unrecognized, power group is prepared to initiate a substantive change in the prevailing system of class relationships.

The slogan of our Walter Mitty revolutionists, as we all know, is "Power to the People!" Ironically, if the American *people* had their way, left-wing militants would be dealt with as the Russian peasants dealt in the nineteenth century with the Narodniks, and they would find themselves in an American equivalent of Siberia. Fortunately, the American people have wisely imposed constitutional restraints on themselves although they express their hostility in other ways—by supporting and electing candidates of the far Right, voting down bond issues for higher education, and calling for more and more suppressive legislation.

Failing in the U.S. to evoke a response from workers, the traditional ally of the Left (at any rate, the kind of response they want—the hooliganism of the hard-hats in New York was, after all, a response), New Leftists have sought a new coalition: of college and university youth, of the poor, and of the minorities.

Now the poor, deplorably numerous though they are—twenty percent in our country—are hardly a formidable army as far as the calculus of power is concerned. That fraction includes the halt and the blind, the superannuated, the incompetent, and a tragic number of children—hardly the stuff of which battalions of insurgents are made.

As for the campus, militants enlist only a fraction of the

student body, a fraction expanded temporarily when the activist strategists provoke the police into overreacting. The very fact that such a stratagem is regarded as necessary—there is nothing inferential about this, by the way; the strategy has been completely spelled out—the very fact that such a stratagem is thought necessary is indicative of the extent to which most students do not share the broader complaints and the deep disillusionment and despair of the radicals. There has been widespread discontent. However, no one really knows the extent to which this discontent was inspired by our participation in a profoundly unpopular war. There is a rejection, concentrated among students in the humanities and social sciences, of what William James once called the "Bitch-goddess, Success," and a repudiation of the values which have dominated what R. H. Tawney called the "acquisitive" society. But for the great majority this is hardly comparable to the total alienation and violent hostility which send enragés to the barricades. I would not minimize the political power of the campus. But the campus will not provide many cadres for a revolution.

There remain the ethnic minorities. But the Chicanos and blacks show few signs of cooperating and, in any case, the great majority of blacks do not think in terms of a violent overthrow of the government. A 1969 *Newsweek* poll of Negroes showed sixty-three percent—as against twenty-one percent—who believed they could win their rights without violence. The very militancy of young Negro intellectuals is proof of progress; militancy does not thrive under conditions of hopelessness. But the same progress that sparks a spirit of revolt in some generates a hope in others that social justice can be achieved within the system.

When Marxists spoke of revolution, they had in mind one or another of the great classes that make up a social system. Marx himself would surely have described the dreams of New Leftists in the United States as sheer adventurism. And, as we all know, the master himself went far astray when he turned to prophecy. The workers of industralized Europe are uninterested in revolution. The progressive deterioration of their condition that Marx predicted has not come about. And that same system of industrial capitalism which was to lead to their progressive impoverishment has, especially in Britain, the Scandinavian countries and, much more tardily and sluggishly in the United States, exhibited some capacity for self-reform. New Left militants are, in fact, anachronisms: they have the misfortune to be ideologues in a day when ideology is, if not dead, as some have said, surely in decline. The Social Democrats of Europe prefer to forget Marx and Marxist dogma and deal with the problems at hand. They are pragmatic rather than doctrinaire. And a similar mood characterizes the major political parties of the United States.

Suppose, however, that the conditions for a revolution *were* present in the United States. Should this be an occasion for self-congratulation? Can anyone who has read about what happened in 1789 or 1917 welcome the blood-letting, the flood of hate, the slaughter of innocent people, the legacy of dictatorship that comes in the wake of such cataclysms? Clearly, some can, some who subscribe, as doctrinaire Marxists mistakenly do, to an iron law of historical progress, whether linear or dialectical, that enables them to believe that something better than what we have now would come of such a bloodbath. For the most part, however, apocalyptic visionaries, preaching that the worse things are the better they are, speak to shrinking audiences.

There is no danger of revolution in the United States. The real danger is that Americans will overreact to those who phantasize about revolution. To fear that "tiny bands of deracinated intellectuals," as Irving Howe has aptly called them, could wage a revolution is to be as divorced from reality as these would-be revolutionaries. Louis B. Lundborg, former board chairman of the Bank of America, perceptively notes the hazard: "I am not afraid the left-wing radicals will win," he observed recently. "I am only afraid of how they will be defeated." He added: "The natural sequel to left-wing radical rebellion is right-wing reaction and repression."[15]

Let us turn from impotent revolutionaries to terrorists. The latter have shown that they do have the power to shut down a great university and virtually incapacitate it. They have shown that they can gut the central section of a city. Their bombs can spread fear even in those great Manhattan temples where the high priests of capitalism normally preside in resplendent comfort and seemingly perfect security. For a time the technique of the terrorist increasingly beckoned black militants intoxicated with the discovery that they could make the streets of an entire city unsafe after dark and who were understandably infuriated by the humiliations they daily encountered.

However, violence or the threat of violence will not further the professed cause of terrorists, even though temporary concessions may be won. The heavy artillery is commanded by those who oppose their view of social justice or will go only part way. Terrify or alarm a man who commands the artillery and he is likely to use it on you, even though he thereby brings about great harm to himself. A frightened man does not act rationally. Arouse his fear and you are lost; your one hope is to appeal to his reason.

Suppose, however, that terrorists are numerous enough to act with impunity. The true idealists among them must ask if they can hope to avoid becoming brutalized by the methods they employ. They must ask if their ends are not fatally compromised by the means used to obtain them. They should, even though they may not, ask themselves if they want to trigger the destructive impulses which, as suggested earlier in the discussion of psychogenic violence, lie latent in the depths of all of us. At what point will they start settling their own notorious differences wih the violence they began by directing at others, as the Robespierres and Stalins of history remind us. Not long ago two UCLA black militants were killed on the campus, not lynched by a white mob—that could never happen in California—but by fellow blacks who had embraced the gospel of militancy and were contesting for leadership.

What assurance have the idealistic militants that the rhetoric some of their comrades use is not a mask for sadists and psychopaths? Earlier, in my discussion of psychogenic violence, I stressed the difficulty encountered in identifying psychopaths, with their deceptive mask of normality. I was thinking of the dilemma in which idealistic militants inevitably find themselves. I am not saying that *they* are psychopaths, although I think that they are often divorced from reality. I am asking how a terrorist can hope to weed out the psychopaths in a kind of undertaking which tends to attract them.

The late Karen Horney, one of the most perceptive writers in the field of psychoanalysis, points out that the compulsive and often fanatical drive to reform others often has sadistic origins springing from the self-loathing of individuals who are unable to measure up to their own idealized image and who externalize their self-contempt by disparaging, humiliating, and ultimately hurting others. Meanwhile they develop a shield of righteousness to protect themselves from their own self-contempt. Some militants should look into Horney's mirror; they may see themselves. Horney's words are worth quoting:

While he (the sadist) violates the most elementary requirements of human decency he at the same time harbors within himself an idealized image of particularly high and rigid moral standard. He is one of those . . . who despairing of ever being able to measure up to such standards, have consciously resolved to be as "bad" as possible. He may succeed in being "bad" and wallow in it with a kind of desperate delight. But by doing so the chasm between the idealized image and the actual self becomes unbridgeable . . . His self-loathing reaches such dimensions that he cannot take a look at himself. He is compelled, therefore, to externalize his self contempt . . . he turns his violent self contempt for himself outward. Since his righteousness prevents him from seeing his share in any difficulty that arises he must feel that he is the one who is abused and victimized. Since he cannot see that the source of all his despair lies within himself he must hold others responsible for it.[16]

I do not say that all or even most militants are sadists, except in the sense that all men may have sadistic tendencies. But what are we to think of the militant journalist who declared that "morality comes out of a gun?" What are we to make of the statement of the committee organized to defend three persons charged with the New York City bombings:

Either the accused did strike a magnificent blow against those who make profit through the destruction of our lives and our world and they are our most courageous and beloved comrades; or they are being framed.[17]

What are we to make of Weatherman leader Bernadine Dohrn's comment on the Sharon Tate murderers, as reported in *The Guardian*, a New Left paper: "Dig it," she said. "First they killed the pigs, then they ate dinner in the same room with them, then they even shoved a fork into a victim's stomach! Wild!" These, like the praise some militants had for the assassin of Robert Kennedy, are extreme cases. But they are not far from comments found not long ago in campus newspapers.

Are we to conclude that violence is never justified? Must relief from oppression always await the tardy and usually negligible response of the oppressor? Is violence never effective? It may be agreed that acts of individual violence may sometimes be justified. I would not *morally* condemn the attempt to assassinate Hitler. On the other hand, I might well question the effectiveness of such an attempt.

Where legal or political remedies are available, individual or mass acts of violence are inexcusable, however great the evils against which they are a protest. Political remedies, painfully slow though they may be, are available in a democracy and, if the answer is made that democracy in the United States is merely a euphemism for the iron rule of a military-industrial establishment, the plain fact is that the great majority of Americans do not agree. Until they do, recourse to *terrorism* is an admission of lack of popular support. If they do, if the people were to come to the conclusion they were ruled by a dictatorship, one might then and only then fall back on Locke's verdict concerning revolution:

> Revolutions happen not upon every little mis-management in public affairs. Great mistakes in the ruling part, many wrong and inconvenient laws, and all the slips of human frailty will be borne by the people without mutiny or murmur. But if a long train of abuses, prevarications and artifices, all tending the same way, make the design visible to the people—and they cannot but feel what they lie under, and see whither they are going—it is not to be wondered that they should then rouse themselves and endeavor to put the rule into such hands which may secure to them the ends for which ancient names and specious forms are so far from being better that they are much worse than the state of nature or pure anarchy.

The weight of Locke's response is even more evident in the following paragraph, which is worth citing in nearly full length. It is one of the most significant passages in the literature of political philosophy.

> Nor let anyone say that mischief can arise from hence as it shall please a busy head or turbulent spirit to desire the alteration of the government. It is true such men may stir whenever they please, but, it will be only to their own just ruin and perdition. For till the mischief be grown general, and the ill designs of the rulers become visible, or their attempts sensible to the greater part, the people, who are more disposed to suffer than right themselves by resistance, are not apt to stir. The examples of particular injustice or oppression of here and there an unfortunate man moves them not. But if they universally have a persuasion grounded upon manifest evidence that designs are carrying on against their liberties, and the general course and tendency of things cannot but give them strong suspicions of the evil intention of their governors, who is to be blamed for it? Who can help

it if they, who might avoid it, bring themselves into this suspicion? Are the people to be blamed if they have the sense of rational creatures . . . ? And is it not rather their fault who put things in such a posture . . . ?[18]

Revolution can, we may agree with Locke, be *morally* justified. But what of its *effectiveness*? The fatal flaw in the use of violence, revolutionary or other, is, as Hannah Arendt has said, that we can never predict the outcome. To be sure, this handicap applies to all efforts to effect social change, and conservatives stress it in order to discourage all attempts at reform. Why, they characteristically ask, give up a known present for an unknown future? They greatly exaggerate, and for the most part they speak more from fear and self-interest than from wisdom. But their point has genuine applicability to the use of violence as an instrument of social change. The architects of the French and Russian revolutions failed utterly to anticipate the consequences of the great upheavals they set in motion. With all the vast agencies of information and intelligence at their disposal, our leaders were unable to predict the outcome of our violent intervention in Vietnam. Too many variables are operative; they baffle the attempts of reason to calculate them. At that point unreason—fear, panic, hysteria, pride ("we have never lost a war")—take over. And so it is with all violence. That is why our militants increasingly embrace the "cult of spontaneity." They sense that reason cannot serve them. Given our feeble powers of long-range prediction in human affairs, even where men and groups of men proceed with some measure of rationality, and given the further and profound enfeeblement of these predictive powers when the forces to be calculated are irrational, those who would predict the outcomes of violence are brash indeed. That is why J. M. Cameron concluded—in my judgment with perfect felicity—that if "the consequences of violence are sometimes happy [this] is a grace of fate and not an illustration of the wisdom of the violent."[19]

It is appropriate to conclude with two reminders, one addressed to the militant Left, the other to the alarmed Right. Militant Leftists might well ponder one of Edmund Burke's sagest observations. Commenting on those who habitually engage in criticism and fault-finding, he said: "By hating vice too much they come to love men too little."

Those on the Right who are unnecessarily alarmed and given to overreacting might be reminded of a fatal flaw in the solution of one of Queen Victoria's possibly less exigent problems. The Crystal Palace, built by Prince Albert, required more than a million square feet of glass. In all, it was six hundred yards long and high enough to enclose the trees which dotted the Hyde Park greensward. With the trees, birds were enclosed—according to one account, quite accidentally. Even if they were enclosed intentionally, the systematic German—Albert is said to have designed the palace himself—could hardly have foreseen that the droppings of the birds would mar the valuable exhibits. The birds had to be destroyed. But the use of shotguns in the glass-enclosed structure was out of the question. The Duke of Wellington was called in. True to his reputation, the hero of Spain and Waterloo had a ready solution. "Try sparrow hawks, ma'am," he said. The historian who tells us this story about the difficulties encountered by the Victorians with their feathered friends neglects to relate how they got rid of the hawks. Before the Right has recourse to hawks it had better solve the problem of how to get rid of them. In the 1930's the German Right failed tragically to solve that problem.

# Notes

[1] H. D. Graham and T. R. Gurr, eds., *The History of Violence in America* (New York: Praeger, 1969), p. xxix.

[2] Hannah Arendt, *On Violence* (New York: Harcourt, Brace & World, 1970), pp. 8, 43.

[3] J. M. Cameron, "On Violence," *New York Review of Books* 15 (2 July 1970): 24.

[4] Robert M. MacIver, *The Ramparts We Guard* (New York: Macmillan Co., 1950), p. 84. See also David Riesman, *The Lonely Crowd* (New Haven: Yale University Press, 1950), pp. 287ff.; and Robert K. Merton, *Social Theory and Social Structure* (Glencoe, Ill.: Free Press, 1957), pp. 161–70.

[5] American Psychiatric Association, *Diagnostic and Statistical Manual: Mental Disorders* (Washington, D.C.: American Psychiatric Association, 1963), p. 38.

[6] Harvey M. Cleckley, "Psychopathic Personality," in *International Encyclopedia of the Social Sciences,* new ed., 13:113.

[7] Ibid., pp. 114, 118, 114.

[8] Those who hold that psychotics are qualitatively different see schizophrenia or other "functional" psychoses as having a clear somatic matrix.

[9] Program of the Executive Committee. See J. B. S. Hardman, "Terrorism," in *Encyclopedia of the Social Sciences,* 1st ed., 14:578.

[10] Richard Hofstadter, "The Future of American Violence," *Harper's Magazine,* April 1970, p. 47.

[11] Irving Howe, "Political Terrorism: Hysteria on the Left," *New York Times Magazine,* 12 April 1970, p. 25.

[12] Friedrich Nietzsche, *The Genealogy of Morals.* In *Complete Works,* ed. Oscar Levy and trans. Helen Zimmermann (New York: Russell & Russell, 1964), p. 24.

[13] Cited by Karl Popper in *The Open Society and Its Enemies* (Princeton: Princeton University Press, 1950), pp. 270, 262.

[14] Jean-Paul Sartre, preface to *The Wretched of the Earth,* by Frantz Fanon, trans. Constance Farrington (New York: Grove Press, 1963), pp. 21–22.

[15] Louis B. Lundborg, speech, Rotary Club of Seattle, 17 June 1970.

[16] Karen Horney, *Our Inner Conflicts* (New York: W. W. Norton & Co., 1945), pp. 203–6.

[17] Cited by Irving Howe "Political Terrorism," p. 28.

[18] John Locke, *An Essay Concerning the True, Original, Extent and End of Civil Government* (Oxford: Basil Blackwell & Mott, 1946) chap. 29, pars. 225, 230.

[19] Cameron, "On Violence," p. 32.

# Violatives: Modes and
# Themes of Violence

SHERMAN M. STANAGE has taught at and served as chairman of the departments of Philosophy at Northern Illinois University, Trinity University, and Bowling Green University. He has also taught at Baker University and served as a visiting professor at the University of Texas at Austin, Hamline University, and the University of New Mexico. Professor Stanage has studied at the University of Connecticut, the University of Pennsylvania, the University of New Mexico, and the Iliff School of Theology. He received the Ph.D. at the University of Colorado in 1959. He was a Fulbright Scholar, a Danforth Scholar, and an Elizabeth Iliff Warren Fellow. His publications include writings on ethics and value theory, phenomenology, and philosophy of the social sciences, especially in the area of political ideology.

# Violatives: Modes and
# Themes of Violence

by Sherman M. Stanage

Georges Sorel wrote, well over sixty years ago, "the problems of violence still remain very obscure."[1] More recently, Hannah Arendt has reiterated this judgment, and has further stated that although violence has always played an enormous role "in human affairs it is . . . rather surprising that violence has been singled out so seldom for special consideration."[2] Behavioral and social scientists are surely remiss in their responsibility to study all aspects of the human condition. But perhaps philosophers are even more culpable in this case.[3]

At least one mandate in philosophy has always been its responsibility to speak to any problem within the human condition in a continuing attempt to assist persons to escape from any form of human bondage. One of these forms of bondage is surely violence, but there have been precious few discussions of violence in the philosophical literature. Even when one comes upon them, they rarely reflect to the credit of philosophers, who should (as central among their other tasks) speak caringly to the problems of what it means to be *human* in the face of the repertoire of repetitive violations of the very *being* of human beings.[4]

The fundamental *philosophical problems* in discussing violence, I believe, are the problems of situating violence, of describing and analyzing its structure or structures, of clarifying the ways in which it is structured, of articulating its modes and themes, and of showing how various kinds of violence may be related. A discussion of all of these problems, and more, is a pathway toward the understanding of the relevance of violence to persons, and the relevance of persons to violence.

In this essay I will try to *situate* the phenomena of violence in terms of some of the principal modes and themes of their manifestation and in terms of some of the language we commonly use in articulating violence.[5] This will involve, first, a discussion of the concepts of *civilization and barbarism* along general Collingwoodian lines.[6] So-called *destructive violence* and *constructive violence* will also be explored, since it has long been a truism that violence is like a two-edged sword which both slays and saves. To investigate the one without the other is to deny the Janus-like and all too human quality of the phenomena of violence. Further, violence will be discussed in relation to harm, power, force, and strength. Following the clarification of some distinctions between violence, harm, power, force, and strength, the essay will offer what I call a *theory of violatives*.[7] These violatives are phenomenological distinctions within occurrences of violence—distinctions that are articulated by our language when this language is carefully explored (and especially when the dictionary is carefully worked, as Austin put it).[8] Finally, the essay will conclude with a section that treats briefly such matters as the perception, measurement, relevance, and definition of violence as situated.

In short, I will try to *situate* violence in civilization and society; within its instrumental uses[9] (as destructive or constructive); as distinguished from harm, power, force, and strength; as an "out-of-order" act or event; as perceived; as measured; and, thus, as defined, or at least as further characterized and clarified for subsequent philosophical explorations. I suggest that the markings along the way in this discussion of violence ought to offer at least presumptive and heuristic grounds for philosophically useful explorations into the phenomena of violence. It is rare to encounter philosophically useful discussions of violence in the meager philosophical literature dealing with the subject.

Finally, it should be noted that I am not attempting here to justify violence of any kind or for any purpose; nor am I concerned with tracing out the "causes," "effects," or particular details of given instances of violence. The former would be a special ideological task, rather than a primarily philosophical one; and the latter ought to be the primary concern of the social scientist, or as I would prefer to say, the *human* scientist.

## I. ON SITUATING VIOLENCE

In most respects the *situationality* of violence makes all the difference in the human world, for questions of violence are fundamentally questions of order and dis-order in the human world. The human world is the only world in which violence takes place or, more literally, takes *a* place.[10] There are occurrences among animals generally, and so-called natural events like earthquakes, floods, volcanic eruptions, tornadoes, hurricanes, locust plagues, droughts, etc., that are frequently classed as violent; but they are not violent per se. They are classed as such, or modified by the adjective "violent," because they intrude upon the lives of human beings in such a way as to reduce the quality of the human condition and of personal lives, or because they destroy human lives.[11] The use of the adjective form seems to be derived from a prior, paradigmatic usage of the term relating to human beings and their violence to one another. The former usages have the force of metaphor, figurative language, and various other licenses within the common uses of language.

*Situating* violence means placing and locating violence, and although these human acts make all the difference in our perceiving and understanding the phenomena of violence, they are no simple tasks to perform.[12] To *situate* violence is to give it a site, a place, or location. It is to locate or place certain phenomena (1) in terms of their relationships to their surroundings, and (2) in terms of their constituent relationships within themselves, e.g. as the *parts* of violence to the *whole* of violence, say, or as an exploration of the modes and themes of violence within the intuited essence of violence.[13] These *situatings* certify some phenomena as violence, or attest their violence.

I shall try to do something on both of these counts in this section, beginning with an examination of the first point. One way to begin to *situate* violence, in the special sense of exploring it within its surroundings, is to call attention to an important passage in Hobbes's *Leviathan*. In this, one of the classic passages in political philosophy, Hobbes states:

> Whatsoever, therefore is consequent to a time of war where every man is enemy to every man, the same is consequent to the time wherein men live without other security than what their own

strength and their own invention shall furnish them withal. In such condition there is no place for industry, because the fruit thereof is uncertain; and consequently no culture of the earth; no navigation nor use of the commodities that may be imported by sea; no commodious building; no instruments of moving and removing such things as require much force; no knowledge of the face of the earth; no account of time; no arts; no letters; no society; *and, which is worst of all, continual fear and danger of violent death*; and the life of man solitary, poor, nasty, brutish, and short.[14]

Cameron writes that "Hobbes was right in seeing violence beyond a certain point as both the sign and the cause of the breakdown of civility."[15]

But consider several points concerning this passage. *First*, if that human condition described by Hobbes where "every man is enemy to every man" is interpreted in a strict and literal sense in the absolute terms of aboriginal living,[16] or as the *absence of any civilization*, then no violence is present, although the life of each person indeed would be (and no doubt was) "solitary, poor, nasty, brutish, and short." The disorder and chaos of that day, the usual, the commonplace of that life, was death, natural and expected.[17] In this strict interpretation, Hobbes can only be writing of "violent death" as a seventeenth-century philosopher, "civilized" by all of *his* past traditions, reading *his* own civility back into a remote past. Thus Hobbes, as a civilized man, was invoking a contemporary perception of violence in describing certain phenomena of a human condition in the past. Hobbes knew violence, but his enemies "to every man" did not, since in a state of nature there is no human order. In the absence of human order there can be no violence, in the strict sense that violence is at least *violative* of some human order. Hopefully, this point will become increasingly clear in the discussion.

*Second*, as a "sign" of civility, the perception of violence in any sense is already an indication of some exception from an ordered process, something as out-of-order. Thus, to be aware of a civil order is at the same time to be aware of exceptions to it. The perception of one heightens the perception of the other.

*Third*, a perception of too much exception (or too many exceptions) to the civil order is a perception of what we might normally call a "breakdown of civility," whether or not we would call the exception the "cause" of this breakdown or not.

As a further means of *situating* violence by placing it within

its surroundings, so to speak, I turn now to a discussion of the
special form of human ordering we call "civilization." It is civilization that surrounds the human being. This move is best
facilitated, I believe, by a discussion of selected portions of
R. G. Collingwood's *The New Leviathan* in which he discusses
the meaning of civilization.

In his preface Collingwood places himself within the tradition
of Hobbes's classical political philosophy, which Collingwood
calls "the world's greatest store of political wisdom." Collingwood sets out "to deal with the same groups of problems in the
same order [as Hobbes placed them in the *Leviathan*], calling
the four parts of [his] book, 'Man,' 'Society,' 'Civilization,' and
'Barbarism'." *The New Leviathan*, he says, is "an attempt to
bring the *Leviathan* up to date, in the light of the advances
made since it was written, in history, psychology, and anthropology."[18] It is an attempt that was begun at the outbreak of
World War II. Collingwood's essay is impressive, a seminal lode
of insight into social and political philosophy largely unmined
even through the present day by either philosophers or theorists
in the appropriate behavioral and social sciences.

From the first line, "What is man?", to the last paragraph of
a remarkable book written as he lay dying, Collingwood argues
through his convictions that philosophers (especially) must
sometimes take off their gloves and labor to change the enslaving human conditions of the world. It is not enough merely to
understand the world; one has to *try* to change the human
world, or, failing in that, at least cackle as the sacred geese of
Rome cackled, heralding the fall of Rome.[19] But Collingwood
does more than cackle. Properly read, I believe, *The New
Leviathan* is a violent book about violence, or in Collingwood's
own terms, about "savagery" and "barbarism," and instances of
violence, harm, power, force, and strength. He was desperately
concerned about human acts and events that he believed to be
directed toward the single purpose of destroying civilization.

My plan at present is not to present Collingwood's whole
argument, that of "a plain man telling a plain story" about
successive barbarisms and the failing of Western culture—
although his argument would be instructive to us all. I will
present only a part of it, a part that helps us to *situate* violence
—to locate and place violence—in a way more relevant philosophically than the usual characterizations of it in the philosophical literature.

Part I, "Man," conducts the reader through successive chapters which examine such topics as the body and mind of human beings, feeling, language, appetite, passion, desire, happiness, and human reason. Part II, "Society," *situates human being in sociation*, discusses community, politics (in its various forms), and concludes with a section on the decline of the classical politics inaugurated by Hobbes.

Who were responsible for this decline? Rousseau, Kant, Hegel, and Marx, primarily. In the first few words of the *Social Contract*, Rousseau raised the problem: "Man is born free, and everywhere he is in chains. How did this happen? I do not know."[20] The significance of this cry went unheeded by both Kant and Hegel; but with Marx it was another story, a story that still unfolds. Parts III and IV of *The New Leviathan* are entitled "Civilization" and "Barbarism", respectively, and these are the parts of the essay that are most relevant to philosophical questions about violence.

Civilization, said Collingwood, is a creation of the mind, the intellectual process of rendering something civil, or the process of becoming civil, or the state of being civil. But there is more. "Civilization is *something which* happens to a community"— that is, to two or more human beings collectively:

> Civilization is a *process of approximation to an ideal state*.
>
> To civilize a thing is to impose on it or promote in it a process; a process of becoming; a process in something which we know to be a community, whereby it approaches nearer to an ideal state which I will call *civility* and recedes farther from its contradictory, an ideal state which I will call *barbarity*.
>
> These are ideal states, not actual states.[21]

> So in the present case, if the process of *civilizing* is at work, the civil elements in the life of the community are gradually predominating and the barbarous elements are being gradually prevailed over, though the community's condition never becomes one of pure civility and the barbarous elements never vanish.[22]

Then Collingwood develops his key terms "civility," "barbarity," "civilize," and "barbarize."

> '*Civility*' is the name I use (following English custom established for several centuries) for the ideal condition into which whoever is trying to civilize a community is trying to bring it.
>
> '*Barbarity*' I use for the condition out of which whoever is trying to civilize a community is trying to bring it.

To *'civilize'* a community is to try to bring it into a condition of civility.

To *'barbarize'* a community means bringing or trying to bring a community into a condition of barbarity.

*'Civilization'* I use, as I find it used, in three senses.

In sense (I) it is used for *the process itself.* . . .

In sense (II) it is used for the *condition to which in a given case it leads*: the result of the process.

In sense (III) it is used as *equivalent to 'civility.'* . . .

For symmetry's sake I admit as justifiable three corresponding senses of the word *'Barbarism.'*

(I) as a name for *the process of barbarizing*; (II) as a name for *the condition to which in a given case that process leads*; (III) as *equivalent to 'barbarity.'*[23]

In subsequent passages it is clear that civilization means agreement between persons, efforts toward cooperative, mutual relations between persons, and "scientific or intelligent exploitation" of the natural world; but most of all it means behaving *civilly* to one another, and

Behaving 'civilly' to a man means respecting his feelings: abstaining from shocking him, annoying him, frightening him, or (briefly) arousing in him any passion or desire which might diminish his self-respect; that is, threaten his consciousness of freedom by making him feel that his power of choice is in danger of breaking down and the passion or desire likely to take charge.[24]

To behave towards a man in such a way as to arouse in him uncontrollable passions or desires, with the resulting breakdown of his will, is to *exercise force over him.*

The ideal of civil behaviour in one's dealings within one's fellow-men, therefore, is the ideal of *refraining from the use of force towards them.*[25]

*Being civilized* means *living, so far as possible, dialectically*, that is, in constant endeavour to convert every occasion of non-agreement into an occasion of agreement. A degree of force is inevitable in human life; but being civilized means cutting it down, and becoming more civilized means cutting it down still further.[26]

The process of civilization is the process of developing a society, and the condition of civilization at a given moment is the condition of a particular society. The civil relations (viz., the civil rights and civil liberties) within a given civilization are equivalent to the system of agreements within community life in which individuals form a continuous and regulatory association for their mutual benefit and protection. Human beings participate in the process of developing a society, are the unique phenomena of a given civilization at a given moment, are *civil* or *uncivil* to one another at a given time.

A society, then, is a collection of human beings composing a community, or many persons collectively, regarded as sharing common characteristics and relationships (e.g. agreements). A society is also a projection of persons' lives together, the attempted harmonious coexistence and action for hoped-for, even planned-for, benefits. Within societies the relatedness of persons becomes the occasion of expectations, customs, rules, regulations, and, most significant of all, *order*. This is expressive of moral order, or morality, and some moral order becomes relatively fixed and codified as law.[27] The Latin terms are instructive here. "Civilization" is derived from *civilis* ("under law," "orderly," and "society" comes from *socius* "partner," "companion," "comrade," "associate"). We can say, then, that civilization and society are related in the special sense that *within and under order, lawful order*, some human beings gather as partners, companions, comrades, or associates; the goal of it all is the creation of persons out of human beings. Collingwood put a similar point in this way:

> Let us get this clear, for it is the most important thing in the book. *Law and order mean strength.* Men who respect the rule of law are by daily exercise building up the strength of their own wills; becoming more and more capable of mastering themselves and other men and the world of nature. They are becoming daily more and more able to control their own desires and passions and to crush all opposition to the carrying-out of their intentions. They are becoming day by day less liable to be bullied or threatened or cajoled or frightened into courses they would not adopt of their own free will by men who would drive them into doing things in the only way in which men can drive others into doing things: by arousing in them passions or desires or appetites they cannot control.[28]

Once in existence, a society *surrounds, situates,* locates human beings as persons. So much so, that, in Marx' words, "It is not men's consciousness that *determines* their existence; on the contrary, it is their social existence that *determines* their consciousness."[29] One does not have to go the full distance of *determinism* with Marx, perhaps, but one must go part way, the way of consciousness. Thus, our feelings, our experiences, our consciousness, the *being of human being*, so to speak, are very much conditioned by our *sociation*, and especially so by the perceived orderings of our *sociation*, our society. We are therefore placed and located in a given space and time, surrounded by the forms of ordering that we and our companions depend upon. Berger and Luckmann have argued in support of a similar claim:

> Man is biologically predestined to construct and to inhabit a world with others. This world becomes for him the dominant and definitive reality. Its limits are set by nature, but once constructed, this world acts back upon nature. In the dialectic between nature and the socially constructed world the human organism itself is transformed. In this same dialectic man produces reality and thereby produces himself.[30]

## II. DESTRUCTIVE AND CONSTRUCTIVE VIOLENCE

Within any society, "destructive" and "constructive" violence may be distinguished.[31] Moreover, within any society there are always some degrees and forms of violence.[32] No society is perfectly ideal in the sense that no violence is present. There are always some marked forms of departure from orderly, civil, lawful behavior on the part of individual persons and groups of persons. Some of these degrees and forms of departure are destructive to the civil order, are moments of barbarism within a society. We call them instances or phenomena of violence. Less commonly acknowledged, however, are particular degrees and forms of departure from the civil order that are violent, but for all their violence are *considered constructive*, or constructive "in the long run." "What counts as violence at a given time is very much a matter of the position and the angle of vision of particular social groups"—or individual persons, we might say —and this is markedly true when considering the distinctions between destructive and constructive violence.[33]

To go in one direction, with destructive violence, is to go with savagery and barbarism, "for where there is violence there is that much less civility and where there is a great deal of violence civility tends to vanish."[34] To go in the other direction is to go with civilization. Both directions, however, are *violative*. The degrees and forms of destructive violence are prima facie violations. The use of violent phenomena toward constructive ends is evidence that some degree and kind of order must be *dis*-ordered in the emergence of some new ordering. Both forms of violence are actually forms of the *instrumental situating* of violence.[35] We shall consider each of these instrumental uses of violence immediately below.

## A. Destructive Violence

Many human acts and events can be agreed upon as being both violent and destructive in some degree or form. Following are some examples of destructive violence: *abusing* a person physically or through cursing him; *breaking* his arm deliberately; *ceasing* support of a friend involved in a fight; *damaging* his cause, or his will to stand for his rights; *defeating* an enemy; *desecrating* a temple of worship; *dishonoring* a person; *disagreeing* to the point of a broken friendship; *disobeying* a commandment; *erupting* in a fit of anger; *exciting* a friend to the point of a paroxysm; *fearing* the act someone is going to commit upon you; *forcing* someone to do something against his will; *harming* a person intentionally; *injuring* a person intentionally; *impairing* a person's ability to function at his best; *impeding* a person seeking a rightful goal; *insulting* a person; *interrupting* a person; *killing* a person; *maltreating* him; *marring* a person's body deliberately; *murdering* a person; *obstructing* someone; *perturbing* a person; *preventing* a person from seeking a legitimate goal; *punishing* a person; *resenting* a person; *spoiling* a child; *stopping* someone from seeking a legitimate goal; *torturing* someone; *thwarting* someone; *wounding* someone. These are all examples of violence in addition to the usual instances like rape, armed assault, assault with intent to commit bodily harm or kill, homicide, kidnaping, making obscene phone calls, etc. We all recognize such instances of violence with little difficulty, and we think of them as destructive.

Destructive violence is generally understood to be violence employed toward non-creative, negative ends, and committed by a person or persons. It may even be, through power, enforced, authorized and/or sanctioned. Destructive violence in some form and in some degree is a form and degree of savagery and barbarism, always *some kind of incivility within civility*, some kind of non-social act or event within *sociation*, some form of uncivilized behavior within civilization. But even destructive violence is "rational to the extent that it is effective in reaching the end that must justify it."[36]

Many of the problems relating to destructive violence concern the questions of the "angle of vision," the social perceptions, and the majority/minority status of the person or persons perceiving given phenomena and evaluating some of these as having no redeeming social value, even "in the long run." One of the most difficult problems concerns the *co-presence* of a civil order and violence in some societies. The fact of this co-presence must be granted in the case of some societies, and it raises certain difficulties. *First*, a civil order may not have been able to rid itself of very much savagery and barbarism. This is the kind of case I have dealt with at some length above. *Second*, there may be such a high degree of violence, and so many kinds of violence, present in a civil order that the phrase "civil order" is simply misapplied. In this case, what is being palmed off as civil order is merely successfully enforced living under the authority of some person or persons, but without the consent of at least the majority of those living under the strictures of the enforcement. *Third*, the perception of violence as indigenous to a civil order is usually the justification for acts of constructive violence directed against that civil order by revolutionaries, rebels, insurrectionists, and mutineers. This is a point I treat below.

## B. Constructive Violence

Constructive violence is violence committed by a person or persons and employed toward creative, positive ends. A person may commit violence in order to protect himself, his wife, and his children; authorized civil authorities may commit violence in protecting their community against those who murder its citizens. There are countless examples of this kind.

But there are other ways in which violence is thought to be put to use toward constructive ends. The fruits of civilization, in fact, are borne along the trunks and branches of violent phenomena. Examples are the development and use of tools and instruments that extend human senses and capabilities. Almost every one of these inventions has violated some previous ordering in a civilization: the telescope and microscope, the spinning jenny, movable type, the automobile, nuclear hardware, computer software, the laser. The development in medical theories and techniques, including both surgical and pharmaceutical treatments, and especially the violent phenomena employed in prolonging the lives of the dying (the form of violence that is the principal focus of contemporary discussions of euthanasia), is another example.

Moreover, we are very familiar with a variety of arguments that attempt either to balance out or to mitigate some of the tragic harvests of war by pointing to the positive benefits brought into civilization through advances that are its special side-effects: the development of medicines, the use of the assembly line, improvements in surgical techniques, the uses of steel superstructure for skyscrapers, the transistor radio, the lawn mower, etc.[37] All of these illustrations of the constructive uses of violence in the furtherance of the objectives of a civilization and society are perhaps self-evident. All of them are a function of persons' tolerance for the extent and the levels of intensity of violent activities and events considered necessary to the continued development of a civilization.

Consider only one further instance of this kind (and perhaps the most ambivalently perceived instance): the steadily increasing use of the automobile even in the face of its violent instrumentality. Violative of an ordered way of life when first introduced, the automobile has surely left its markings along the ways of civilization. And, on the whole, while it remains a violative instrumentality, is its violence used more in the interest of destructive, or constructive, ends? This is a prime question in all contemporary ecological debates. As a matter of fact, most current ecological debate concerns the many degrees and forms of violence brought into human ordering via instrumentality per se, viz., in the embodied extensions of our capabilities through tools, machines, and today's almost total technological orientation.

We have considered briefly the degrees and kinds of constructive violence that are the effects of technology and of the planning and waging of war. Quite different in form, though no less determinative as instrumental uses of violence toward constructive purposes, are the human acts and events directed toward the dis-ordering and the re-ordering of society (in the process of civilization). We call these acts revolution, rebellion, insurrection, or mutiny. This kind of violence is employed by persons who are not in office, and is used as an instrument against the uses (and abuses) of violence by those who are.

Witness a passage in *Report from Iron Mountain*:

Lasting peace, while not theoretically impossible, is probably unattainable; even if it could be achieved it would almost certainly not be in the best interests of a stable society to achieve it.[38]

And Cameron has called attention to the same problem:

Mob violence and police violence are equally characteristic of some modern societies. But those who use the former phrase may well avoid the latter; and those who use the latter may be inclined to view the roughest demonstration as a kind of Quaker meeting. . . . It is precisely this moment, both in the metropolitan countries and in the relatively underdeveloped countries, that violence in many forms causes us to question the staying power and the moral value of that civility which exists alongside injustice.[39]

Maurice Merleau-Ponty states:

*The contingency of the future, which accounts for the violent acts of those in power, by the same token deprives these acts of all legitimacy, or equally legitimates the violence of their opponents.* The right of the opposition is exactly equal to the right of those in power.[40]

Merleau-Ponty points precisely to the target of the revolutionary act or event of constructive violence. The revolutionary act or event is aimed at those power centers that are perceived by persons to be violent at their very core, or perceived to be such pervasive and efficient carriers of violence that it is difficult to distinguish between a given existing civil order and the express sanctioning of destructive violence by persons in office.

Because of these perceptions (feelings, experiences, thoughts, as well) some persons are led to formulate revolutionary goals. Revolutionaries do not invent violence. In Merleau-Ponty's words, they "find it already institutionalized, [but] for the moment the question is not to know whether one accepts or rejects violence, but whether the violence with which one is allied is 'progressive' and tends towards its own suspension or toward self-perpetuation."[41]

What many revolutionaries direct their actions against is precisely the articulation of the philosophy of the state and the civil order presented by Machiavelli. Machiavelli's *The Prince* offers the classic account in political philosophy of violence put to constructive uses in establishing the bases of power, authority, and the legitimate employment of force. *The Prince* continues to be the book containing the recipes of power for those in power who intend to remain in power.[42] It is a bald account of presumed constructive uses of raw power, and no doubt most political scientists today find little justification for refuting most of its principal claims.

But Marx, Nietzsche, Sorel, and many modern revolutionaries on the Left offer persuasive, relevant accounts of the uses of constructive violence against the state. In varying ways and degrees, they offer accounts of the uses of violence intended radically to alter law and order within a society and civilization. There are countless examples. Sartre wrote in the preface to Fanon's *The Wretched of the Earth*, "violence, like Achilles' lance, can heal the wounds that it has inflicted."[43]

No doubt the classic philosophical account of violence (in fact, it comprises a philosophy of violence) is still that of a self-styled "non-philosopher," Georges Sorel, in his *Reflections on Violence*. Sorel argued for a special constructive violence, a genuine violence with a special charismatic excitement associated with a sublime far-off end, the rule of the proletariat. "It is very difficult," he wrote, "to understand proletarian violence as long as some think of it in terms of the ideas disseminated by middle-class philosophers; according to this philosophy, violence is a relic of barbarism which is bound to disappear with the influence of enlightenment."[44] But distinctive violence is often exacerbated and sanctioned by the state.

Sorel devoutly believed that the world would be saved from "barbarism" (i.e., the civilization and society espoused by the ruling classes) by "proletarian violence, carried on as a pure and simple manifestation of the sentiment of the class war." Thinking of the conditions of tomorrow, he argued that such violence was a "very fine and heroic thing . . . at the service of the immemorial interests of civilization."[45] His philosophy of violence has been a most important contribution to all degrees and shades of revolution. He praised, most of all,

the development of specifically proletarian forces, that is to say, with violence enlightened by the idea of the general strike. . . . the bond which I pointed out in the beginning of this inquiry between Socialism and proletarian violence appears to us now in all its strength. It is to violence that Socialism owes those high ethical values by means of which it brings salvation to the modern world.[46]

Sorel derived much of what he wrote from his reading of the works of Marx, Nietzsche, and, in particular, Bergson. More recent examples of constructive violence abound in the writings and the actions of Mao, Ho Chi Minh, Castro, Che Guevara, and countless Third World revolutionaries. But the most important of these modern examples may be the writings of Fanon, whose explorations into the phenomena of violence were forced upon his consciousness during his experience of French colonialism, and the subsequent war, in Algeria. Moreover, his own eloquence was supported by Sartre, and of course by his own camaraderie with many of the French intellectuals in their struggle against French policies in Algeria. Thus Fanon, aided and abetted by Sartre, has provided the most eloquent *recent* testimony attesting the values of the constructive violence of revolution, rebellion, insurrection, and mutiny. Indeed, Fanon believed that violence is necessary to the *understanding of social truths*:

Violence alone, violence committed by the people, violence organized and educated by its leaders, makes it possible for the masses to understand social truths and gives the key to them. Without that struggle, without that knowledge of the practice of action, there's nothing but a fancy-dress parade and the blare of trumpets. There's nothing save a minimum of readaptation, a few reforms at the top, a flag waving: and down there at the bottom an undivided mass, still living in the middle ages, endlessly marking time.[47]

But Sorel still stands alone in his eloquent testimony supporting constructive violence that is directed against the barbarism built into civility itself:

Everything may be saved, if the proletariat, by their use of violence, manage to re-establish the division into classes, and so restore to the middle class something of its former energy; that is, the great aim towards which the whole thought of men—who are hypnotized by events of the day, but who think of the conditions of tomorrow—must be directed. Proletarian violence, carried on as a pure and simple manifestation of the sentiment of the class war, appears thus as a very fine and a very heroic thing; it is at the service of the immemorial interests of civilization; it is not perhaps the most appropriate method of obtaining immediate material advantages, *but it may save the world from barbarism.*[48]

## III. THE LANGUAGE OF VIOLENCE: HARM, POWER, FORCE, AND STRENGTH

Within a civil order, the most pervasive medium of civility is the language of the people. Language is the most distinctive human activity, that activity whereby persons become conscious of their feelings.[49] Collingwood wrote, "it ought not to surprise you to be told that emotions may turn into thoughts or that thoughts may originate in emotions."[50] He stated that this comes about as persons *name* their feelings and continue to talk about them: "To name the feeling awakens [a person's] consciousness of the feeling."[51] Collingwood records as one of Hobbes's "greatest achievements" his claim that language "is an activity prior to knowledge itself, without which knowledge could never come into existence."[52] He quotes Hobbes:

> [T]he noblest and most profitable invention of all other, was that of SPEECH, consisting of *Names* or *Appellations*, and their Connexion; whereby men register their thoughts; recall them when they are past; and also declare them to one another for mutuall utility and conversation; without which, there had been amongst men, neither Common-wealth, nor Society, nor Contract, nor Peace, no more than amongst Lyons, Bears, and Wolves.[53]

This is not the proper place to enter a full discussion of the nature and function of language.[54] It is enough to say with both Hobbes and Collingwood that without language there could be no civil order. Language not only records our feelings, it presents and articulates our perceptions as well. The language of violence is of great importance, for (1) it articulates both the textures of the civil order and departures from the civil order; (2) it is that distinctive human activity which makes possible the dialectical living necessary to the civil order; and (3) it is a way of removing or meliorating conditions under which violence is likely to occur.[55]

But the language of violence also situates persons in the world in special ways. The word "violence" (or one of its forms) is always used in traditional grammar as one of four distinct parts of speech: (1) It may be used as a noun in terming a human action or event an instance of *violence*. (2) It may be used as an adjective in qualifying a human act or event as *violent*. (3) It may be used as an adverb in modifying the meaning of a verb, an adjective, or other adverb, in the sense that one speaks of someone coughing *violently*. (4) It may be used as a verb in the archaic construction *to violence* something or someone. ·

Used in any one of the first three ways, "violence," "violent," and "violently" are sometimes thought to be synonymous with harm, power, force, and/or strength. After a few words on the mind-body problem, I will try to show in the remainder of Section III that these words do not always mean harm, power, force, and/or strength; that none of these words performs the full promise of the meaning of "violence" or any of its forms. In Section IV, I will discuss the fourth use of the word "violence" and its forms, its use as a verb, and offer a *theory of violatives* that suggests certain ways in which the meanings of violence might be explored fruitfully.

## A. Excursus on Violence and the Mind-Body Problem

Most discussions of violence involve analyses of notions of harm, power, force, strength, and other notions often thought to be synonyms, or near-synonyms, for violence.[56] These are physicalistic or body-oriented concepts. Their constant employment, not only in philosophical essays on violence, but in the common language, takes no account of one of the most serious philosophical problems in any philosophy of language: the problem of situating violence in terms of the human mind and body.

I cannot be certain of this, but *I believe that Collingwood stands alone among philosophers in his deliberate attempts to explore, clarify, and analyze the mind-body problem consciously as a prelude and propaedeutic to his analysis of violence*.[57] I believe that one ought to be able to find at random discussions of violence that do more than merely (at their very best) tell us half the story—and only the "physical" half, at that. It is not, however, possible to do so.

A recent article raises this question quite forcefully. In a well-argued essay, Ronald B. Miller writes:

> the phrase 'physical violence' is redundant. Violence just is the *physical* overpowering of a person or object with the intent to injure, or destroy. There is no such thing as non-physical violence.[58]

Surely there is ample testimony within the theory and practice of psychotherapy to rebut—even to refute—this claim. But this point remains to be investigated. Still, the problems of the physicalistic foundations of supposed synonyms for violence are ever-present in the philosophical literature on violence.

Assuming that mind and body are separate (a position I do not myself hold), how is it possible that one part of my person (my body) may be violated, while another part of my person (my mind) may not be violated through the commission of the same act? Is it possible to argue that physical harm against my body (say, through the loss of both my arms through war injuries) is *not*, appositely, a harm against my mind? Or is it possible to argue that a harm to my mind (say, in the form of some acute mental instability) is not, appositely, a harm to my body? How is it possible to present a tenable view of either physical or mental violence if these two are mutually exclusive? But where are the arguments that are based *either* on the assumption of some degree and kind of fusion of the mind and body, *or* upon some previously argued account of a "solution" to the mind-body problem? And if someone believed that persons are reducible to material or physicalistic bases, he would be prone to argue that physical violence is the more telling form of violence, that it would be more significant—more violative, so to speak—than mental or psychological violence (whatever, in such a view, the latter two kinds of violence could be).

I do not intend in this essay to resolve all of the problems I have cited above, although I am certain that what I say immediately below will suffer somewhat because of my failure to do so. Even so, I hope that the reader will pay more careful attention to all discussions (my own included) of violence and physicalistically oriented notions thought to be synonymous with it.

## B. Harm

I may *harm* a person without doing him violence, without displaying power toward him, without forcing him, or without displaying any strength toward him. Consider this example: I am in a playful mood. I trip my friend intentionally. Immediately he falls to the ground and breaks his arm. Surely I have *harmed* my friend. But how could it be argued that I displayed any power, force, or strength toward him, unless one wishes deliberately to qualify my simple case by saying that I tripped my friend "powerfully," "forcefully," or "with strength"? But I can trip my friend in delicate ways involving none of these. Almost anyone else can do likewise. This example (and many more like it) suggests that harm can be done to a person with no violence whatsoever, *if* by violence one means power, force, or strength. Still, I believe that I have done violence to my friend in tripping him, and while not all harm may involve violence, all violence must involve harm, in the sense of some hurt, injury, damage, or other kind of violation of his person.

## C. Power

Power is an ability to act or to affect someone or something strongly enough to move the person or thing in some sense. It is physical, mental, or moral strength, might or vigor. Power is an enabling process. It is energy, character, effectiveness. Power is an active principle in animate beings. Power is control, or command, over others. It is domination, rule, influence, authority (as residing in some, or over some, person, office, or group of persons). Power may be the limits within which actions may take place. It may be influence in the form of personal and social ascendancy, or influence in the form of political ascendancy—influence in the government of a country or state.

Power may be legal ability, capacity, or authority to act, especially in the sense of delegated authority, authorization, commission, or faculty. A document, or a clause within a document, might even *be* a power, as well as *give* a power. Or perhaps a power is one who *has* the power. There are many other uses of the term as well. A power might well be a body of fighting men, a fighter, or even a large number of persons, a large quantity, a great deal, etc.

The term is also used in the sciences, especially in mathematics, mechanics, and optics, but all of the earliest references seem to point to an anthropomorphic intentionality. Persons are, have, and perform power, and so power becomes useful in other areas as an analogue taken over by these other disciplines.

Finally, in harmony with many examples found in the *Oxford English Dictionary*, Arendt concludes:

> *Power* corresponds to the human ability not just to act but to act in concert. Power is never the property of an individual; it belongs to a group and remains in existence only so long as the group keeps together. When we say of somebody that he is "in power" we actually refer to his being empowered by a certain number of people to act in their name. The moment the group, from which the power originated to begin with (*potestas in*

*populo*, without a people or group there is no power), disappears, "his power" also vanishes. In current usage, when we speak of a "powerful man" or a "powerful personality," we already use the word "power" metaphorically; what we refer to without metaphor is "strength."[59]

Most instances of power—probably all—could be presented quite apart from instances of violence. Power and violence are simply not the same phenomenon. The confusing claim that they are, or are in some degree, is a confusion of (1) the bases of authority, the sources of authority, and the sanctions of authority (that is, power), and (2) the measurement of the uses and abuses of this power in terms of deviations from the orderly, expected uses of power.

Consider the following sentence: "Although the king held the power of the throne, he did not have sufficient power to quell the rebellion of the noblemen, nor did he want to resort to violence." The responsibility for civil order resides with the power of the office of the king. If the king has instituted no civil order other than his own whim and fancy, then the king cannot deviate from the civil order; and there can be no violence from the king's side, only the exercise of his power. His subjects know precisely what to expect: a life that might well be nasty, brutish, and short.

But if the king has laid out a civil order not entirely dependent upon himself, one that includes the irrevocable delegation of power(s) to other offices, then he may well have the *necessary* power to quell the rebellion, but lack *sufficient* power. Alas, poor king! What shall he do? In neither case does he have sufficient power. But to try to quell the rebellion in the *first* case is never to engage in violence, but only in the uses and abuses of power more clarified, refined, and pure. And to try to quell the rebellion in the *second* case is not to use the power of his office (for although he holds the necessary power, he lacks sufficient power), but to do violence: it is to commit the unexpected, the *dis*-ordering, *un*-civil act of taking back unto himself the powers he had irrevocably delegated to others.

## D. *Force*

Consider one of Collingwood's examples of the use of force:

There is a *society*, A, of which the surgeon B and the patient C are members, each of his own free will, and whose joint enterprise is the removal of C's appendix by B. It is this society as a whole that authorizes B to take out C's appendix.

*Authority is a relation between a society and a part of that society to which the society assigns the execution of a part of its joint enterprise.* This may involve the use of force by one part upon another part of the society. As thus exercising force upon C, B is not ruling the society; the society, as always, is ruling itself; B is a part of itself which it is using in the course of its rule over itself to exercise force on another part of itself. This force is exercised by authority of the society; and therefore according to the free will of every member of the society, including C.

The patient may be a child; in which case the decision to remove its appendix will be jointly made not by surgeon and patient but by surgeon and patient's parent. The child is not a party to that decision. From the child's point of view the removal of its appendix is an act of *force* jointly exercised upon it by parent and surgeon. The child as undergoing this joint or social force is a *dependent* upon the society.

The word 'force' in political contexts never means 'physical force', as when a stronger man 'forces' open a weaker man's fingers and 'makes' him let go what he is holding. It always means 'moral force' or mental strength.

Moreover it is a relative term. It signifies not mental strength as such but one man's superiority in mental strength to another. When A is said to exercise force upon B, what is meant is that A is strong relatively to B, and uses this superiority to make B do what he wants.[60]

The example is a good one. It presents a prima facie case of force that is unrelated to violence. Again, as with the case of power, the presence of violence would mean the deviation from the normally expected, the ordered, the lawful. To meet this condition of violence, the example would have to be amended: the surgeon would have to be someone not certified to do the operation, drunk while performing the operation, or otherwise unable (for a variety of possible reasons) to perform the operation according to the procedures normally laid down by medical science. Or perhaps the example would have to include the case where the child was restrained through the use of so much strength, and so much against his will, that the restraining process became hurtful to his person.

Collingwood's remarks about "force" in the political context are also instructive, for they (together with his example) show that our language offers a distinction—a notion distinct from harm, power, and strength—that is still not violence per se.

Thus, force is power that is either stronger or weaker than some other power in a given situation. Although force is relative strength in a given situation, it is still not violence.

## E. Strength

Arendt argues that violence "phenomenologically . . . is close to strength, since the implements of violence, like all other tools, are designed and used for the purpose of multiplying natural strength until, in the last stage of their development, they can substitute for it."[61] I believe that Arendt is very close to the mark. Violence is closer to strength in its usage than it is to any of the other concepts I have discussed in this section. Strength is the quality or property of being stronger, whether in terms of muscular power or force, or in terms of mental or moral character, or in terms of capacities for instrumental uses of power or force. Thus, strength is not a separate notion from the rest. It is, however, a distinction, a way of speaking in *measuring* terms about such matters as harm, power, and force. But it assumes some base, some foundation, some norm, some order, such that it can be said that some instance of power or force is greater or less than another one, or that some harm is more or less harmful than some other harm.

The above explorations into the uses of these several words that are often argued as synonyms for violence—or sometimes as paradigms of violence—suggest certain tentative conclusions, which should at another time be carefully investigated:

(1) Violence is *never* pure harm, power, force, or strength.

(2) Although violence is always a degree and kind of harm, it need not necessarily be associated with any degree or kind of power or force, although it *sometimes* is.

(3) Harm, power, force, and strength need not necessarily be associated with one another, although they *sometimes* are.

(4) When violence is associated with either power or force, or with both, it is never associated with either one per se. It is always used in association as a qualification (and thus used as an adjective or adverb) of power or force, or both, as: (a) harmful, (b) out-of-order, (c) stronger than usual, (d) more intense than usual.

(5) "Violence" used as a noun is always a variation of (4) above—in the sense, for example, that someone may say "a violence of rage" rather than use the word "paroxysm."

## IV.  THE LANGUAGE OF VIOLENCE: *Violatives*

Thus far I have tried to show that violence is a human act, or event within a human ordering, that departs from that human ordering in some measurable ways; that violence is equated with the paradigms of neither harm, power, force, nor strength; and that the paradigm of violence is in fact found in departure-from-order, in un-order, in dis-order, or in the out-of-order. Violence occurs in differing degrees and kinds. Violent acts are always *violative* in some degree, and violent acts are always some kind of *violative*. Thus, violence as a class concept is the class all of whose members are *violatives*; as a generic concept, violence is a genus whose species are *violatives*, and whose generic essence (and variable attribute) is dis-order.[62]

In this section I wish to offer a very rudimentary description of certain *violatives*, which results from a careful working of the dictionary following the guidelines of what can be termed a "linguistic phenomenology."[63] This involves a discussion of the *fourth* use of the word violence, its use as a verb. In this case "violence" means "to do violence," "to violate." Its use as a verb was quite common in the seventeenth century, although the *Oxford English Dictionary* lists this usage as now obsolete. The sentences given in the *OED* as examples, however, are most enlightening: "The one was so farre from violencing the other, as one could not stand without the other" (1612); "The most Sacred things are violenced, and the most Profane Licenced" (1650); "In doing otherwise he would thwart and violence his own conscience, and be self-condemned" (1677); "Sure 'twill not be thought reasonable that these two shall be forced and violenced to consent to that" (1647); "They have done what they could to violence him from his Religion" (1648). Moreover, the sentences "He violated the woman" and "He violenced the woman" mean the same thing.

I suggest below a *few* examples of English verbs connoting violence, words commonly used to articulate many distinctions within the phenomena of violence. I trust the reader to provide the further, *situative* contexts in which each of these words (within the reader's own feeling, experience, and consciousness) does indeed intend violence in some degree, and of some kind. I also suggest the correlative modes of violence, or *violative modes*, for each of these verbs.

| Verbs Connoting Violence in Kind and Degree | *Violative Modes* in Kind and Degree |
|---|---|
| Abuse | Abusives |
| Break | Breakives |
| Cease | Ceasives |
| Damage | Damagives |
| Defeat | Defeatives |
| Desecrate | Desecratives |
| Dishonor | Dishonorives |
| Disagree | Disagreeives |
| Disobey | Disobeyives |
| Embarrass | Embarrassives |
| Erupt | Eruptives |
| Excite | Excitives |
| Fear | Fearives |
| Force | Forcives |
| Harm | Harmives |
| Humiliate | Humiliatives |
| Injure | Injurives |
| Impair | Impairives |
| Impede | Impedives |
| Insult | Insultives |
| Interrupt | Interruptives |
| Kill | Killives |
| Maltreat | Maltreatives |
| Mar | Marives |
| Murder | Murderives |
| Obstruct | Obstructives |
| Perturb | Perturbives |
| Prevent | Preventives |
| Punish | Punishives |
| Resent | Resentives |
| Spoil | Spoilives |
| Stop | Stopives |
| Torture | Torturives |
| Thwart | Thwartives |
| Wound | Woundives |

This is a very brief list of English verbs constitutive of our standard vocabulary of violence. They all call attention to instances of violence; they are all violations, *violative* modes, or simply, *violatives*. I am certain that many verbs—some even more appropriate—have been omitted, and that imaginative and resourceful philosophers could offer a far richer list. I invite them to do so, and to further construct and apply, with me, this *theory of violatives*.

The wonder is that such commonly-used *violatives* have gone largely unexplored in the limited philosophical literature on violence. Not all of them have gone unexplored, however. Within the list, no doubt those that have received the fullest treatment include: abuse, damage, force, harm, injure, kill, and murder. I suggest that it would be more profitable in the philosophical literature henceforth to offer phenomenological, exploratory accounts of modes of violence, or *violatives*, such as *abusives, damagives, forcives, harmives, injurives, killives, murderives*, etc. Of course this would require that academic philosophers remove their purely academic gowns and gloves and resume their human tasks once more. This is the sort of descriptive work engaged in by Collingwood at the beginning of World War II, and by Sartre, Fanon, Camus, and Merleau-Ponty, for example, during the French-Algerian War.

Paying close phenomenological attention to the language of violence means already to focus upon distinguishable *violative* modes. They are distinguishable from one another because: (1) They are *violatives* that are specified in our speaking. The *violative* modes are a part of a rich, distinguishing repertoire of terms commonly in use, and with a deeply rooted and consistent etymology. (2) They are relevantly spoken of by one or more persons within a civil community of persons, since they are among the paradigm cases of common moral and ethical customs and traditions and legal codifications. (3) They are words used to call attention to, to present, and to state cases of violence agreed upon, or accepted, as acts of violence within a civil community.

There is no question, moreover, but what these words—and a host of other words of equal significance for the articulation of violent phenomena—are distinctive expressions within the English language for violatives. They have arisen within the language as persons within the community have attempted to speak of the variegated ways in which the civil order is intruded upon or interrupted, or where the civil order can be broken toward achieving *dis*-order or *re*-order.

Moreover, these are among the most relevant words in the

language in the sense that they always raise the question of what it means to be human, to be the person I am, or the person someone else is; they raise repeatedly the question of distinctions between one person's treatment of another person. These words denote the more extreme cases of breaking the bonds of civil treatment of one person by another, which communities must mend if they are to progress toward *dialectical* life in the civil community.

These words (and many more like them) are expressions of prima facie violence, the *violatives* of the human civil order. They are linguistic situatings in spatial and temporal terms. They are among the measures of violence, the measures to which violence extends. They are the calibrated, scaled departures from an established civil order. They are the modulated articulations of violent phenomena felt, experienced, and known by persons who use the language. Most persons know the difference between an *abusive* and a *killive*, for example, and it might be possible, upon a good deal of reflection, to situate these violatives on a scale showing their degree of departure from civil order.[64]

## V. CONCLUSION

Many problems can now be raised as a result of this exploration into the phenomena of violence. In closing, I will briefly state some of those I consider most important for immediate philosophical research.

(1) Neither harm, power, force, nor strength is a paradigm of violence. Each is co-extensive with violence only on certain occasions. This conclusion is perhaps easier to draw through the use of a *theory of violatives* wherein the paradigm of violence is seen to be a given deviation from a given civil order. It would be most useful for the theories and practices of a host of social sciences (e.g. philosophy, anthropology, geography, economics, history, psychology, sociology) to cooperate in investigations of the particular and unique *violatives* in which harm, power, force, and/or strength are co-extensive with violence. The conclusions of such investigations might, for example, have a profound influence upon the theory and the practice of law.

(2) It is not particularly fruitful to continue to speak of "moral violence," "political violence," "religious violence," or "economic violence," as we sometimes do. Given instances of *violatives* may be all of these together. A more useful analysis

and explanation is provided by an understanding of the particular *violatives* per se, but not as moral, economic, etc.

(3) Explorations into violence surely raise a prime metaphysical issue: the mind-body question. A given analysis of violence is always dependent upon some philosophical posture regarding this problem (if in fact it is a problem), but one looks vainly through the literature for any resolution to it. Thus, many discussions of the problem of violence lose their persuasiveness precisely at the point where authors are forced to a virtual psycho-physical parallelism, separating physical violence *and* psychological violence, or denying one or the other.[65]

(4) All questions of *non-violence* arise within the context of an understanding of violence. The theory and the practice of non-violence have meaning only on the grounds of the prior meaning of violence. And varying perceptions of violence will necessarily dictate particular perceptions of non-violence. The use of something like the *theory of violatives* that I have presented would suggest specific degrees and forms of non-violent theory and practice as most relevant to specific degrees and forms of the theory and practice of violence.

(5) It is within the law that the theory of *violatives* should prove most useful. Indeed, reflection upon the law, and the investigation of statutes and precedents might well attest the presence of something very like an *implicit theory of violatives*. But even so, an *explicit* statement of the theory fed back into not only the theory but also the practice of law ought to be of considerable worth.

Finally, if persons are to become less *violative* of one another, violence must cease to be our principal bondage, must come to be less sensational and mysterious to each of us. Violence should be accepted forthrightly for what it is: human acts and human events *violative* in the human world—acts and events which must be corrected by humane, dialectical ordering within the world.

I close with a passage from Spinoza:

If the way which I have pointed out as leading to this result seems exceedingly hard, it may nevertheless be discovered. Needs must it be hard, since it is so seldom found. How would it be possible, if salvation were ready to our hand, and could without great labor be found, that it should be by almost all men neglected? But all things excellent are as difficult as they are rare.[66]

# Notes

1 Georges Sorel, "Introduction to the First Publication," *Reflections on Violence*, trans. T. E. Hulme and J. Roth (Glencoe, Ill.: Free Press, 1950; New York: Collier Books, 1961), p. 60.

2 Hannah Arendt, *On Violence* (New York: Harcourt, Brace & World, 1970), p. 8; see also p. 35.

3 *The Encylopedia of Philosophy*, for example, contains no article on violence, although it does contain discussions of power and force.

4 The question of violence surely concerns the most human question of all, *Who am I?*, for reflection upon the being of human being surely necessitates reflection upon violations of this being.

5 I shall try to do this along the lines of what can be termed a "linguistic phenomenology," following the usage of this phrase by J. L. Austin and Herbert Spiegelberg. See J. L. Austin, *Philosophical Papers* (Oxford: Clarendon Press, 1961), p. 130; also Herbert Spiegelberg, "Linguistic Phenomenology: J. L. Austin and Alexander Pfänder," *Memorias del Congreso International de Filosofía*, vol. 9 (Mexico, D.F.: Universidad Nacional Autonoma de Mexico, 1964), pp. 511–20; also Sherman M. Stanage, "Linguistic Phenomenology and 'Person-Talk'," *Philosophy and Rhetoric* 2 (1969): 81–90.

6 See Robin G. Collingwood, *The New Leviathan* (Oxford: Clarendon Press, 1942).

7 The suffix "-ive" is sometimes used in forming adjectives and substantives in modern Romance languages and in English in adapting Latin words. The suffix connotes "having a tendency to," "having the nature, character, or quality of," or "given to some action." It implies a permanent or habitual quality or tendency. Thus, any use of the term *violative* intends the nature, character, or quality of violence, or the permanent or habitual quality or tendency toward violence. The further importance of this term (as it is built into a theory of violatives) will become evident in the following pages, and especially so in Section IV, entitled "The Language of Violence: *Violatives*."

8 See J. L. Austin, *How To Do Things with Words* (Cambridge: Harvard University Press, 1962). See also n. 5 above.

9 Arendt, *On Violence*, pp. 4, 79.

10 See Arendt: "Neither violence nor power is a natural phenomenon, that is, a manifestation of the life process; they belong to the political realm of human affairs whose essentially human quality is guaranteed by man's faculty of *action*, the ability to begin something new" (*On Violence*, p. 82 [my italics]). See also J. M. Cameron: "In all periods what is taken to be unalterable, a part of the natural order, is not singled out as violence" ("On Violence," *New York Review of Books* 15 [2 July 1970]: 24).

11 When we speak of the violence of the earthquake, the volcanic eruption, the tornado, or the hurricane, we mean something felt, experienced, or known, or perhaps a recorded account of the natural event. The feeling, the experiencing, and the recording are human matters. The eruption per se was simply what it was. But it may have been felt or

experienced by those who lived near it. Perhaps the earthquake was recorded by seismographs and measured on the Richter scale, etc. A given natural event was a happening in the lives of some, perhaps only in the lives of the villagers, or perhaps recorded in terms of the most advanced scientific theory and instrumentation. Whatever the form, within its *humanly perceived life* (as distinct from its own occurring) the event was a violative happening, with greater or lesser intensity.

[12] *Situationality* is an important concept in this essay. I intend it in the sense given to it in both Dewey's *pragmatic philosophy* and in Merleau-Ponty's *existential phenomenology*. See John Dewey: "For we never experience or form judgments about objects and events in isolation, but only in connection with a contextual whole. The latter is what I call a 'situation'" (*Logic: The Theory of Inquiry* [New York: Henry Holt & Co., 1938], p. 66). See also Maurice Merleau-Ponty: "I never encounter face to face another person's consciousness any more than he meets mine. I am not for him, nor is he for me, a pure existence for itself. We are both for one another *situated* beings, characterized by a certain type of relation to men and the world, by a certain activity, a certain way of treating other people and nature" (*Humanism and Terror* [Boston: Beacon Press, 1969], p. 108; my italics; see also idem, *The Phenomenology of Perception* [London: Routledge & Kegan Paul, 1962], passim, but esp. pp. 443 ff.).

[13] Is violence a class concept or a generic concept? For an important discussion of these two kinds of concepts, see Robin G. Collingwood, *An Essay on Philosophical Method* (Oxford: Clarendon Press, 1932), esp. chaps. 2 and 3. This is a point I also discuss in Section IV of this essay.

[14] Thomas Hobbes, *Leviathan: Parts I and II*, ed. Herbert W. Schneider, (Indianapolis: Bobbs-Merrill Co., 1958), p. 107.

[15] Cameron, "On Violence," p. 25.

[16] From *ab origine*, "from the beginning."

[17] Although one wonders what form "expectations" would have taken in such a life world.

[18] Collingwood, *New Leviathan*, pp. iii, iv.

[19] See Robin G. Collingwood, *An Essay on Metaphysics* (Oxford: Clarendon Press, 1940), p. 343.

[20] Quoted by Collingwood in *New Leviathan*, p. 269.

[21] Ibid., p. 283.

[22] Ibid., p. 284.

[23] Ibid., p. 286. Cf. p. 307.

[24] Ibid., p. 291.

[25] Ibid., p. 292. Collingwood is making the same point as Cameron. See Cameron: "Violence is strictly brutish in that it comes about through a falling away from what men have it in them to become, free and rational agents. Agreement in rationality and fraternity mark out the distinctive human community; in so far as social relationships are determined by habit, passion, and force, they are in that degree less than human, if one may think of *humanitas* as a concept used to prescribe as well as to describe" ("On Violence," p. 30).

[26] Collingwood, *New Leviathan*, p. 326. Cf. Cameron: "It is precisely at this moment, both in the metropolitan countries and in the relatively underdeveloped countries, that violence in many forms causes us to question the staying power and the moral value of that civility which exists alongside injustice" ("On Violence," pp. 25–26).

[27] See Collingwood, *New Leviathan*, chap. 39, "Law and Order." But there are many kinds of "order" within modern society. Examples are economic order, social order, political order, religious order, scientific order, historical order, artistic order, etc. These are distinctions which progressively come to be made as a civilization develops, and as its episodes become distinguishable and unique as societies. All of these are articulated as specific degrees and kinds of laws within a society.

[28] Ibid., p. 332.

[29] Ibid., pp. 136–37; italics mine. Collingwood is quoting a passage from Marx's *Kritik der Politischen Ökonomie*, 5th ed. (Stuttgart, 1910), p. lix, "being no. 4 of the 'propositions' set forth in the *Introduction*."

[30] Peter L. Berger and Thomas Luckmann, *The Social Construction of Reality: A Treatise in the Sociology of Knowledge* (Garden City, N.Y.: Doubleday & Co., 1967), p. 183.

[31] This section could have had a different title, e.g. "Negative/Positive Violence," "Unjust/Just Violence," "Bad/Good Violence," "Illegitimate/Legitimate Violence," "Illegal/Legal Violence." But in general the focus would have been the same: Some degrees and kinds of violence have always been unacceptable, whereas some degrees and kinds of violence have always been acceptable in civilizations. The particular degrees and kinds, of course, have differed. There has always been a constant ground, however, for the evaluation of destructive violence. This has been the ground or the foundation of law and order, or the *situatings* performed by the legal codifications of the orderings of civility within a civilization. Perhaps the grounds have been near-legal codifications. Here, of course, questions of authority and sanctions, and harm, power, force, and strength are among the primary ones. Just as important are questions of the majority/minority perceptions of what constitute law and order within the *civility* of a given society.

[32] In fact, I believe that scales that fuse degrees and kinds of violence within a given culture can—and should—be developed by social and political philosophers and by philosophers of culture. I do not explicitly attempt this in this essay, but I do believe that projects of this nature should be carried out, and soon. They should follow, in my judgment, a philosophical method of a scale of forms suggested by R. G. Collingwood in his *Essay on Philosophical Method;* see chaps. 2 and 3 especially. Any given society could be investigated through the collection of empirical data of violent phenomena articulated by the society's language in use. The results of this kind of study should be situated on a philosophical scale of forms of violence specific to that given society. No doubt anthropologists do something like this as a part of their special work, but philosophers, anthropologists, sociologists, psychiatrists, historians, and indeed all of the "social sciences," should cooperate in these kinds of projects.

[33] Cameron, "On Violence," p. 30.

[34] Ibid., p. 25.

[35] See n. 9 above.

[36] Arendt, *On Violence*, p. 79.

[37] See Leonard C. Lewin (pseud.), *Report from Iron Mountain: On the Possibility and Desirability of Peace* (New York: Dial Press, Dell Publishing Co., 1967), p. 53.

[38] Ibid., p. x. Of course, this little book is a "spoof" written pseudonymously by a well-known American. But the claim that violence may well

be present at the very center of a society is made by many critics. The charges that racist and sexist violence are indigenous to the civil order within American society are special variations on this theme.

39 Cameron, "On Violence," pp. 25–26.

40 Merleau-Ponty, *Humanism and Terror*, p. xxxvi.

41 Ibid., p. 1; cf. p. xxxvi. Both those *in* power and those *out* of power who are using constructive violence to gain power plan for the future.

42 Note the orientation toward the future that is built into *The Prince*.

43 Jean-Paul Sartre, Preface to *The Wretched of the Earth*, by Frantz Fanon, trans. Constance Farrington (New York: Grove Press, 1968), p. 30.

44 Sorel, *Reflections on Violence*, p. 80.

45 Ibid., p. 98.

46 Ibid., p. 249.

47 Fanon, *Wretched of the Earth*, p. 87.

48 Sorel, *Reflections on Violence*, p. 98.

49 Here, as in many other places in this essay on violence, it should be observed that a clarification of violence requires a prior clarification of very many other problems of the human condition. Thus, explorations into language and speech-acts—special cases of action theory—are vital to an understanding of violence, for reasons to be given below.

50 Collingwood, *New Leviathan*, p. 344.

51 Ibid., p. 42.

52 Ibid., p. 43.

53 Ibid., p. 43 (quoting the *Leviathan*, p. 12).

54 Cf. Collingwood, *New Leviathan*, pp. 40–46. See also idem, *The Principles of Art* (Oxford: Oxford University Press, 1938), pp. 225–69.

55 A classic illustration of this point is offered by Herman Melville in *Billy Budd, Foretopman*. See Rollo May's account: "When an age is in the throes of a profound transition, the first thing to disintegrate is the language. This, as Auden rightly says, leads directly to the upsurge of violence. Billy Budd, at his trial after he had killed the master-at-arms with his fist, exclaims: 'Could I have used my tongue, I would not have struck him. . . . I could only say it with a blow.' Not being able to find his tongue (because of his severe stuttering) he could only speak by physical means of the physical expression of his passion" (*Power and Innocence: A Search for the Sources of Violence* [New York: W. W. Norton & Co., 1972], p. 64).

The columnist Sydney J. Harris reported that the Human Engineering Laboratory in Boston "sees a one-to-one correlation between vocabulary and violence: If the level of verbal expression is low, the only other form of expression is physical" (*Louisville Times*, 1 May 1972).

The same point is the central premise of the need for international communities of government such as the United Nations and the earlier League of Nations.

56 See Jerome A. Shaffer, ed., *Violence* (New York: David McKay Co., 1971). This volume contains four award-winning essays in the Council for Philosophical Studies Competition. The essays are by Robert Audi, Bernard Harrison, Robert L. Holmes, and Ronald B. Miller.

57 Collingwood, *New Leviathan*, pp. 1–26. Perhaps Hobbes stands with him, but Collingwood's *New Leviathan* is a much more deliberate analysis of violence.

[58] Ronald B. Miller, "Violence, Force, and Coercion," in *Violence*, ed. Shaffer, pp. 11–44. Of course, Miller may mean that whatever else violence is, it is at least, or also, *physical violence*.

[59] Arendt, *On Violence*, p. 44.

[60] Collingwood, *New Leviathan*, pp. 141–42.

[61] Arendt, *On Violence*, p. 46.

[62] See n. 32 above.

[63] See n. 5 above.

[64] See n. 32 above.

[65] See Section III A above.

[66] Benedict de Spinoza, *The Chief Works of Benedict De Spinoza*, trans. R. H. M. Elwes (New York: Dover Publications, 1951), pp. 270–71.

# BIBLIOGRAPHY

# Bibliography

Aiken, Henry David. "Violence and the Two Liberalisms." *Social Theory and Practice* 2 (1972): 47–66.

Allen, J. L. "The Relation of Strategy and Morality." *Ethics* 73 (1963): 167–78.

Amir, Menachem. *Patterns in Forcible Rape*. Foreword by Marvin E. Wolfgang. Chicago: University of Chicago Press, 1971.

Anscombe, Elizabeth. "War and Murder." In *War and Morality*, edited by Richard A. Wasserstrom. Belmont, Calif.: Wadsworth Publishing Co., 1970.

Arendt, Hannah. "Civil Disobedience." *New Yorker* 46 (12 September 1970): 70–105.

———. *On Revolution*. New York: Viking Press, 1968.

———. *On Violence*. New York: Harcourt, Brace & World, 1970.

———. "Reflections on Violence." *Journal of International Affairs* 23 (1969): 1–35.

———. "Thinking and Moral Considerations." *Social Research* 38 (1971), 417–46.

Audi, Robert. "On the Meaning and Justification of Violence." In *Violence*, edited by Jerome A. Shaffer. New York: David McKay Co., 1971.

Auineri, Shlomo. "The Problem of War in Hegel's Thought." *Journal of the History of Ideas* 22 (1961): 463–74.

Barth, Karl. *The Church and the War*. New York: Macmillan Co., 1944.

Bayles, M. "Considerations on Civil Disobedience." *Review of Metaphysics* 24 (1970): 3–20.

Bedau, Hugo Adam. "Civil Disobedience and Personal Responsibility for Injustice." *Monist* 54 (1970): 517–35.

———. "The Death Penalty as a Deterrent: Argument and Evidence." *Ethics* 80 (1970): 205–17.

———. "On Civil Disobedience." *Journal of Philosophy* 58 (1961): 653–65.

Berardo, Felix M., and Pauline B. Bart, special issue editors. "Violence and the Family." *Journal of Marriage and Family* 33 (November 1971): 621–731.

Berger, John. *Art and Revolution*. New York: Pantheon Books, 1969.

———. *A Painter of Our Time*. Baltimore: Penguin Books, 1965.

Berrigan, Philip. *Prison Journals of a Priest Revolutionary*. Edited by Vincent McGee. New York: Holt, Rinehart & Winston, 1970.

Black, Hugh. "By Their Toys Ye Shall Know Them?" *Journal of Thought* 4 (1969): 139–41.

Blackstone, William T. "Civil Disobedience: Is It Justified?" *Southern Journal of Philosophy* 8 (1970): 233–50.

Boas, George. "Warfare in the Cosmos." *Diogenes* 78 (1972): 38–51.

Bonars, Joseph C. "Response to Willers." *Philosophy of Education: Proceedings* 26 (1970): 241–42.

Bourne, Randolph S. *Towards Enduring Peace*. New York: American Association for International Conciliation, 1916.

Bradlee, Benjamin. "Ritual Violence and the Crisis in Education: A Symposium." *Antioch Review* 29 (1969): 159–97.

Brandt, Richard B. "Comment on 'Reform, Violence, and Personal Integrity'." *Inquiry* 14 (1971): 314–17.

Bronowski, Jacob. *The Face of Violence*. New York: George Braziller, 1955.

Browing, Frank. "They Shoot Hippies, Don't They?" Introduction by Tom Hayden. *Ramparts* 9 (November 1970): 14–23.

Brown, Norman O. *Life Against Death*. Middletown, Conn.: Wesleyan University Press, 1959.

Brun, Jean. "Formalisation, violence et érotisme." *Etudes philosophiques* 23 (1968): 11–30.

Buber, Martin. *Pointing the Way*. Translated and edited by Maurice Friedman. New York: Harper & Brothers, 1957.

Burke, Edmund. *Reflections on the Revolution in France*. 1790. Reprint. London: Everyman's Library, 1910.

Bychowski, Gustar. *Evil in Man: The Anatomy of Hate and Violence*. New York: Grune & Stratton, 1968.

Cameron, J. M. "On Violence." *New York Review of Books* 15 (2 July 1970): 24–32.

Camus, Albert. "Lettre au directeur des *Temps modernes*." *Temps modernes* 8 (1952): 317–33.

———. *The Rebel*. Translated by Anthony Bower. New York: Random House, Vintage Books, 1954.

Castañeda, Hector-Neri, and George Nakhnikian. *Morality and the Language of Conduct*. Detroit: Wayne State University Press, 1963.

Cattaneo, Mario. *Il Concetto di rivoluzione nella scienze del diritto*. Milan and Varese: Istituto Editoriale Cisalpino, 1960.

Chase, S. "Violence in Labor Conflicts." *World Tomorrow* 10 (March 1927): 108–11.

Chatelet, François. "Remarques sur le concept de violence." *Etudes philosophiques* 23 (1968): 31–38.

Chomsky, Noam. *American Power and the New Mandarins*. New York: Pantheon Books, 1969.

————. *At War with Asia*. New York: Pantheon Books, 1970.

————. *For Reasons of State*. New York: Pantheon Books, 1973.

————. "Philosophers and Public Philosophy." *Ethics* 79 (1968): 1–9.

————. "The Responsibility of Intellectuals." *New York Review of Books* 8 (26 January 1967): 16–26.

Cleaver, Eldridge. "The Death of Martin Luther King: Requiem for Non-Violence." In *Eldridge Cleaver: Post-Prison Writings and Speeches*, edited by Robert Scheer. New York: Random House, 1967, pp. 73–79.

————. *Soul on Ice*. New York: McGraw-Hill Book Co., 1968.

Cohn-Bendit, Daniel, et al. *The French Student Revolt*. Translated by B. R. Brewster. New York: Hill & Wang, 1968.

Collingwood, Robin G. *The New Leviathan*. Oxford: Clarendon Press, 1942.

Conio, Caterina. "Il Concetto Gandhiano di vomo e società." *Rivista di filosofia neo-scolastica* 62 (1970): 176–84.

Coradi, Gemma. *Philosophy and Coexistence*. Preface by P. F. Carcano. Leyden: A. W. Sijthoff, 1966.

Cranston, M. "Sartre and Violence." *Encounter* 29 (1967): 18–24.

Davis, Angela, and Michael Myerson. "Angela Davis: A Prison Interview." *Ramparts* 9 (February 1971): 20–25.

de Beauvior, Simone. "Merleau-Ponty et le pseudo-Sartrisme." *Temps modernes*, 114–15 (1955): 207–12.

————. *Pour une morale de l'ambiguïté*. Paris: Librairie Gallimard, 1947.

Debray, Regis. *The Border and A Young Man in the Know*. Translated by Helen R. Lane. New York: Grove Press, 1968.

De Greef, Jan. "Le concept de pouvoir éthique chez Levinas." *International Philosophical Quarterly* 10 (1970): 252–75.

Dekker, Andre G. "Gewald en Recht." *Tijdschrift voor Filosofie* 30 (1968): 675–94.

Delhomme, Jeanne. "Du Transcendental comme empirique." *Etudes philosophiques* 23 (1968): 3–10.

Dellinger, David. *Revolutionary Nonviolence*. Garden City, N.Y.: Doubleday & Co., Anchor Books, 1971.

Dellinger, David, and Isaac Deutscher. "Marxism and Nonviolence." In *The Movement toward a New America*, edited by Michael Goodman. New York: Alfred A. Knopf, 1970.

Denisoff, R. Serge. *Great Day Coming: Folk Music and the American Left*. Urbana: University of Illinois Press, 1972.

Desan, Wilfrid. *The Marxism of Jean-Paul Sartre*. Garden City, N.Y.: Doubleday & Co., 1965.

Dewey, John. "Force and Coercion." *International Journal of Ethics* 26 (1916): 359–67.

Dhondt, Jacques. "Violence et histoire." *Etudes philosophiques* 23 (1968): 39–46.

Dietze, G. "Will the Presidency Incite Assassination?" *Ethics* 76 (1965): 14–32.

Dwight, Van de Vate, Jr. "Violence and Persons." *Philosophy Forum* 7 (1969): 3–31.

Dworkin, A. G., ed. "Symposium on Violent Confrontation." *Sociological Quarterly* 12 (1971): 291–406.

Earle, William. "The Political Responsibilities of Philosophers." *Ethics* 74 (1968): 10–13.

Edelman, Murray, and Rita James Simon. "Presidental Assassinations: Their Meaning and Impact on American Society." *Ethics* 79 (1969): 199–221.

Ehrmann, Jacques, ed. *Literature and Revolution.* Boston: Beacon Press, 1967.

Ellul, Jacques. *Violence: Reflections from a Christian Perspective.* Translated by C. G. Kings. New York: Seabury Press, 1969.

Endleman, Shalom, ed. *Violence in the Streets.* Chicago: Quadrangle Books, 1968.

Erasmus, Desiderius. *Erasmus against War.* Edited by Lewis Einstine, with an introduction by J. W. MacKail. Boston: Merrymount Press, Humanist Library, 1907.

Fanon, Frantz. *Black Skins, White Masks.* Translated by Charles L. Markmann. New York: Grove Press, 1967.

——. *A Dying Colonialism.* Translated by Haakon Chevalier, with an introduction by Adolfo Gilly. New York: Grove Press, 1967.

——. *Toward the African Revolution.* Translated by Haakon Chevalier. New York: Grove Press, 1969.

——. *The Wretched of the Earth.* Translated by Constance Farrington, with a preface by Jean-Paul Sartre. New York: Grove Press, 1968.

Fogelson, Robert M. *Violence as Protest: A Study of Riots and Ghettos.* Garden City, N.Y.: Doubleday & Co., Anchor Books, 1971.

Ford, John C. "The Morality of Obliteration Bombing." In *War and Morality,* edited by Richard A. Wasserstrom. Belmont, Calif.: Wadsworth Publishing Co., 1970.

Fortas, Abe. *Concerning Dissent and Civil Disobedience.* New York: New American Library, 1968.

Foucault, Michel. *Madness and Civilization.* New York: Pantheon Books, 1965.

Fowlie, Wallace. *Climate of Violence: The French Literary Tradition from Baudelaire to the Present.* New York: Macmillan Co., 1967.

Franchini, Farraello. "Della Violenza." *Rivista di studi Crociani* 21 (1971): 72–75.

Fraser, J. "An Art of Violence." *Partisan Review* 36 (1969): 363–87.

Friedrich, Carl J. "Opposition, and Government, by Violence." *Government and Opposition* 7 (1972): 3–19.

——, ed. *Revolution*. New York: Atherton Press, 1966.

Gandhi, Mohandas K. *Non-Violent Resistance*. New York: Schocken Books, 1961.

Garver, Newton. "Philosophy and Pacifism." *Philosophy Today* 11 (1967): 142–47.

——. "What Violence Is." *The Nation*, 24 June 1968, pp. 817–22.

Genet, Jean. "Here and Now for Bobby Seale." Translated by Judy Aringer. *Ramparts* 8 (June 1970): 30–31.

Gert, B. "Justifying Violence." *Journal of Philosophy* 66 (1969): 616–28.

Gillan, Garth. "Word—Spectacle—Mask." *Philosophy Today* 12 (1968): 130–37.

Gilula, Marshall E., and David N. Daniels. "Violence and Man's Struggle to Adapt." *Science* 164 (1969): 396–405.

Godfrey, Erwina E. "Student Unrest versus Student Violence." *Journal of Thought* 4 (1969): 306–12.

Goldman, Emma. "Preparedness: The Road to Universal Slaughter." *Mother Earth*, December 1915.

Goldstone, Peter J. "Philosophical Analysis and the Revolution." *Philosophy of Education: Proceedings* 26 (1970): 220–28.

Gomez, Samuel. "Violence, Persons, Communications: A Transactional Model." *Philosophy Forum* 7 (1969): 49–56.

Goodman, Michael, ed. *The Movement toward a New America: The Beginnings of a Long Revolution*. New York: Alfred A. Knopf, 1970.

Gray, J. Glenn. *On Understanding Violence Philosophically and Other Essays*. New York: Harper & Row, 1970.

——. *The Promise of Wisdom*. Philadelphia: J. B. Lippincott Co., 1968.

——. *The Warriors: Reflections on Men in Battle*. Introduction by Hannah Arendt. New York: Harper & Row, 1967.

Harris, Errol E. "The Power of Reason." *Review of Metaphysics* 22 (1969): 621–39.

Harrison, Bernard. "Violence and the Rule of Law." In *Violence*, edited by Jerome A. Shaffer. New York: David McKay Co., 1971.

Hart, H. L. A. *The Concept of Law*. Oxford: Clarendon Press, 1961.

——. *Law, Liberty, Morality*. Stanford, Calif.: Stanford University Press, 1963.

Hartigan, R. S. "Saint Augustine on War and Killing: The Problem of the Innocent." *Journal of the History of Ideas* 27 (1966): 195–204.

Hersh, Seymour M. *Cover-Up*. New York: Random House, 1972.

——. *My Lai 4: A Report on the Massacre and Its Aftermath*. New York: Random House, Vintage Books, 1970.

Hoffmann, S. "Rousseau on War and Peace." *American Political Science Review* 57 (1963): 317–33.

Holmes, Robert L. "Violence and Nonviolence." in *Violence*, edited by Jerome A. Shaffer. New York: David McKay Co., 1971.

Honeywell, J. A. "Revolution: Its Potentialities and Its Degradations." *Ethics* 80 (1970): 251–65.

Hood, C. Ellsworth. "Violence and the Myth of Quantification." *International Philosophical Quarterly* 9 (1969), 590–600.

Hook, Sidney. "The Ideology of Violence." *Encounter* 34 (1970): 26–38.

Israel, A. "The Aesthetic of Violence: Rimbaud and Genet." *Yale French Studies* 17 (1971) 415–31.

Jacobs, Paul. "The Varieties of Violence." *Center Magazine* 2 (1969): 17–19.

Jaffe, Raymond. "Conservatism and the Praise of Suffering." *Ethics* 77 (1967): 254–67.

Jaspers, Karl. *The Future of Mankind*. Chicago: University of Chicago Press, 1961.

Jeanson, Francis. "Albert Camus ou l'âme revoltée." *Temps modernes* 7 (1952): 207–209.

―――. *Le Problème moral et la pensée de Sartre*. Paris: Editions du Seuil, 1965.

Jones, LeRoi. "What Does Nonviolence Mean?" *Home: Social Essays*. New York: William Morrow & Co., 1966, 133–54.

Kant, Immanuel. *The Metaphysical Elements of Justice*. Translated by John Ladd. Indianapolis: Bobbs-Merrill Co., 1965.

Kelsen, Hans. *The Communist Theory of Law*. London: Stevens & Sons, 1955.

―――. *General Theory of Law and State*. Translated by Anders Wedberg. Cambridge: Harvard University Press, 1945.

Kent, Edward, ed. *Revolution and the Rule of Law*. Englewood Cliffs, N.J.: Prentice-Hall, 1971.

Klein, Alexander, ed. *Dissent, Power, and Confrontation*. New York: McGraw-Hill Book Co., 1971.

Koestler, Arthur. *Darkness at Noon*. Translated by Daphne Hardy. London: Jonathan Cape, 1940.

Kosik, Karel. "Reason and History." *Telos* 2 (1969): 64–71.

Krickers, R. J. "On the Morality of Chemical/Biological Warfare." *Journal of Conflict Resolution* 9 (1965): 200–10.

Kunen, James Simon. *The Strawberry Statement: Notes of a College Revolutionary*. New York: Avon, 1969.

Kuykendall, Eleanor. *Philosophy in the Age of Crisis*. New York: Harper & Row, 1970.

Laing, Ronald D. and R. G. Cooper. *Reason and Violence*. New York: Random House, Vintage Books, 1971.

Lang, B. "Civil Disobedience and Nonviolence: A Distinction with a Difference." *Ethics* 80 (1970): 156–59.

Lawrence, John S. "The Moral Attractiveness of Violence." *Journal of Social Philosophy* 1 (1970): 5–6.

———. "Violence." *Social Theory and Practice* 1 (1970): 31–49.

Lenin, V. I. *The State and Revolution.* In *Selected Works.* New York: International Publishers, 1935.

Levinas, Emmanuel. *Totality and Infinity.* Translated by Alphonso Lingis. Pittsburgh: Duquesne University Press, 1969.

Lifaserson, Max. "Revolution und Recht." *Zeitschrift für öffentliches Recht* 8 (1930): 553–70.

Loewenberg, Jacob. "Ethics and the War." *Mills Quarterly* 1 (1969): 6–9.

———. "Judgments of Fact and of Value in Relation to the War." In *The Meaning of the War to the Americas: Lectures Delivered under the Auspices of the Committee on International Relations on the Los Angeles Campus of the University of California.* Berkeley and Los Angeles: University of California Press, 1941.

Lorenz, Konrad. *On Aggression.* New York: Harcourt, Brace & World, 1966.

Lowenthal, R. "Unreason and Revolution." *Encounter* 33 (1969): 22–34.

Lukacs, Georg. "On the Responsibility of Intellectuals." *Telos* 2 (1969): 123–31.

———. *Realism in Our Time: Literature and the Class Struggle.* Translated by John and Necke Mander. New York: Harper & Row, 1964.

McBride, William L. *Fundamental Change in Law and Society: Hart and Sartre on Revolution.* The Hague: Moulton & Co., 1970.

———. "Reflections on Reflections on Revolution." *The New Journal* (student publication, Yale University) 2 (8 December 1968): 13–17.

———. "Sartre and the Phenomenology of Social Violence." In *New Essays in Phenomenology,* edited by James M. Edie. Chicago: Quadrangle Books, 1969.

Maccallum, Gerald C. "Reform, Violence, and Personal Integrity." *Inquiry* 14 (1971): 301–14.

McDade, Jesse. "Frantz Fanon: The Ethical Justification of Revolution." Ph.D. dissertation, Boston University, 1970.

MacFarlane, Leslie J. "Justifying Political Disobedience." *Ethics* 79 (1968): 24–55.

McKeon, Richard. "Mankind: The Relation of Reason to Action." *Ethics* 74 (1964): 174–85.

McWilliams, W. E. "On Violence and Legitimacy." *Yale Law Journal* 79 (1970): 623–46.

Madden, E. H., and Peter H. Hare. "Reflections on Civil Disobedience." *Journal of Value Inquiry* 4 (1970): 81–95.

Malcolm X. *The Speeches of Malcolm X at Harvard.* Edited by Archie Epps. New York: William Morrow & Co., 1968.

Malinowski, Bronislaw. *Crime and Custom in Savage Society.* London: Routledge & Kegan Paul, 1926.

Marcuse, Herbert. "Dear Angela:" *Ramparts* 9 (February 1971): 22.

———. *An Essay on Liberation.* Boston: Beacon Press, 1969.

———. "Ethics and Revolution." In *Revolution and the Rule of Law,* edited by Edward Kent. Englewood Cliffs, N.J.: Prentice-Hall, 1971.

———. *One-Dimensional Man.* Boston: Beacon Press, 1964.

———. "The Problem of Violence and the Radical Opposition." In his *Five Lectures: Psychoanalysis, Politics and Utopia.* Translated by J. J. Shapiro and Shierry M. Weber. Boston: Beacon Press, 1970.

———. *Reason and Revolution: Hegel and the Rise of Social Theory.* Boston: Beacon Press, 1960.

———. Review of *Poverty of Historicism,* by Karl R. Popper. *Partisan Review* 26 (1959): 117–29.

———. "Socialist Humanism?" In *Socialist Humanism: An International Symposium,* edited by Erich Fromm. Garden City, N.Y.: Doubleday & Co., Anchor Books, 1966.

Martin, Rex. "Civil Disobedience." *Ethics* 80 (1970): 123–37.

Marty, W. R. "Nonviolence, Violence and Reason." *Journal of Politics* 33 (1971): 3–24.

Megill, Kenneth. "In Defense of Revolution." *Telos* 5 (1970): 190–96.

Menninger, Karl. *The Crime of Punishment.* New York: Viking Press, 1968.

Merkl, Adolf. "Das Problem der Rechtskontinuität und die Forderung des einheitlichen rechtlichen Weltbildes." *Zeitschrift für öffentliches Recht* 5 (1926): 497–527.

Merleau-Ponty, Maurice. *Les Aventures de la dialectique.* Paris: Librairie Gallimard, 1955.

———. *Humanism and Terror.* Translated by John O'Neill. Boston: Beacon Press, 1969.

———. *The Primacy of Perception and Other Essays.* Edited by James M. Edie. Evanston, Ill.: Northwestern University Press, 1964.

———. *Signs.* Translated by Richard C. McCleary. Evanston, Ill.: Northwestern University Press, 1964.

———. "The War Has Taken Place." In *Sense and Non-Sense,* translated by Hubert L. Dreyfus. Evanston, Ill.: Northwestern University Press, 1964.

Miller, Ronald B. "Violence, Force and Coercion." In *Violence,* edited by Jerome A. Shaffer. New York: David McKay Co., 1971.

Monastero, Xavier O. "Camus and the Problem of Violence." *New Scholasticism* 44 (1970): 199–222.

Monte, Anita and Gerald Leinwald, eds. *Riots*. New York: Washington Square Press, 1970.

Morgan, Douglas N. "On Justifying Political Action." *Ethics* 71 (1961): 155–74.

Munro, Thomas. "Art and Violence." *Journal of Aesthetics and Art Criticism* 27 (1969): 317–22.

Murphy, Jeffrie G. "Allegiance and Lawful Government." *Ethics* 79 (1968): 56–69.

———. "Violence and the Rule of Law." *Ethics* 80 (1970): 319–21.

Muste, A. J. *The Essays of A. J. Muste*. Edited by Nat Hentoff. New York: Simon & Schuster, 1967.

———. *Non-violence in an Aggressive World*. New York: Harper & Brothers, 1940.

Nelson, John O. "The Anachronisms of the Group-Psyche and War." *Ramparts Journal* 4 (1968): 89–95.

———. "The Two Opposed Theories of Freedom in Our Philosophical Heritage." *Ramparts Journal* 3 (1967): 1–18.

Nelson, Truman. *The Right of Revolution*. Boston: Beacon Press, 1968.

Niebuhr, Reinhold. *Moral Man and Immoral Society*. New York: Charles Scribner's Sons, 1941.

Nielsen, Kai. "Remarks on Violence and Paying the Penalty." *Philosophy Forum* 2 (1970): 3–14.

Olivercrona, Karl. *Law as Fact*. Copenhagen: Einau Munksgaard, 1939.

Organ, Troy. "The Anatomy of Violence." *Personalist* 51 (1970): 417–33.

Orth, S. P. "Law and Force in International Affairs." *International Journal of Ethics* 26 (1916): 339–46.

Palter, R. M. "The Ethics of Extermination." *Ethics* 74 (1964): 208–18.

Perry, Charner. "Violence—Visible and Invisible." *Ethics* 81 (1970): 1–21.

Petrie, Hugh G. "Response to Goldstone." *Philosophy of Education: Proceedings* 26 (1970): 229–33.

Piccone, Paul. "Students' Protest, Class Structure, and Ideology." *Telos* 2 (1969): 106–22.

Pollock, Robert C. "Dream and Nightmare: The Future as Revolution." In *American Philosophy and the Future*, edited by Michael Novak. New York: Charles Scribner's Sons, 1968.

Popper, Karl R. "Utopia and Violence." *Hibbert Journal* 46 (1948): 109–16.

Porterfield, Austin Larimore. *Cultures of Violence*. Fort Worth: Leo Patishman Foundation, 1965.

Posse, E. H. Review of *Réflexions sur la violence*, by Georges Sorel. *Historische Zeitschrift* 141 (1930): 542–43.

Potter, Paul B. *War and Moral Discourse.* Richmond, Va.: John Knox Press, 1969.

Prosch, Harry. "Toward an Ethics of Civil Disobedience." *Ethics* 72 (1967): 176–91.

Raines, J. C., and Thomas Dean, eds. *Marxism and Radical Religion: Essays toward a Revolutionary Humanism.* Philadelphia: Temple University Press, 1970.

Ramsey, Paul. *War and the Christian Conscience.* Durham: Duke University Press, 1961.

Ranly, Ernest W. "Defining Violence." *Thought* 47 (1972): 415–27.

Rapoport, David C. "Coup d'Etat: The View of the Men Firing Pistols." In *Revolution,* edited by Carl J. Friedrich. New York: Atherton Press, 1966.

Rawls, John. "Justice as Fairness." *Philosophical Review* 67 (1958): 164–94.

———. "The Justification of Civil Disobedience." In *Revolution and the Rule of Law,* edited by Edward Kent. Englewood Cliffs, N.J.: Prentice-Hall, 1971.

———. *A Theory of Justice.* Cambridge: Harvard University Press, 1971.

———. "Two Concepts of Rules." *Philosophical Review* 64 (1955): 3–52.

Regan, Thomas. "A Defense of Pacifism." *Canadian Journal of Philosophy* 2 (1972): 73–86.

Riga, Peter D. "Toward a Theology of Protest." *Thomist* 33 (1969): 229–50.

———. "Violence: A Christian Perspective." *Philosophy East and West* 19 (1969): 143–53.

Roberts, Adam. "Civilian Defense and the Inhibition of Violence." *Philosophy East and West* 19 (1969): 181–93.

Rose, Thomas, ed. *Violence in America.* Foreword by Paul Jacobs. New York: Random House, Vintage Books, 1969.

Ross, Alf. *On Law and Justice.* Berkeley and Los Angeles: University of California Press, 1959.

Rovatti, Pier Aldo. "A Phenomenological Analysis of Marxism." *Telos* 5 (1970): 160–73.

Rubinoff, M. Lionel. *The Pornography of Power.* New York: Ballantine Books, 1967.

Sacksteder, William. "Person, Communication, and Violence." *Philosophy Forum* 7 (1969): 35–46.

Sander, Fritz. "Das Faktum der Revolution und die Kontinuität der Rechtsordnung." *Zeitschrift für öffentliches Recht* 1 (1919/1920): 132–64.

Santoni, Ronald E. "Man First and Philosophers Afterward: A Response to Kuntz and Ryle." *International Philosophical Quarterly* 9 (1969): 601–604.

————. "A Reply to Professor Garver on Philosophy and Pacifism." *Philosophy Today* 11 (1967): 147–50.

Sartre, Jean-Paul. *Critique de la raison dialectique*. Vol. 1. Paris: Librairie Gallimard, 1960.

————. "Genocide." In *The Movement toward a New America*, edited by Michael Goodman. New York: Alfred A. Knopf, 1970. (From *Ramparts* 6 [February 1968]: 36–42.)

————. "Merleau-Ponty." In *Situations*, by Maurice Merleau-Ponty, translated by Benita Eisler. New York: George Braziller, Fawcett World Library, 1965.

————. Preface to *The Wretched of the Earth*, by Frantz Fanon, translated by Constance Farrington. New York: Grove Press, 1968.

————. "Reply to Albert Camus." In *Situations*, by Maurice Merleau-Ponty, translated by Benita Eisler. New York: George Braziller, Fawcett World Library, 1965.

————. *Saint Genet*. New York: Alfred A. Knopf, 1963.

Sartre, Jean-Paul, and J. C. Garot. "Intellectuals and Revolution: Interview with Jean-Paul Sartre." Translated by Bruce Rice. *Ramparts* 9 (December 1970): 52–55.

Schorstein, Joseph. "The Metaphysics of the Atom Bomb." *Philosophical Journal* 1 (1964): 33–46.

Seale, Bobby. *Seize the Time*. New York: Random House, 1968.

Shaffer, Jerome A., ed. *Violence*. New York: David McKay Co., 1971.

Short, James F., and Marvin E. Wolfgang, eds. *Collective Violence*. Chicago: Aldine & Atherton, 1971.

Sibley, Mulford Q. "Nonviolence and Revolution." *Humanist* 28 (1968): 3–6.

Silber, John R. "Soul Politics and Political Morality." *Ethics* 79 (1968): 14–23.

Simpson, Evans. "Social Norms and Aberrations: Violence and Some Related Social Facts." *Ethics* 81 (1970): 22–35.

Smith, C. I. "Hegel on War." *Journal of the History of Ideas* 26 (1965): 282–85.

Smith, John. "The Inescapable Ambiguity of Nonviolence." *Philosophy East and West* 19 (1969): 155–58.

Somerville, John. "The Key Problem of Current Political Philosophy: The Issue of Force and Violence." *Philosophy of Science* 19 (1952): 156–65.

————. "Violence, Politics, and Morality." *Philosophy and Phenomenological Research* 32 (1971): 241–49.

Sorel, Georges. *Reflections on Violence*. Translated by T. E. Hulme and J. Roth. Glencoe, Ill.: Free Press, 1950.

Storr, Anthony. *Human Aggression*. New York: Atheneum, 1968.

Struckmeyer, Frederick R. "The 'Just War' and the Right of Self-Defense." *Ethics* 82 (1971): 48–55.

Students for a Democratic Society. *The Port Huron Statement*. New York: Students for a Democratic Society, 1964.

Talman, J. L. "The Legacy of Georges Sorel." *Encounter* 34 (1970): 47–60.

Thakur, Shivesh C. "Gandhi's God." *International Philosophical Quarterly* 11 (1971): 485–95.

Toch, Hans H. *Violent Men: An Inquiry into the Psychology of Violence*. Chicago: Aldine Publishing Co., 1969.

Trotsky, Leon. *Literature and Revolution*. Ann Arbor: University of Michigan Press, 1960.

———. *Stalin*. Translated by Charles Malamuth. New York: Grosset & Dunlap, 1941.

———. *Terrorism and Communism: A Reply to Karl Kautsky*. With foreword and translation by Max Shachtman. Ann Arbor: University of Michigan Press, 1961.

Upadhyaya, R. N. "The Bhagavad-Gita on War and Peace." *Philosophy East and West* 19 (1969): 159–69.

Vandenberg, Donald. "Non-Violent Power in Education." *Educational Theory* 19 (1969): 49–57.

Van Den Haag, Ernest. "On Deterrence and the Death Penalty." *Ethics* 78 (1968): 280–88.

Ver Eecke, Wilfried. "Law, Morality, and Society: Reflections on Violence." *Ethics* 80 (1970): 140–45.

Vidal-Naquet, Pierre. *Torture, Cancer of Democracy: France and Algeria, 1954–62*. Translated by Barry Richard. Baltimore: Penquin Books, 1963.

"Violence." *20th Century* 173 (Winter 1964/1965): 3–130.

Wade, Francis C. "Comments and Criticism on 'On Violence'." *Journal of Philosophy* 68 (1971): 369–77.

Wallis, N. "Seeking the Storms." *Spectator* 212 (6 March 1964): 314–16.

Waltz, K. N. "Kant, Liberalism and War." *American Political Science Review* 56 (1962): 331–40.

Walzer, Michael. *Obligation: Essays on Disobedience, War, and Citizenship*. Cambridge: Harvard University Press, 1970.

———. "The Obligation to Disobey." *Ethics* 72 (1967): 163–75.

———. "War and Revolution in Puritan Thought." *Political Studies* 12 (1964): 220–29.

Wasserstrom, Richard A. "Disobeying the Law." *Journal of Philosophy* 58 (1961): 641–53.

———. "Three Arguments Concerning the Morality of War." *Journal of Philosophy* 65 (1968): 578–90.

———, ed. *Morality and the Law*. Belmont, Calif.: Wadsworth Publishing Co., 1970.

———, ed. *War and Morality*. Belmont, Calif.: Wadsworth Publishing Co., 1970.

Weaver, G. R., and J. H. Weaver, eds. *The University and Revolution*. Englewood Cliffs, N.J.: Prentice-Hall, 1969.

Weil, Eric. "The State and Violence." (In Hebrew.) *Iyyun* 20 (1969): 60–70.

Weinberg, Arthur, and Lila Weinberg, eds. *Instead of Violence*. New York: Grossman Publishers, 1963.

Wells, Donald A. "How Much Can the Just War Justify?" *Journal of Philosophy* 66 (1969): 819–29.

———. "Is Just Violence Like Just War?" *Social Theory and Practice* 1 (1970): 26–38.

———. *The War Myth*. New York: Pegasus, 1967.

———. "What Does the Conviction of Calley Imply?" *Journal of Social Philosophy* 2 (1971): 2–5.

Wertham, Frederick. *A Sign for Cain: An Explanation of Human Violence*. New York: Macmillan Co., 1966.

*When All Else Fails: Christian Arguments on Violent Revolution*. Edited by IDOC Staff. Philadelphia and Boston: Pilgrim Press, 1970.

Wilhelmsen, Frederick D., and Jane Bret. *The War in Man: Media and Machines*. Athens, Ga.: University of Georgia Press, 1970.

Willers, Jack C. "Violence—An Educational Dilemma." *Philosophy of Education: Proceedings* 26 (1970): 234–40.

Wolff, Robert Paul. *In Defense of Anarchism*. New York: Harper & Row, 1970.

———. "On Violence." *Journal of Philosophy* 66 (1969): 601–16.

———. *The Poverty of Liberalism*. Boston: Beacon Press, 1968.

Wolff, Robert Paul, Barrington Moore, Jr., and Herbert Marcuse. *A Critique of Pure Tolerance*. Boston: Beacon Press, 1968.

Yglesias, José. "Deaths I have Known." *Ramparts* 10 (May 1972): 42–47.

Zinn, Howard. *Disobedience and Democracy: Nine Fallacies on Law and Order*. New York: Random House, 1968.